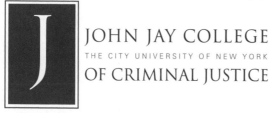

JOHN JAY COLLEGE
THE CITY UNIVERSITY OF NEW YORK
OF CRIMINAL JUSTICE

RHETORIC, RESEARCH, AND STRATEGIES

THIRD EDITION

Excerpts taken from:

The Longman Pocket Writer's Companion, Second Edition
by Chris M. Anson, Robert A. Schwegler, and Marcia F. Muth

Research Writing Across the Disciplines: The Essential Guide,
Third Edition
by James D. Lester and James D. Lester, Jr.

Writing Proposals: Rhetoric for Managing Change
by Richard Johnson-Sheehan

The Longman Pocket Writer's Companion, First Edition
by Chris M. Anson, Robert A. Schwegler, and Marcia F. Muth

*Citing Cyberspace: A Quick-Reference Guide to Citing Electronic
Sources in MLA and APA Style,* Second Edition
by James D. Lester

Learning Solutions

New York   Boston   San Francisco
London   Toronto   Sydney   Tokyo   Singapore   Madrid
Mexico City   Munich   Paris   Cape Town   Hong Kong   Montreal

Cover Art: Courtesy of Corbis

Excerpts taken from:

*The Longman Pocket Writer's
Companion*, Second Edition
by Chris M. Anson, Robert A.
Schwegler, and Marcia F. Muth
Copyright © 2006 by Pearson
Education, Inc.
Published by Longman
New York, New York 10036

*Research Writing Across the
Disciplines: The Essential Guide*,
Third Edition
by James D. Lester and
James D. Lester, Jr.
Copyright © 2005 by Pearson
Education, Inc.
Published by Longman

*Writing Proposals: Rhetoric for
Managing Change*
by Richard Johnson-Sheehan
Copyright © 2002 by Pearson
Education, Inc.
Published by Longman

*The Longman Pocket Writer's
Companion*, First Edition
by Chris M. Anson, Robert A.
Schwegler, and Marcia F. Muth
Copyright © 2003 by Pearson
Education, Inc.
Published by Addison Wesley
Boston, Massachusetts 02116

*Citing Cyberspace: A Quick-Reference
Guide to Citing Electronic Sources in
MLA and APA Style*, Second Edition
by James D. Lester
Copyright © 2000 by Pearson
Education, Inc.
Published by Longman

Pearson Learning Solutions, 501 Boylston Street, Suite 900, Boston, MA 02116
A Pearson Education Company
www.pearsoned.com

Printed in the United States of America

1 2 3 4 5 6 7 8 9 10 V0CR 15 14 13 12 11 10

000200010270592075

NM

ISBN 10: 0-558-83486-8
ISBN 13: 978-0-558-83486-9

Contents

INTRODUCTION xiii

Chapter 1 WRITING AND READING 1

1a Writing and Reading in Communities 1
    Understanding Your Writing Situation 2
    Moving from Reading to Writing 3
    Paying Attention to the Writing Process 4

1b Developing a Thesis 5
    Creating a Thesis Statement 5
    Designing an Appropriate Thesis 6

1c Providing Support and Reasoning Clearly 6
    Reasoning Critically 6
    Providing Support 7
    Evaluating Support 8

1d Paragraphing for Readers 8
    Focusing Paragraphs 8
    Making Paragraphs Coherent 9
    Developing Paragraphs 10

1e Matching Style and Strategy to a Community of Readers 11
    Recognizing a Community's Style 11
    Adjusting to a Community's Style 12
    Recognizing a Community's Expectations 12

1f Designing Documents for Readers 13
    Planning Your Document 13
    Laying out Your Document 14
    Using Type Features 14
    Using Visuals 15
    Sample Documents 15

1g Constructing an Argument 16
    Identifying an Issue 16
    Developing an Argumentative Thesis 18
    Developing Reasons and Supporting Evidence 19
    Presenting Counterarguments 20
    Reasoning Logically 20

Chapter 2 FINDING A SCHOLARLY TOPIC   23

2a Generating Ideas and Focusing the Subject   24
Relating Your Personal Ideas to a Scholarly Problem   24
Talking with Others to Find and Refine the Topic   27
Using Electronic Sources   28
Using Textbooks and Reference Books   29

2b Writing a Thesis, Enthymeme, or Hypothesis   30
Thesis Statement   30
Enthymeme   31
Hypothesis   32

2c Drafting a Research Proposal   33
Writing a Short Research Proposal   33
Writing a Detailed Research Proposal   34

Chapter 3 CONDUCTING RESEARCH   37

3a Planning and Conducting Research   37
Recognizing Research Communities   37
Recognizing Research Topics   38
Identifying Keywords   38
Developing Research Questions   39
Developing Search Strategies   39
Selecting Resources for a Working Bibliography   40
Keeping Track of Your Sources and Notes   41
Pulling Your Research Materials Together   41

3b Finding Library and Database Resources   42
Finding Library Resources   42
Using Library Resources   43
Finding Research Databases   43
Using Research Databases   43

3c Finding Web and Internet Resources   44
Developing an Online Search Strategy   44
Finding Web and Internet Resources   45
Searching Efficiently   46
Using Web Resources   47

3d Reading and Evaluating Sources   48
Summarizing and Paraphrasing   48
Synthesizing and Questioning   49
Evaluating Sources Critically   50
Evaluating Online Sources Critically   51
Turning Inquiry into Writing   54

3e Integrating and Crediting Sources   54
Documenting Sources for Your Audience   55
Using Quotations   55
Integrating Sources into Your Text   57
Avoiding Plagiarism   57
Deciding What to Document   58
Presenting Sources   59

Chapter 4 FIELD RESEARCH: COLLECTING DATA OUTSIDE THE LIBRARY 61

4a Conducting Research within a Discipline 61
    The Social Scientists 61
    The Physical Scientists 61
    The Applied Scientists 62
    The Humanists 62
4b Investigating Local Sources 63
    Interviewing Knowledgeable People 63
    Writing Letters and Corresponding by E-mail 63
    Reading Personal Papers 64
    Attending Lectures and Public Addresses 65
    Investigating Government Documents 65
4c Examining Audiovisual Materials, Television, and Radio 66
4d Conducting a Survey with a Questionnaire 66
4e Conducting Experiments, Tests, and Observation 67

Chapter 5 UNDERSTANDING AND AVOIDING PLAGIARISM 71

5a Using Sources to Enhance Your Credibility 71
5b Identifying Bias in a Source 72
5c Honoring Property Rights 73
5d Avoiding Plagiarism 73
    Common Knowledge Exceptions 75
    Borrowing from a Source Correctly 76
5e Seeking Permission to Publish Material on Your Web Site 79

Chapter 6 FINDING AND READING THE BEST SOURCES 81

6a Understanding the Assignment 81
    Guide to Academic Sources 82
6b Identifying the Best Source Materials 83
    Scholarly Book 83
    Biography 84
    Scholarly Article 84
    Sponsored Web Site 85
    Interview 85
    Experiment, Test, or Observation 85
    Trade Book 85
    Encyclopedia 85
    Popular Magazine 86
    Newspaper 86
    E-mail Discussion Group 86
    Individual Web Site 86
    Internet Chat Conversations 87

6c Evaluating a Source   87
  Relevance   87
  Authority   87
  Accuracy   88
  Currency   88

Chapter 7 ORGANIZING IDEAS AND SETTING GOALS   89

7a Using the Correct Academic Model (Paradigm)   89
  A General, All-Purpose Model   89
  Academic Pattern for the Interpretation of Literature and Other
    Creative Works   90
  Academic Pattern for the Analysis of History   90
  Academic Pattern for Advancing Philosophical
    and Religious Ideas   91
  Academic Pattern for the Review of a Performance   91
  Academic Pattern for Advancing Your Ideas and Theories   92
  Academic Pattern for Argument and Persuasion Papers   93
  Academic Model for a Comparative Study   93
  Academic Pattern for a Laboratory Investigation
    or Field Report   94
  Academic Pattern for Scientific Analysis   94
  Academic Pattern for a Report of Empirical Research   95

7b Using Your Thesis to Control the Outline   96
  Argument   96
  Cause and Effect   96
  Evaluation   96
  Comparison   97

7c Writing an Outline   97
  Topic Outline   98
  Sentence Outline   99

Chapter 8 WRITING EFFECTIVE NOTES   101
  Honoring the Conventions of Research Style   101

8a Writing Personal Notes   102

8b Writing Direct Quotation Notes   103
  Quoting the Primary Sources   104
  Quoting the Secondary Sources   104

8c Writing Paraphrased Notes   105

8d Writing Summary Notes   106
  Use the Summary to Review Briefly an Article or Book   106
  Use the Summary to Write an Annotated Bibliography   107
  Use the Summary in a Plot Summary Note   107
  Use the Summary to Create an Abstract   107

8e Writing Notes from Field Research 108

8f Using Your Notes to Write an Annotated Bibliography 108

8g Using Your Notes to Write a Review of the Literature 111

Chapter 9 DRAFTING THE PAPER
IN AN ACADEMIC STYLE 121

9a Writing for Your Field of Study 121

    Academic Style in the Humanities 122

    Academic Style in the Social Sciences 122

    Academic Style in the Physical and Medical Sciences 123

9b Focusing Your Argument 124

    Persuading, Inquiring, and Negotiating 124

    Maintaining a Focus with Ethical and Logical Appeals 125

    Focusing the Final Thesis Sentence or Hypothesis 125

9c Designing an Academic Title 127

9d Drafting the Paper 128

    Writing with Unity and Coherence 129

    Writing in the Proper Tense 129

    Using the Language of the Discipline 129

    Using Source Material to Enhance Your Writing 130

    Writing in the Third Person 130

    Writing with the Passive Voice in an Appropriate Manner 130

    Placing Graphics Effectively in a Research Essay 130

    Avoiding Sexist and Biased Language 131

9e Creating an Introduction, Body, and Conclusion 132

    Writing the Introduction 132

    Writing the Body of the Research Paper 134

    Writing the Conclusion of the Paper 135

9f Revising the Rough Draft 136

    Editing before Printing the Final Manuscript 136

    Using the Computer to Edit Your Text 137

    Participating in Peer Review 137

    Proofreading 138

9g Writing With Style 139

Overview 139

Good Style Is a Choice, Not an Accident 139

What Is Style? 139

Writing Plain Sentences 141

    Guideline 1: The subject should be what the sentence is
        about 142

    Guideline 2: Make the "doer" the subject 143

Guideline 3: State the action in the verb   143
Guideline 4: Put the subject early in the sentence   144
Guideline 5: Eliminate nominalizations   145
Guideline 6: Avoid excessive prepositional phrases   145
Guideline 7: Eliminate redundancy   146
Guideline 8: Make sentences "breathing length"   146
A Simple Method for Writing Plainer Sentences   147

Writing Plain Paragraphs   148
The Elements of a Paragraph   148
Aligning Sentence Subjects in a Paragraph   150
The Given/New Method   152

Persuasive Style   156
Elevating the Tone   157
Using Similes and Analogies   158
Using Metaphors   159
Changing the Pace   160
Last Word   161

Chapter 10 WRITING CORRECTLY   163

10a Fragments   163
Recognizing Sentence Fragments   164
Editing Sentence Fragments   165
Using Partial Sentences   165

10b Comma Splices and Fused Sentences   166
Recognizing Comma Splices   166
Recognizing Fused Sentences   166
Editing Comma Splices and Fused Sentences   167

10c Pronoun Reference   168
Recognizing Unclear Pronoun Reference   168
Editing Pronoun Reference   169

10d Agreement   170
Recognizing Agreement   171
Editing Subject-Verb Agreement   171
Editing Pronoun-Antecedent Agreement   174

10e Correct Forms   174
Recognizing and Editing Verb Forms   174
Editing for Clear Tense Sequence   177
Recognizing Pronoun Forms   177
Editing Pronoun Forms   178
Recognizing Adjectives and Adverbs   179
Editing Adjectives and Adverbs   179
Recognizing and Editing Comparisons   182

Chapter 11 WRITING CLEARLY   183

11a Clear Sentences   183
Recognizing Unclear Sentences   184
Editing for Clear Sentences   184
11b Mixed Structures   186
Recognizing Mixed and Incomplete Sentences   186
Editing Mixed and Incomplete Sentences   187
11c Dangling and Misplaced Modifiers   188
Recognizing Misplaced Modifiers   188
Editing Misplaced Modifiers   189
11d Unnecessary Shifts   190
Recognizing Shifts in Person and Number   190
Editing Shifts in Person and Number   191
Recognizing Shifts in Tense   191
Editing Shifts in Tense   191
11e Parallelism   192
Recognizing Faulty Parallelism   192
Editing for Parallelism   192
11f Coordination and Subordination   193
Recognizing Coordination   194
Recognizing Subordination   194
Editing for Coordination and Subordination   196
11g Conciseness   196
Recognizing Common Types of Wordiness   197
Editing for Conciseness   198
11h Language Choices   198
Recognizing and Editing Language Varieties   199
Recognizing and Editing Disrespectful Language   199

Chapter 12 WRITING WITH CONVENTIONS   201

12a Commas   202
Recognizing Commas That Join Sentences   202
Editing Commas That Join Sentences   202
Recognizing Commas That Set Off Sentence Elements   203
Editing Commas That Set Off Sentence Elements   203
Editing Disruptive Commas   205
Editing Commas with Words in a Series   205
12b Semicolons and Colons   207
Recognizing Semicolons That Join Sentences   207
Editing Semicolons That Join Sentences   207

Editing Semicolons in a Complex Series 208
Recognizing and Editing Colons 208

12c Apostrophes 209
Recognizing Apostrophes That Mark Possession 209
Editing Apostrophes That Mark Possession 209
Recognizing Apostrophes That Mark Contractions 210
Editing Apostrophes That Mark Contractions 210

12d Quotation Marks 211
Recognizing Marks That Set Off Quotations 211
Editing Marks That Set Off Quotations 211
Editing Quotation Marks With Titles of Short Works 212

12e Italics and Underlining 213
Recognizing Conventions for Italics (Underlining) 213
Editing for Conventions That Show Emphasis 213

12f Capitals 214
Recognizing Capitals That Begin Sentences 214
Editing Capitals That Begin Sentences 214
Editing Capitals That Begin Words 215

12g Abbreviations 216
Recognizing and Editing Abbreviations 217
Editing to Use Abbreviations Sparingly 218

12h Numbers 218
Recognizing When to Spell or Use Numerals 219
Editing Numbers in General Text 219

12i Hyphens 219
Recognizing Hyphens That Join Words 220
Editing Hyphens That Join Words 220
Editing Hyphens That Divide Words 221

12j Spelling 221
Using the Computer to Proofread for Spelling 221
Recognizing and Editing Spelling Errors 221

12k Other Marks and Conventions 223
Recognizing and Editing Parentheses 224
Recognizing and Editing Dashes 224
Recognizing and Editing Brackets 224
Recognizing and Editing Ellipses 225
Recognizing and Editing Slashes 225
Recognizing and Editing End Marks 226
Recognizing and Editing Electronic Addresses 227
Combining Marks 227

Chapter 13 GRAMMAR AT A GLANCE 229

How Can You Recognize a Sentence? 229
How Do Sentence Patterns Work? 230
    Five Basic Predicate Structures 230
    Four Sentence Structures 230
    Four Sentence Purposes 231
What Are the Principal Parts of Verbs? 231
What Are the Tenses of Verbs in the Active Voice? 231
    Present, Past, and Future (Showing Simple Actions) 232
    Present, Past, and Future Perfect (Showing Order of Events) 232
    Present, Past, and Future Progressive (Showing Action
      in Progress) 232
    Present, Past, and Future Perfect Progressive (Showing the
      Duration of Action in Progress) 233
How Can You Recognize Active and Passive Verbs? 233
What Are Verbal Phrases? 233
What Are the Forms of Some Common Irregular Verbs? 234
What Do Pronouns Do? 234
What Are the Forms of Comparatives and Superlatives? 235
    Adjectives 235
    Adverbs 235
    Negative Comparisons (Adjectives and Adverbs) 235
    Irregular forms 236

Chapter 14 QUICK TIPS FOR WRITERS, READERS, AND SPEAKERS 237

    Tips for Academic Writers 237
    Taking It Online 237
    Tips for Workplace Writers 238
    Taking It Online 238
    Tips for Public Writers 238
    Taking It Online 239
    Tips for Readers 239
    Taking It Online 240
    Tips for Speakers 240
    Taking It Online 241
    Tips for Collaborative Writers 241
    Taking It Online 242
    Tips for Online Writers 242

Taking It Online   243
Tips for Online Researchers   243
Taking It Online   243

Appendix: Glossary of Manuscript Style   245

Abbreviations   245
Accent Marks   245
Ampersand   245
Arabic Numerals   246
Bullets, Numbers, and Indented Lists   247
Capitalization   247
Comma   247
Figures and Tables   248
Foreign Cities   248
Headings   248
Indenting   248
Margins   249
Monetary Units   249
Names of Persons   249
Numbering Pages   250
Roman Numerals   250
Running Heads   250
Shortened Titles in the Text   250
Spacing   250
Titles within Titles   250
Underscoring (Italicizing)   251
Word Division   251

Glossary of Usage and Terms   253

Symbols for Revising and Editing   267

Index   269

Why You Need This Handbook

WHY YOU NEED THIS HANDBOOK

Four words of advice: don't sell this book! At the end of every semester, students typically sell some of their books back to the bookstore. This is one book you will want to keep throughout your undergraduate years. You will use this book not only in your freshmen composition courses but also in courses you take across the curriculum and in your major. So, keep it on your bookshelf next to your dictionary for handy consultation. And remember, you don't have to rely on this book alone for help with your writing. John Jay has a writing center, a Learning Enhancement Center and a Center for English language Support (CELS), all staffed with skilled tutors who can work with you to improve your writing or to handle a particularly difficult assignment. So use all the guides available to you—print and human—to succeed as a student writer at John Jay College.

Jane P. Bowers, Ph.D.
Provost

In the last few years the college has taken on a number of initiatives aimed at invigorating the writing and research strengths of our students. From a revision of the curriculum for the composition courses, to the Subway Series on-line writing project, to the increased focus on Writing Intensive Courses, to the annual publication of the best student writing in *John Jay's Finest*, all of our students have access to and are required to fulfill a broad and productive set of writing experiences. This increased focus on writing is a profoundly important change, as students' success in college and in subsequent careers is more than ever tied to their ability to control language, to relay what they know in spoken and written words, and to write and read words in an ever more complex literacy landscape.

As we continue to focus on advancing our students' literacy in the era of hypertext, tweets and interactive media, our John Jay Handbook remains a crucial piece of the support mechanisms students need to achieve success in writing and research. Regardless of where, how and what they write, all good writers have resources they turn to for direction when writing something new, or as a reference text when under deadline, or as a way to answer a nagging question about a single sentence's structure. This handbook provides that steady and versatile resource for all of our student writers.

As a required purchase, it also offers faculty in all disciplines a way to quickly and actively direct students to focus on particular writing issues by referencing a section in the handbook. If the handbook is consistently introduced and referenced by faculty in all disciplines at John Jay, the students will come to see the handbook as a useful tool to enhance their writing.

I encourage all John Jay faculty and students to use the John Jay Handbook early and often.

Anne Lopes, Ph.D.
Dean of Undergraduate Studies

How do you get to graduation day? You write your way there. From the first class to the last, college students have to reveal what they know, express their ideas, discuss what they believe, explain their research, design what can work, and show their vision of the world—all in written words! This handbook will help you gain control of the language and the writing process you need to be able to tell your stories to the waiting audience of your peers, your faculty and to the world beyond the walls of John Jay.

Writing well is hard work, but it doesn't have to be lonesome work. As with many of the support services for writing we offer to students, this writing resource attempts to dispel the myth of the single writer going blow-for-blow with the blank page. Writing time doesn't have to be frustrating, unhappy and too often unproductive work. The handbook takes away the mystery of what to write, how to begin, where to research, what to revise, and how to edit and proofread. Ultimately, especially when used in conjunction with a class, the handbook can lessen the pain and increase the gain of writing sessions.

By purchasing this book, you are making the first of many steps toward college writing success.

Tim McCormack
Director of Writing Programs

Welcome to John Jay College! For freshmen, college can seem overwhelming in so many ways. As the director of First Year Experience, I have watched many new students struggle with the amount and quality of writing they have to do in the first year. The John Jay Handbook is one way to relieve some of the stress you may feel as you approach assignments that are radically different than high school. The handbook offers advice and methods for all steps of the writing process from the first thought to the last correction. It also can be used as a reference text for grammar, citation style and paper format.

The John Jay Handbook is one of a number of valuable resources available to you to help you make a smart start to your college experience. The First year Experience office sponsors other writing initiatives that can also help you make a smart start to college. The Subway Series offers you a chance to win prizes by completing writing assignments: http://johnjay.jjay.cuny.edu/subway. We also host an active blogspot where students can read and write about their first year at John Jay and offer support to each other during this exciting time. Join the blog at: http://www.myfirstyearatjohn jay.blogspot.com. To find out more about the programs and services we offer to help you make a smooth transition to college life academically and socially visit us in person in room 100 of the Westport building or "friend us" on Facebook.

Kate Szur
Director of First Year Experience

Although it is unlikely that any handbook can answer all the composing conundrums a student may face, this handbook should offer undergraduates a place to consult, self assess, and question their writing and research competencies. As students continually develop their writing abilities, this handbook can help them understand what they know and don't know about their composing abilities. Using the handbook as a useful point of departure, students can then direct their more specific challenges to the appropriate tutor, mentor or faculty member. In the end, this handbook also offers faculty useful teaching resources to help their students over the difficult humps of learning and writing. Concurrently, when instructors identify a student's challenge, they can direct students to the handbook section that will resolve their difficulty.

The John Jay Handbook, required of all incoming freshmen, is a productive resource for the college, which as an academic community is by definition a writing community.

Professor Mark McBeth, Ph.D.
English Department

This handbook represents an attempt to create a standard manual on writing and stylistic form for all John Jay College students to use throughout their college years and in classes throughout the curriculum. The handbook was also designed with the hope that it could be equally valuable to John Jay faculty, as a common writing resource to be assigned in their courses.

The handbook marks an important innovation at the college, one that we hope will strengthen student writing throughout the curriculum for years to come. It is also symbolic of the power of faculty and staff dialogue and collaboration, and the potential that can develop from such collaborations.

Professor Jose Luis Morin, JD
Latin American and Latina/o Studies

JOHN JAY COLLEGE COMPOSITION COURSES

There are three writing courses in the composition sequence at John Jay College.

ENGW 100: Literacy Inquiries

This course introduces students to the literacy skills, habits, and conventions necessary to succeed at college-level work. While offering students techniques and practices of invention and revision, the course also teaches the students the historical and educational aspects of literacy as a scholarly topic.

ENG 101 College Composition I: Exploration and Authorship: An Inquiry-Based Writing Course

This composition course introduces students to the skills, habits, and conventions necessary to prepare inquiry-based research for college. While offering students techniques and practices of invention and revision, this theme-based composition course teaches students the expectations of college-level research, academic devices for exploring ideas, and rhetorical strategies for completing investigative writing.

ENG 201: Composition II: Disciplinary Investigations: Exploring Writing Across the Disciplines

This composition course introduces students to the rhetorical characteristics of cross-disciplinary writing styles. Instructors choose a single theme and provide students with reading and writing assignments that address the differing literacy conventions and processes of diverse fields. Students learn how to apply their accumulated repertoire of aptitudes and abilities to the writing situations presented to them from across the disciplines.

Progression

Entering students are placed into the appropriate writing course based on a placement exam (CUNY Assessment Test in Writing) or other qualifying factors.

To move from one level of composition to the next level requires a passing grade in the previous course.

All John Jay students must also pass the CUNY Proficiency Examination (CPE) between 60 and 75 credits.

JOHN JAY COLLEGE WRITING CENTER

2450 North Hall   212.237.8569
http://web.jjay.cuny.edu/~writing/

The writing center is a free service offered to all matriculated undergraduate and graduate students of John Jay College of Criminal Justice who desire assistance in writing. Any student of any level of ability or from any discipline may come to the Writing Center for help from our trained tutors. The Writing Center offers these services:

- One-on-one tutoring with trained and experienced peer tutors.
- Workshops on writing for specific academic situations (i.e. the response paper)
- Workshops on writing for specific disciplines (i.e. Literature, Sociology)
- Workshops on specific writing topics (i.e. using quotes, making an argument)
- Workshops to prepare for CUNY exams (i.e. ACT, CAAW, and CPE)
- CUNY Proficiency Exam (CPE) Tutorials
- Workshops on writing for your career (i.e. cover letter and resume)
- Synchronous On-line tutoring

Since tutors strive to develop and improve the writing abilities of their tutees, the Writing Center recommends long-term tutoring one or more times per week for a part of the semester or for an entire semester or more. Although some hours are reserved for "walk-ins," the best way for students to use the center is to plan to attend a number of sessions on a regular basis. The ideal situation is for students to come to the Writing Center and arrange appointments when a paper is first assigned to them or use weekly appointments to focus on particular writing issues.

JOHN JAY COLLEGE CENTER FOR ENGLISH LANGUAGE SUPPORT (CELS)

1201 North Hall   Phone: 212.237.8231
http://web.jjay.cuny.edu/~esl/

Students who learned English as a second language can use the free services of the Center for English Language Support (CELS).

- Individual tutoring in academic writing and grammar from instructors who have a Master's degree in Teaching English as a Second Language
- Workshops on academic reading and writing, grammar, and oral presentations
- Computer programs for learning grammar and vocabulary
- Advice and Counseling for ESL students
- Interactive, online tutorials on the E-Resource Center (http://jjc.jjay.cuny.edu/erc/)

    The E-Resource Center has tutorials for: writing, grammar, CUNY Assessment Tests in Writing and Reading and the CUNY Proficiency Exam (CPE), and for specific courses (Sociology 101, Criminal Justice 01, and Government 101).

The English Department offers reading and writing courses for students who are learning English as a Second Language (ESL).

CELS helps place students into these English courses.

- English for Academic Purposes (EAP) 121
- English for Academic Purposes (EAP) 131
- English (ENGW) 100, Section for Non-Native Speakers

Students need to complete ENGW 100 (or get special permission from their instructor) before they can re-take the CUNY Assessment Test in Writing.

Once students have passed the CUNY Assessment Test in Writing, they can continue with the composition sequence by taking the required English courses, English 101 and English 201. Alternatively, students can fulfill the same requirement by taking the ESL versions of these courses.

- English 101 / Section for Non-Native Speakers
- English 201 / Section for Non-Native Speakers

These courses are identical in content to all other sections, however, they are taught by faculty with advanced training to work with ESL students. Students who would like to register for these sections should contact the Director of CELS, Christopher Davis at cdavis@jjay.cuny.edu.

1

Writing and Reading

WRITING AND READING IN COMMUNITIES   1

DEVELOPING A THESIS   5

PROVIDING SUPPORT AND REASONING CLEARLY   6

PARAGRAPHING FOR READERS   8

MATCHING STYLE AND STRATEGY TO A COMMUNITY OF READERS   11

DESIGNING DOCUMENTS FOR READERS   13

CONSTRUCTING AN ARGUMENT   16

Voices
from the Community

"Every story is an act of trust between a writer and a reader; each story, in the end, is social. Whatever a writer sets down can harm or help the community of which he or she is a part." —Barry Lopez, "A Voice,"
About This Life: Journeys on the Threshold of Memory

1a Writing and Reading in Communities

Writing grows from the relationship between writers and readers. Whether you are drafting a history paper, a memo at work, or a neighborhood flyer, try to envision the **community of readers and writers** you are addressing—people with shared, though not necessarily identical, interests, goals, and preferences. Their expectations help you decide how best to shape ideas, information, and experiences you want to share with them.

1

Participating in academic, work, and public communities means talking, reading, and especially writing. As you communicate in these broad communities, you'll find that they share some preferences— such as favoring clear, specific writing—and differ on others, such as addressing the reader as *you*. Understanding such preferences can help you recognize readers' expectations and likely responses as well as writers' opportunities and choices.

Understanding Your Writing Situation

Begin by "reading" your situation, often a specific task, occasion, project, or assignment.

- What is your purpose? What do you want or need to achieve?
- How will you relate to readers? What will they expect?
- What is your subject? What do you know, or need to know, about it?

STRATEGY   Pinpoint your writing task.

Look over your task or assignment. Draw a straight line under words (usually nouns) that specify a **topic.** Put a wavy line under action words (verbs) that tell what your writing needs to *do*, its **purpose.**

> **Assignment:** Analyze a magazine ad for hidden cultural assumptions. Describe what happens in the ad, noting camera angle, color, and focus.

Whatever your task and whatever your broad community (academic, work, or public), you need to address your specific readers, actual or potential. Always ask, "Exactly what do my readers expect?"

STRATEGY   Analyze your readers.

> **Who?** How large is your audience? How well do you know them? Are they close or distant?
>
> **Expectations?** Which expectations of readers are typical of the community in which you are writing?

THREE COMMUNITIES OF READERS AND WRITERS			
	ACADEMIC	**WORK**	**PUBLIC**
GOALS	Create or exchange knowledge	Solve problems, inform, promote	Persuade, participate, inform
FORMS	Analysis, interpretation, lab report, proposal, article, bibliography	Memo, letter, ad, report, minutes, proposal, instructions	Letter, flyer, newsletter, position, paper, fact sheet
WRITING CHARACTERISTICS	Reasoning, analysis, insights, evidence, detail, fair exploration	Clarity, accuracy, conciseness, focus on problem	Advocacy, evidence, shared values, recognition of others

Knowledge? What are your readers likely to know about your topic? What do they want or need to know?

Background? What defines your readers socially, culturally, or educationally? How do they think?

Relationships? Are your readers peers or superiors? What do they expect you to do? What do you expect them to do?

Moving from Reading to Writing

Good writing is often inspired by what others have written. Critical reading techniques will help you understand a text and respond to it by developing your own ideas and insights.

Reading Critically

Critical reading begins with understanding that leads to analysis and interpretation. Before you begin reading, review the table of contents, abstract, or headings. Scan the text for key ideas and concepts. Note any background information about the author, the intended audience, or the occasion for which the text was written.

As you read, draw on the following techniques.

- Skim each section after you have read it, reviewing major points and their connections.
- Take note of what you have learned and what you find puzzling or confusing. Reread at a later time to clarify your understanding.
- Try to sum up or restate the text's main points or ideas in your own words.
- List the major insights, opinions, or ideas.

During and after reading, interact with a text in ways that help you develop your own insights and ideas.

STRATEGY Interact with a text.

- **Question.** What do you want or need to know?
- **Synthesize.** How does the text relate to other views? What other views does it acknowledge (or fail to anticipate)?
- **Interpret.** What does the writer mean or imply? What do you conclude about the text's outlook or bias?
- **Assess.** How do you evaluate its value and accuracy? How does it compare to other texts being read in the community?

Turning Reading into Writing

Try putting your responses to a text into informal kinds of writing that you can later develop into essays or reports. Some techniques include the following.

- **Marginal comments.** In the margins of a text (if it belongs to you) or on a photocopy, write your interpretations, questions, objections, evaluations, or applications (to a class, service learning project, civic activity, or work task).

- **Journal entries.** In a journal or on note cards, respond to your reading, noting what you think or where you agree or disagree with the author.

Paying Attention to the Writing Process

Experienced writers know that paying attention to all parts of the writing process generally leads to more effective writing.

Discovering and Planning

To identify and develop a promising topic, use techniques such as these.

- **Freewrite** quickly by hand or at the computer for five or ten minutes. Don't stop; just slip into engaging ideas.
- Try **focused freewriting,** exploring a specific idea.
- Ask **strategic questions** to stir memories and suggest what to gather. Begin with *what, why,* and *why not.* Next try *who, where, when, how.*
- Use **interactive prompts** from the Web, computer lab, tutoring center, or your software.

To focus and organize your writing, try the following strategies. They can help you create a design or structure to guide your drafting.

- Try **clustering.** Write an idea at the center of a page, and jot down random associations. Circle key ideas; add lines to connect them.
- **List ideas and details** you want to discuss.
- **Chunk** related points and material in computer files (organized by topic or by section of the paper).
- Consider a **formal outline** (numbered and lettered sections) or a **working outline** (introduction, body, conclusion) to order points.

Drafting

Begin drafting once you have a main idea (or **thesis**) and a general structure. Draft quickly; don't worry about perfect sentences. Or try **semidrafting,** writing until you stall out, noting *etc.* or a list instead of full text, and moving on to the next point.

Revising, Editing, Proofreading

Revision means critically *reading* and *reworking.* It precedes **editing** to fine-tune sentences or **proofreading** to check for small errors.

> **REVISING, EDITING, AND PROOFREADING**
>
> **Major revision.** Redraft passages, reorganize, add, and delete.
>
> **Minor revision.** Adopt a reader's point of view. Rework illogical, wordy, or weak passages.
>
> **Collaborative revision.** Ask peers to suggest improvements.
>
> **Editing.** Improve clarity, style, and economy; check grammar, sentence structure, wording, punctuation, and mechanics.
>
> **Proofreading.** Focus on details and final appearance, especially spelling, punctuation, and typing errors.

1b   Developing a Thesis

Most writing needs a clear **thesis**—a main idea, insight, or opinion that you wish to share. Announcing it in a **thesis statement** helps readers follow your reasoning and helps you organize and maintain focus.

Creating a Thesis Statement

You may choose to state your thesis near the beginning to guide readers, perhaps after introducing your topic and giving any needed background. Begin with a **rough thesis,** a sentence (or two) that identifies your perspective and states your assertion, conclusion, or opinion.

VAGUE TOPIC	Ritalin
STILL A TOPIC	The use of Ritalin for kids
STILL A TOPIC (NO ASSERTION)	Problems of Ritalin for kids with attention-deficit disorder (ADD)
	READER'S REACTION: But what should parents do?
ROUGH THESIS (ASSERTION)	Parents should be careful about Ritalin for kids with ADD.

Extend a rough thesis, making it more precise and complex. For example, what stance should parents take: Avoid Ritalin? Use it cautiously?

EXTENDED THESIS	Although Ritalin is widely used to treat children with ADD, parents should not rely too heavily on such drugs until they have explored both their child's problem and all treatment options.

STRATEGY   Sharpen your thesis until your final draft.

Treat your thesis as tentative. Refine it to offer a clear assertion—focused, limited, and yet complex enough to warrant readers' attention.

Designing an Appropriate Thesis

Refine your thesis to suit your purpose or readers.

General Thesis

Readers will expect to discover your conclusions or special perspectives.

Sooner or later, teenagers stop listening to parents and turn to each other for advice, sometimes with disastrous results.

Informative Thesis

Readers will expect to learn why this information is of interest and how you'll organize it.

When students search for online advice about financial aid, they can find help on three very different kinds of Web sites.

Argumentative Thesis

Readers will expect your opinion, perhaps with other views on the issue, too.

Although bioengineered crops may pose some dangers, their potential for combating worldwide hunger justifies their careful use.

Academic Thesis

Readers will expect you to state your specific conclusion and a plan to support it in terms that fit the field.

My survey of wedding announcements in local newspapers from 1960 to 2000 indicates that religious background and ethnicity have decreased in importance as factors in mate selection.

1c   Providing Support and Reasoning Clearly

Whether exploring an academic topic, making a recommendation at work, or urging people to take a stand on an issue, the path your thinking takes is called a **chain of reasoning.** Readers will find your writing logical and convincing if it's careful and critical, providing details and support suitable for your subject, purpose, and community.

Reasoning Critically

What processes support critical reasoning?

- Exploring a question, problem, or experience
- Uniting ideas and information to reach a conclusion
- Focusing on the end point of the chain of reasoning—the main conclusion—often your thesis statement

> **TYPES OF CONCLUSIONS YOU MIGHT DRAW**
>
> **Interpretations** of meaning (experience, literature, film), importance (current event, history), or causes and effects (problem, event)
>
> **Analyses** of elements (problem, situation, phenomenon, subject)
>
> **Propositions** about an issue, problem, or policy
>
> **Judgments** about "rightness" or "wrongness" (action, policy), quality (performance, creative work), or effectiveness (solution, course of action)
>
> **Recommendations** for guidelines, policies, or responses
>
> **Warnings** about consequences of action or inaction

CRITICAL REASONING IN THREE MAJOR COMMUNITIES			
	ACADEMIC	**WORK**	**PUBLIC**
GOAL	Analysis of text, phenomenon, or creative work to interpret, explain, or offer insights	Analysis of problems to supply information and propose solutions	Participation in democratic processes to contribute, inform, or persuade
REASONING PROCESS	Detailed reasoning leading to specific conclusions	Accurate analysis of problem or need with clear explanation of solution	Plausible reasoning to support own point of view without ranting
EVIDENCE	Specific references to detailed evidence, with citations of others' work	Sufficient evidence to show the problem's importance and justify a solution	Relevant evidence, often local, to substantiate views and probabilities
EXAMPLE	Present and support new explanation of Alzheimer's	Describe marketing strategy for Alzheimer's drug	Propose new community facility for Alzheimer's patients

STRATEGY   Focus on your conclusions.

List all your conclusions, interpretations, or opinions. What others come to mind? Which are main and which secondary? What explanation or evidence connects these points? Does each lead logically to the next?

Providing Support

A convincing chain of reasoning gives readers information that supports generalizations. **Information** includes facts of all kinds—examples, data, details, quotations—that you present as reliable, confirmable, or generally undisputed. **Generalizations** are conclusions based on and supported by information. Information turns into **evidence** when it's used to persuade a reader that an idea is reasonable.

> **TYPES OF EVIDENCE**
>
> **Examples** of an event, idea, person, or place, brief or extended, from personal experience or research
>
> **Details** of an idea, place, situation, or phenomenon
>
> **Information** about times, places, participants, numbers, consequences, surroundings, and relationships
>
> **Statistics,** perhaps presented in tables or charts
>
> **Background** on context, history, or effects
>
> **Quotations** from experts, participants, or other writers

Evaluating Support

Assess evidence critically. How **abundant** is it? Is it **sufficient** to support conclusions? Is it **relevant, accurate,** and **well documented?**

STRATEGY Align your evidence with your thesis.

General thesis. Supply evidence that fits your claim and readers' expectations: statistics, interviews, examples from experience.

Informative thesis. Give evidence showing a subject's elements.

Argumentative thesis. Supply information, examples, and quotations to support your stand, answer objections, and refute opposing views.

Academic thesis. Provide evidence that meets the discipline's standards; cite contributions of others.

1d Paragraphing for Readers

Every time you indent to begin a new paragraph, you signal academic, workplace, or public readers to watch for a shift in topic or emphasis.

Focusing Paragraphs

A **focused paragraph** has a clear topic and main idea that guide readers through the specifics of your discussion.

STRATEGY Check your paragraph focus.

- What is your main point in this paragraph?
- How many different ideas does it cover?
- Does it elaborate on the main idea? Do details fit?
- Have you announced your focus to readers? Where?

Help readers recognize a paragraph's focus by stating your topic and main idea or perspective in a **topic sentence.** Place this sentence at a paragraph's end, leave it unstated but clearly implied, or add a clarifying sentence to explain further. When you want readers to grasp the point right away, put this sentence first.

> When writing jokes, it's a good idea to avoid vague generalizations. Don't just talk about "fruit" when you can talk about "an apple." Strong writing creates a single image for everyone in the crowd, each person imagining a very similar thing. But when you say "fruit," people are either imagining several different kinds of fruit or they aren't really thinking of anything in particular, and both things can significantly reduce their emotional investment in the joke. But when you say "an apple," everyone has *a clear picture*, and thus a feeling.
>
> —Jay Sankey, "Zen and the Art of Stand-Up Comedy"

Making Paragraphs Coherent

A paragraph is **coherent** if each sentence leads clearly to the next, forming an easy-to-understand arrangement. When sentences are out of logical order or jump abruptly, readers may struggle to follow the thought.

STRATEGY   Check your paragraph coherence.

- Does the paragraph repeat key words and synonyms naming the topic and main points? Do these words begin or end sentences, or are they buried in the middle?
- What transition words relate sentences?
- What parallel structures emphasize similar ideas?
- Are ideas and details arranged logically?

Place key words to keep readers aware of the arrangement of ideas.

> **People married for a long time** often develop similar **facial features. Younger couples** display only chance resemblances between their **faces.** Because **they** share emotions for many years, however, **older couples** acquire similar **expressions.**

USEFUL TRANSITIONS FOR SHOWING RELATIONSHIPS

Time and sequence: next, later, after, meanwhile, while, immediately, earlier, first, second, third, shortly, in the future, subsequently, soon, since, finally, last, as long as, at that time

Comparison: likewise, similarly, also, again, in comparison

Contrast: in contrast, on the one hand . . . on the other hand, however, although, yet, but, nevertheless, at the same time, regardless

Examples: for example, for instance, such as, thus, namely, specifically, to illustrate

Cause and effect: as a result, consequently, due to, for this reason, accordingly, if . . . then, as a consequence

Place: next to, above, behind, beyond, between, here, there, opposite, to the right, in the background, over, under

Addition: and, too, moreover, in addition, besides, next, also, finally

Concession: of course, naturally, granted, it is true that, certainly

Conclusion: in conclusion, as a result, as the data show

Repetition: in other words, once again, to repeat

Summary: on the whole, to sum up, in short, therefore

Developing Paragraphs

Paragraph development provides the informative examples, facts, details, explanations, or arguments readers expect to support a conclusion.

UNDERDEVELOPED

Recycling is always a good idea—or almost always. Recycling some products, even paper, may require more energy from fossil fuels and more valuable natural resources than making them the first time.

READER'S REACTION: I need to know more before I agree. Which products? How much energy does recycling take? What resources are consumed?

STRATEGY Check your paragraph development.

Highlight the material that develops your paragraph. Do you present enough to *inform* readers? Do you adequately *support* generalizations?

Patterns for development help you accomplish tasks in ways that readers will easily recognize.

PATTERNS FOR PARAGRAPH DEVELOPMENT

Narrating: tell a story or anecdote; recreate events
Describing: provide detail about a scene, object, character, or feeling
Comparing and contrasting: explore similarities or differences; evaluate alternatives
Explaining a process: provide directions; explain how a mechanism, procedure, or natural process operates
Dividing: separate into parts; explore their relationships
Classifying: sort into groups; explain their relationships
Defining: explain a term; illustrate a concept
Analyzing causes and effects: consider why something did or might happen

Matching Style and Strategy to a Community of Readers

Should you use *I* or *we*—or *you*? Should you add technical terms? Such choices depend less on your "voice" than on **community style**—preferences taken for granted by communities of readers and writers. Likewise, the goals and strategies you choose should reflect an understanding of the community of writers and readers you are addressing.

Recognizing a Community's Style

Consider the following to help you understand your options as a writer.

Formality

Do readers expect writing that is formal, complicated, and technical or relaxed and direct?

Writer's Stance

How do writers identify themselves, readers, and the topic: *I, we, you, he, she, it, they*?

Language

What **diction**—word choices—do readers favor: vivid or neutral phrases, logical or informal links, technical or everyday terms?

STYLE IN THREE MAJOR COMMUNITIES			
	ACADEMIC	**WORK**	**PUBLIC**
FORMALITY	Formality supports analytical approach and values of the field	Informality reflects or builds teamwork or closeness	Informality reveals personal involvement with serious issues
WRITER'S STANCE	Observer (*he, she, it*) or participant (*I, we*)	Team member (*we*) with personal concern (*I, you*)	Involved person (*I, you*) or representative (*we, you*)
LANGUAGE	Technical terms and methods of the field	Plain or technical terms but little vivid, figurative wording	Lively and emotional; few technical terms and little slang
DISTANCE	Objective and dispassionate, not personal or emotional	Supportive, committed closeness with mutual respect	Passionate and personal about cause, issue, or group
EXAMPLE	Presentation of data and findings from experiment	Instructions for new marketing campaign	Pamphlet encouraging people to join recycling program

Distance

Is a writer typically distant or involved, an insider or outsider, a participant or observer?

Adjusting to a Community's Style

Examine your community's style as you read typical documents. For example, academic writers tend to rely on formal analysis using a discipline's terms and methods. Often distant observers, they may use *I*, depending on the field, but seldom address readers directly. In contrast, work communities share values such as efficiency and service, often using *we* to build teamwork. In public exchanges, writers may be dedicated partisans, speaking individually (*I*) or collectively (*we*).

Recognizing a Community's Expectations

The strategies you employ in your writing should take into account your audience's expectations. The following tips may help you understand the ways readers approach your work and the ways you can address their expectations.

What Academic Readers Expect

In general, academic readers will ask you to do the following.

- Analyze or interpret a text or an event.
- Review and cite related theory and research.
- Reason logically and critically about a question.
- Bring fresh insights, and draw your own conclusions.

> **STRATEGY**   Tips for academic writing.
> - State your thesis and main points clearly.
> - Use pertinent detail to support your views.
> - Write clearly and logically, even on a complex topic.
> - Acknowledge other views as you explore a topic.

What Workplace Readers Expect

Workplace readers will expect your writing to accomplish objectives such as these.

- Provide or request information
- Analyze problems
- Recommend actions or solutions
- Identify and evaluate alternatives

STRATEGY Tips for workplace writing.

- Focus on the task, problem, or goal.
- Present the issue clearly and accurately.
- Organize efficiently, and summarize for busy readers.
- Use concise, clear, direct prose.

What Public Readers Expect

Members of an organization, possible supporters of a cause, public officials, community activists, local residents, and other public audiences will look to you to do the following.

- Provide issue-oriented information, especially local background, data, and evidence.
- Encourage civic involvement and decision making.
- Persuade others to support a cause or issue.

STRATEGY Tips for public writing.

- Persuade, enlighten, alert, or energize readers to act.
- Recommend policies, actions, or solutions.
- Be an advocate for your cause.
- Present relevant evidence to support your position.
- Recognize the interests and goals of others.

1f Designing Documents for Readers

What makes your research report, essay, or letter memorable—clear, persuasive, and easy to read? The answer often lies in document design, considering the look of the page or screen and the processes of readers.

Planning Your Document

To design effective documents, sketch sample pages containing design features or prepare a list of specifications that answers these questions.

- What kind of format or document do my readers expect?
- How will I lay out the pages?
- How will I highlight the organization? Will I provide a table of contents? Will I use color?
- What font, typeface, and type size will I use?
- Will I integrate visual aids? Which ones?
- What are the copyright or legal issues when using others' materials?

Laying out Your Document

Layout is the arrangement of words, sentences, lists, tables, graphs, and pictures on a printed page or screen. Supply visual cues for readers, but don't overwhelm your text.

STRATEGY   Highlight to direct the reader's eye.

- Use **boldface**, *italics*, shading, <u>rules</u>, and boxes to signal distinctions, to connect, and to divide.
- Set off items in lists with numbers, letters, or bullets.
- Use CAPITALS, exclamation points (!!), and other cues sparingly for emphasis. Limit <u>underlining</u> (especially in Web pages with links).
- Use color to meet goals (such as warning), prioritize, trace a theme or sequence, or code symbols.
- Leave **white space**—open space not filled by other design elements—to break dense text into chunks.

Headings are phrases that forecast content or structure. Often larger and darker, they catch a reader's eye and lead to information.

STRATEGY   Design useful headings.

- Orient headings to your task or readers: **Deducting Student Loan Interest,** not **Student Loans.**
- Position headings uniformly (for example, center one level but begin another at the left margin).
- Add white space between headings and text.
- Define heading levels consistently with visual features (font, style, position such as left margin or centered).
- Keep the wording of each level of heading parallel whenever possible.

Using Type Features

Consider readers' expectations as you judiciously use software options.

Type Size and Weight

Both 10- and 12-point type are easy to read; the latter is most common in academic papers. Save sizes above 12 points for special purposes (visuals, flyers, posters). Type weight (letter width and stroke thickness) can also be used to highlight.

8 point   10 point   12 point   16 point

Typefaces

Serif fonts have "little feet" or small strokes at the end of each letterform. Sans serif fonts lack them.

N   **Serif**   N   **Sans serif**

Readers tend to find serif type easier to read in text while sans serif works well in titles, headings, labels, and material onscreen. Reserve decorative fonts for brochures, invitations, or posters.

Using Visuals

Drawings, diagrams, and photographs can speed communication. **Tables** order text or numbers in columns and rows. **Graphs** rely on two labeled axes (vertical and horizontal), using lines or bars to relate variables. **Pie charts** show percentages of a whole.

STRATEGY   Integrate visuals with text.

- Choose simple visual aids that make a point; avoid decorative filler.
- Place a visual near related text; connect it verbally.
- Label all graphics as figures (except for tables), number them, and supply short, accurate captions.
- Credit sources for all borrowed graphics, and respect copyright.

Sample Documents

The following samples show document design in action.

Sample Academic Paper with Illustration, MLA Format

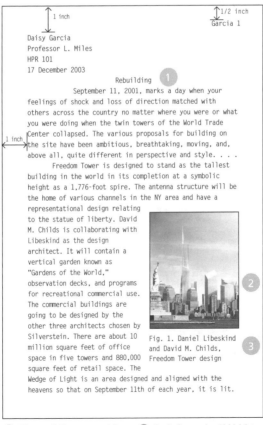

1 inch   1/2 inch
                                                          Garcia 1

Daisy Garcia
Professor L. Miles
HPR 101
17 December 2003

                        Rebuilding   ❶
            September 11, 2001, marks a day when your
feelings of shock and loss of direction matched with
others across the country no matter where you were or what
you were doing when the twin towers of the World Trade
Center collapsed. The various proposals for building on
1 inch ▶the site have been ambitious, breathtaking, moving, and,
above all, quite different in perspective and style. . . .
            Freedom Tower is designed to stand as the tallest
building in the world in its completion at a symbolic
height as a 1,776-foot spire. The antenna structure will be
the home of various channels in the NY area and have a
representational design relating
to the statue of liberty. David
M. Childs is collaborating with
Libeskind as the design
architect. It will contain a
vertical garden known as
"Gardens of the World,"
observation decks, and programs
for recreational commercial use.
The commercial buildings are
going to be designed by the
other three architects chosen by
Silverstein. There are about 10   Fig. 1. Daniel Libeskind
million square feet of office   and David M. Childs,
space in five towers and 880,000   Freedom Tower design
square feet of retail space. The
Wedge of Light is an area designed and aligned with the
heavens so that on September 11th of each year, it is lit.

❶ Title centered with no extra space before or after

❷ Integrates illustration next to discussion in text

❸ Supplies figure number with label that properly credits the artist, and identifies work's title and location or source

Sample Workplace Résumé

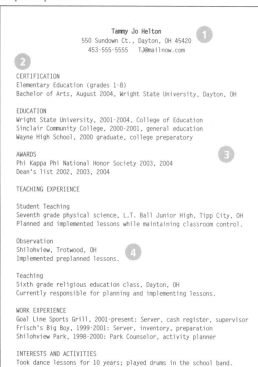

Tammy Jo Helton
550 Sundown Ct., Dayton, OH 45420
453-555-5555   TJ@mailnow.com

CERTIFICATION
Elementary Education (grades 1-8)
Bachelor of Arts, August 2004, Wright State University, Dayton, OH

EDUCATION
Wright State University, 2001-2004, College of Education
Sinclair Community College, 2000-2001, general education
Wayne High School, 2000 graduate, college preparatory

AWARDS
Phi Kappa Phi National Honor Society 2003, 2004
Dean's list 2002, 2003, 2004

TEACHING EXPERIENCE

Student Teaching
Seventh grade physical science, L.T. Ball Junior High, Tipp City, OH
Planned and implemented lessons while maintaining classroom control.

Observation
Shilohview, Trotwood, OH
Implemented preplanned lessons.

Teaching
Sixth grade religious education class, Dayton, OH
Currently responsible for planning and implementing lessons.

WORK EXPERIENCE
Goal Line Sports Grill, 2001-present: Server, cash register, supervisor
Frisch's Big Boy, 1999-2001: Server, inventory, preparation
Shilohview Park, 1998-2000: Park Counselor, activity planner

INTERESTS AND ACTIVITIES
Took dance lessons for 10 years; played drums in the school band.

References available on request.

1. Centers name, address, phone, and email address
2. Uses capitals for main headings
3. Separates page into sections using white space
4. Uses short lines for compressed information
5. Centers closing information

1g Constructing an Argument

In argumentative writing, you present and endorse an outlook, opinion, or course of action. You persuade by focusing on reasons, evidence, and values to encourage readers to agree with your opinion or proposal.

Identifying an Issue

At the heart of occasions calling for argumentative writing is an **issue,** that is, a topic about which you and your audience can recognize two (or more) clearly differing, worthwhile opinions. Many arguments address **existing issues,** ongoing disagreements about either

Sample Newsletter, Designed by Student

Thursday
July 8th, 2003

Volume XX
Issue 2

The Daily Moose

North America's Only Newspaper Devoted to Moose Lovers Everywhere. Twenty-Two Years and Growing

Big Moose Comes From Small Dreams

Staff Reporter: Andrea White

Growing up, your favorite animal may have been a cat, dog, or turtle. Even as exotic as parrots, giraffes and elephants. But in areas north of Chicago and Boston, children wish for pets like deer, caribou and even moose. Moose usually occupy areas in the northern United States and Canada, finding them in southern California is quite unusual. However, traveling to Orange County, California you might see dozens, even hundreds of these winter-weather giants. Mainly Seconds, a craft/antique store in Orange County, has a display of numerous moose paraphernalia all collected by the "Moose" himself, Mike Bonk.

In 1982, Mike's first store opened and received a gift from his wife and former employees. It was a corduroy moose head with a plaque inscribed, "The Moose is Loose". This present hangs on the wall near the entrance next to painted words, *The Moose Museum.* The museum started when Mike put his personal items on display around the store. It seemed that as the store increased and prospered, his collection did also. Soon there was so much moose collectibles, it formed itself into a museum.

This museum is not like any other. Set in the back section of the store, it consists of about fifty cases and 10 aisles of various products either resembling or being moose associated. "If it's moose, it's in here" Mike said during a recent interview. And it's true (Cont. on page 2).

The Moose Museum Located at Mainly Seconds.

*The Moose Museum
Cordially Invites You …*

To Explore the Wide
World of Moose

Come experience the
Northern Wilderness in
Sunny California.
New Exhibits! More Moose!

789 S. Tustin Avenue   555-9876

Warning: Moose X-ing

Travel columnist: Caroline Cesserta

My family and I always agonize about where to travel for our yearly summer vacation. This year, my daughter and I agreed on a nice mountain lodge in Colorado while my husband and other daughter sided on a tropical getaway to Mexico. To compromise, we decided to tour California starting from the Mexican border up to Oregon. One of my personal favorite spots is very unusual store I discovered when we were stopped at a rest stop and someone noticed my moose decal on the back window. (Cont. Pg. 2)

① Selects varied typefaces and sizes for a system of headings

② Uses single page column for lead story

③ Integrates photograph and text

④ Uses double-column format for additional text

⑤ Encloses highlighted text in oval "box"

broad issues (e.g., gun control or global warming) or specific concerns (e.g., a new campus drinking policy or local limits on development). To identify **potential issues,** try evaluating the consequences of a policy, questioning the "taken for granted" ("Do diesels always pollute?") or questioning widely held opinions (*Opinion:* Early decision programs benefit college applicants. *Response:* Do they really?)

	PUBLIC	WORK	ACADEMIC
GENERAL	Genetically altered foods Violence and sex on television	Child care at work Ethnically targeted marketing	Standardized testing Affirmative action in college admissions
LOCAL	A local crusade against a television series	Discipline policies at Abtech's ChildCare	Housing regulations at Nontanko River U

Developing an Argumentative Thesis

To argue effectively, you need to identify your own opinion (your **claim**) and communicate it to readers in an **argumentative thesis statement.**

Explore and Clarify Your Perspective

Begin by articulating your opinion to yourself to focus your ideas, values, and feelings. Write informally about your intuitive reactions to your chosen issue. Does the issue make you feel scorn, pity, fear, or outrage? List the specific elements of the issue to which you respond most strongly and sum up your responses. Identify facts, examples, and ideas that support your opinions. Then think about objections to your view, and list them.

Focus and Revise Your Claim

Limit the scope of your argument by identifying a specific claim and its purpose. Do you want to argue that an activity or belief is good or bad? If so, you are asking readers to agree with a **value judgment.** Do you want to persuade them to support a course of action? If so, you are asking them to agree with a **policy.** Do you want readers to agree with an explanation? If so, you are asking them to endorse an **interpretation.**

STRATEGY   State and revise your claim in memos to yourself.

Write a memo explaining the claim and your purpose for writing.

To: Self
From: Me

I find using roadblocks to catch drunk drivers really disturbing. I know it is important to keep drunk drivers off the road, but I think this remedy is extreme. I guess I want readers to agree that roadblocks violate civil liberties and should be banned.

Revise your claim to reflect what you discover through your research. Then write yourself a second memo.

Create (and Revise) a Thesis Statement

An explicit thesis makes your claim clear to readers and helps them follow your reasoning by

1. Identifying a specific issue and your opinion.
2. Providing a clear and logical statement of your argumentative claim.
3. Suggesting a general direction for your argument.
4. Indicating related claims or opinions.

STRATEGY Revise your thesis statement.

- **State your thesis** in a sentence (or two), using sentence patterns like "*X* should be altered/banned/approved because . . ."; "I propose this plan/ policy/action because . . ."; or "*Y* is beneficial/ineffective/harmful because . . ."
- **Check your tentative thesis** to see whether it blurs your specific purposes for arguing or makes illogical assumptions.

BLURRED AND ILLOGICAL	Police should stop conducting unconstitutional roadblocks and substitute more frequent visual checks of erratic driving to identify people who are driving while intoxicated.

- **Revise to focus** your thesis on a clear issue, a single claim, or two related claims you will argue in appropriate order.

SINGLE PROPOSITIONS	Roadblocks used to identify drunk drivers are unconstitutional because they violate important civil liberties.
	Frequent visual checks for erratic driving can effectively identify intoxicated drivers.

Developing Reasons and Supporting Evidence

To encourage readers to agree with your argumentative claim, you need to give them a series of reasons, each followed by evidence.

TENTATIVE THESIS	Coursework for certification should continue after people start teaching because this efficient approach can increase the number of dedicated new teachers.
REASON 1	People learn a skill or activity best while doing it.
	EVIDENCE: comparisons to medical internships and residencies; reports on innovative teacher training
REASON 2	Practicing teachers are often more motivated learners than are pre-service teachers.
	EVIDENCE: information from scholarly article comparing responses of participants in pre-service and in-service courses
REASON 3 (COUNTER-ARGUMENT)	New teachers will succeed in their first jobs, especially if their schools supervise and support them.

Varied evidence helps develop your reasons effectively by

- Providing logical justification for your opinions and reasoning.
- Encouraging readers to trust your conclusions and proposals and helping them understand your reasoning and connect it with their experiences and values.
- Helping readers envision a proposed course of action or new policy.

Examples from your own or others' experience—events, people, ideas, objects, feelings, stories, images, and texts—can support a claim and draw readers to your point of view. Quotations and ideas from authorities on a subject or issue add to the reasons for readers to agree with your point of view. Detailed information available on most issues includes statistics, technical information, results of surveys and interviews, background information, and historical detail. Visual evidence is of two kinds: (1) details, facts, and statistics in graphs, tables, or other figures, and (2) photographs or drawings that are evidence in themselves. Visuals can present complex evidence, highlight key points, and appeal to values and emotions. Coloring sections of a map red to indicate regions with severe environmental problems can make a powerful statement, for example.

Presenting Counterarguments

Traditional argument is like debate: you imagine an adversary who doesn't go along with your ideas and then you try to undermine that adversary's points or **counterarguments.** In most contemporary arguments, you should acknowledge alternate points of view not so much to "win" as to convince others of the validity of your views.

STRATEGY   Develop counterarguments.

Divide a sheet of paper into three columns. On the left, list the main points supporting your opinion. Write opposing points in the middle column as if you oppose your original stance. On the right, list possible defenses to these counterarguments. Note any sources that would support your argument.

Reasoning Logically

Effective argument assembles your opinions and supporting evidence in an order that reflects a chain of reasoning and avoids flaws in logic.

- **Reasoning from consequences.** You argue for or against an action or outlook, based on real or likely consequences, good or bad.
- **Reasoning from comparisons.** You argue for or against a policy or point of view based on similar situations, problems, or actions.
- **Reasoning from authority and testimony.** You draw evidence from recognized experts or from people with relevant experience.
- **Reasoning from examples and statistics.** You draw on events, situations, and problems presented as illustrations or as statistics.

Data-Warrant-Claim Reasoning

This form of reasoning, proposed by philosopher Stephen Toulmin, identifies several kinds of statements reasonable people make when they argue: *data* correspond to your evidence, *claim* to your conclusion, and *warrant* to the mental process by which a reader connects the data to the claim. It answers the question "How?"

Suppose you are examining the relative safety of cars. As data, you have a study on the odds of injury in different models of cars. To argue effectively, you need to show readers *how* the data and your claim are connected, what patterns (probable facts—warrants) link the data to your claim.

DATA
Ratings of each car model by likelihood of injury (scale: 1–10)

CLAIM
For the average consumer, buying a large car is a good way to reduce the likelihood of being injured in an accident.

WARRANT
- The cars in the ratings fall into three easily recognized groups: small, medium, large. (probable fact)
- The large cars as a group have a lower average likelihood of injury to passengers than either of the other groups. (probable fact)
- Although some other cars have low likelihood of injury, almost all the large cars seem safe. (assertion + probable fact)
- Few consumers will go over the crash ratings to see which models get good or poor scores. (assertion)

Logical and Emotional Appeals

Logical and emotional appeals can enhance your credibility as a writer if you take the time to consider your readers and arrange your reasons and evidence in ways that most people will accept as reasonable and convincing. Emotional strategies focus on the values, beliefs, and emotions that can engage readers and motivate them to care about an issue. However, such appeals are generally best accepted when they are also supported by logical strategies—reasoning based on likely good or bad consequences, relevant comparisons, authoritative experts, trustworthy testimony, pertinent illustrations, and statistics. Watch for logical fallacies or flaws in reasoning as you evaluate your evidence and shape your argument.

A **logical fallacy** is a flaw in reasoning that undermines your argument. Logical fallacies take some common forms.

- **Faulty Cause-Effect Relationship** (*post hoc, ergo propter hoc* reasoning—"after this, therefore because of this"): attempts to persuade you that because one event follows another, the first causes the second.

The increase in violence on television is making the crime rate soar.
READER'S REACTION: This *may* be true, but no evidence here links the two situations.

- **False Analogy:** compares two things that seem, but aren't, comparable.

Raising the speed limit is like offering free cocktails at a meeting of recovering alcoholics.
READER'S REACTION: I don't see the connection. Most drivers aren't recovering from an addiction to high-speed driving.

- **Red Herring:** distracts readers from the real argument.

Gun control laws need to be passed as soon as possible to decrease domestic violence and accidents. The people who think guns should not be controlled are probably criminals themselves.
READER'S REACTION: The second sentence doesn't follow logically or add support. It's just a distracting attack on people who disagree.

- **Ad Hominem:** attacks the person, not the issue.

Of course Walt Smith would support a bill to aid farmers—he owns several farms in the Midwest.
READER'S REACTION: I'd like to hear reactions to his ideas, please.

- **Begging the Question:** presents assumptions as facts.

Most people try to be physically fit; obviously, they fear getting old.
READER'S REACTION: I don't see any evidence that people fear aging—or that they are working on their physical fitness, either.

- **Circular Reasoning:** supports an assertion with the assertion itself.

The university should increase funding of intramural sports because it has a responsibility to back its sports programs financially.
READER'S REACTION: So the university should fund sports because it should fund sports?

Finding a Scholarly Topic

You will seldom go in search of a topic so much as you will focus a preexisting general subject, one given to you by the instructor or one that you have wanted to explore but had no reason for doing so. As you move from class to class, keep your focus on the issues of each course. A health class might suggest this topic to somebody who smokes and who has a family to worry about: "Secondhand Smoke: Is It a Firsthand Danger?" A literature instructor might require you to explore Nathaniel Hawthorne's fiction, which is nineteenth-century material, but you can make it contemporary: "Hester Prynne in the Twenty-First Century: Who Wears the Scarlet Letter Today?" Notice how two students focused their topics.

- Valerie Nesbitt-Hall saw a cartoon about a young woman saying to a man, "Sorry—I only have relationships over the Internet. I'm cybersexual." Although she laughed, Valerie knew she had discovered a good topic in "online romance." Upon investigation, she found her scholarly focus: Matching services and chat rooms are like the arranged marriages from years gone by.

- Jamie Johnston, while watching reports on the Iraqi War, noticed the bitterness of the fighting and the cruelty practiced on both sides of the conflict. Shocking to him was the abuse of prisoners by American forces. He raised a crucial question that pointed him toward his research: How can civilized people in this day and age act with such violence against fellow human beings? He began by investigating prehistoric warfare. Ultimately, his title expressed his thesis: "Prehistoric Wars: We've Always Hated Each Other."

These topics meet the expectations of composition instructors as well as those of instructors in health, sociology, political science, education, and many other disciplines. Consider the following list of possible topics:

EDUCATION:	The Visually Impaired: Options for Classroom Participation
POLITICAL SCIENCE:	The Impact of the Presidential Electoral College
HEALTH:	The Effects of Chemicals on Athletic Performance
SOCIOLOGY:	Parents Who Lie to Their Children: Psychological Consequences

2a Generating Ideas and Focusing the Subject

You can generate ideas for research and focus on the issues with a number of techniques:

- Relate your personal ideas to a scholarly problem.
- Talk with others.
- Examine electronic sources.
- Read textbooks and reference books.

Relating Your Personal Ideas to a Scholarly Problem

Draw on yourself for ideas, keep a research journal, ask yourself questions, and get comfortable with new terminology.

Personal Ideas

Draw on yourself for inspiration and direction. Contemplate the issues and generate ideas worthy of investigation. At a quiet time, begin writing, questioning, and pushing on the buttons of your mind for your feelings and attitudes. The research paper should reflect your thinking in response to the sources. It should not merely report what others have said. If possible, combine a personal interest with one aspect of your academic studies:

ACADEMIC SUBJECT:	Health, especially sports medicine
PERSONAL INTEREST:	Skiing
POSSIBLE TOPICS:	Protecting the Knees
	Therapy for Strained Muscles
	Skin Treatments

You might also consider social issues that affect you and your family:

ACADEMIC SUBJECT:	Education

PERSONAL INTEREST:	The behavior of my child in school
POSSIBLE TOPICS:	Calming Children Who Are Hyperactive
	Should Schoolchildren Take Medicine to
	Calm Their Hyperactivity?

Your cultural background can prompt you toward detailed research into your roots, your culture, and the mythology and history of your ethnic background:

ACADEMIC SUBJECT:	History
ETHNIC BACKGROUND:	Native Americans
PERSONAL INTEREST:	History of the Apache tribes
POSSIBLE TOPIC:	The Indian Wars from the Native
	American's Point of View

A Research Journal

Unlike a diary of personal thoughts about your daily activities or a journal of creative ideas, such as poems, stories, and scenarios, the research journal enables you to list issues, raise questions, create notes, and develop pieces of free writing. In fact, you should build the journal primarily with **free writing** as well as **keywords and phrases** that come to mind. These establish primary categories for your research. One student listed several terms and phrases about the use of midwives in the rural Southeastern mountains:

natural childbirth	disinfectants	recovery time
prenatal care	medicines	delivery
hardships	complications	sterilization
delivery problems	deaths	cost

In her research journal, she began writing notes on these topics, like this:

The cost of delivery by a midwife in the mother's home differs so greatly from the cost of a doctor and a hospital that we can only appreciate the plight of those using this procedure.

The research journal is also a place for preliminary outlining to find the major and minor issues, as shown here:

Midwives in the Rural Southeast Mountains

Preparation:	Delivery:	Recovery:	Cost:
prenatal care	natural childbirth	after delivery	one fee
sterilization	medicines	recovery time	
disinfectants	delivery techniques	deaths	

Questions

Asking questions in your research journal can focus your attention on primary issues, and your subsequent notes in answer to the questions can launch your investigation. For example, having read Henry Thoreau's essay "Civil Disobedience," one writer posed these questions:

What is civil disobedience?
Is dissent legal? Is it moral? Is it patriotic?
Is dissent a liberal activity? Conservative?
Should the government encourage or stifle dissent?
Is passive resistance effective?

Answering the questions can lead the writer to a central issue or argument, such as "Civil Disobedience: Shaping Our Nation."

Academic disciplines across the curriculum invite questions that might provoke a variety of answers and give focus to the subject, as with "sports gambling."

ECONOMICS:	Does sports gambling benefit a college's athletic budget? Does it benefit the national economy?
PSYCHOLOGY:	What is the effect of gambling on the mental attitude of the college athlete who knows that huge sums hang in the balance on his/her performance?
HISTORY:	Does gambling on sporting events have an identifiable tradition?
SOCIOLOGY:	What compulsion in human nature prompts people to gamble on athletic prowess?
POLITICAL SCIENCE:	What laws exist in this state for the control of illegal sports gambling? Are they enforced?

Terminology

Each discipline has its own terminology. For example, in researching a paper on retail marketing you might learn to refer to "the demographics" of a "target audience." In psychological research, you might learn to use the phrases "control group" and "experimental group." One student found essential words for her paper on diabetes:

diabetes	diabetes mellitus	glucose
insulin	metabolize	hyperglycemia
pancreas	ketoacidosis	ketones

She learned the meaning of each term and applied it properly in her paper, giving her work a scholarly edge.

Talking with Others to Find and Refine the Topic

Sometime early in your project, go outside yourself to get feedback on your possible topic and its issues. You can accomplish this task with personal interviews, participation in e-mail discussion groups, and, on a limited basis, in Internet chat forums.

Personal Interview

A personal interview, either face to face, by telephone, or by e-mail, allows you to consult with experts and people in your community for ideas and reactions to your subject. Explore a subject for key ideas while having coffee or a soda with a colleague, relative, or work associate. For example, Valerie Nesbitt-Hall researched online matchmaking. She knew of one married couple who had met while chatting on the Internet. She requested an interview by e-mail, secured it, and made that interview a vital part of her paper.

HINT: Casual conversations that contribute to your understanding of the subject need not be documented. However, a formal interview or an in-depth discussion with an expert demands credit in your text and a citation in the Works Cited page at the end of your paper.

Local E-mail Discussion Group

Many instructors establish e-mail discussion groups for their courses to meet the demands of special interest groups. These discussion boards are popular with online courses, especially those using the Blackboard software for course management. These are private sites reserved for class members and the instructors, so they focus on the specific interests of the group. Thus, you can get input from your peers as well as your instructor, and you can make pertinent queries about your subject matter.

Internet Discussion Group

During an online chat conversation, you might find a few ideas on your topic; however, *heed this warning:* participants use fictitious names, provide unreliable sources, are highly opinionated in most instances, and therefore *they cannot be quoted in your paper.* The best you might gain is marginal insight into the ideas of people who are often eccentric and who hide behind their anonymity.

Using Electronic Sources

The library is your best source for electronic articles. Start with the library's academic databases and its electronic book catalog. After that, search the World Wide Web. You might also examine CDs and videotapes.

Library Databases

Go to the reliable databases available through your library, such as InfoTrac, PsychINFO, UMI ProQuest, Electric Library, and EBSCO-host. You can reach these from remote locations at home or the dorm room by connecting to your library with your personal identification number. The library has monitored Internet sites filtered by editorial boards and peer review. Many articles on these databases appeared first in print. In many cases, you can read an abstract of the article before reading the full text. You can also print the article without going into the stacks. However, libraries vary in their access to electronic databases, so be sure to consult with the reference librarians.

Electronic Book Catalogs

Use your library's computerized index to find books, film, DVD holdings, and similar items. Entering a keyword, such as "George W. Bush," yields a listing of relevant books—in this case, books by and about the president. The book catalog does not index the titles to articles in magazines and journals, but it can tell you which periodicals are housed in the library and whether they are in a printed volume, on microforms, or in an electronic database (see immediately above). Instructors want you to consult books during your research, so follow these steps:

1. Enter a keyword, such as "nutrition," that will generate a reasonably sized list.
2. Examine the entries in detail, starting with the most recent, to find books related to your topic.
3. In the stacks, find and examine each book for relevance. *Tip*: While in the stacks examine nearby books, which may well treat the same subject.

World Wide Web

Articles on the Internet offer ideas about how other people approach the subject, and these ideas can help you refine your topic. Use the subject directory on a browser, such as Google, to probe from a general topic to specific articles (Health > Diseases > Blood disorders > Anemia). Use a keyword search when you already have a specific topic. Thus, entering the keyword "anemia" will send you immediately to various Web articles.

CD-ROM, DVD, VHS

Encarta, Electronic Classical Library, Compton's Interactive Encyclopedia, and other reference diskettes are available. Browsing at one of these sources will give you a good feel for the depth and strength of the subject and suggest a list of narrowed topics. Check with a librarian, a department office, and your instructor for disks and videos in a specialty area, such as mythology, poetry, or American history. These media forms can sometimes be found in local bookstores or purchased over the Internet.

Using Textbooks and Reference Books

Dipping into your own textbooks can reward you with topic ideas, and a trip to the library to examine books and indexes in the reference room can also be beneficial.

Library Books and Textbooks

With your working topic in hand, do some exploratory reading. Carefully examine the **titles** of books, noting key terminology. Search a book's **table of contents** for topics. A history book on the American Civil War might display these headings:

The Clash of Amateur Armies
Real Warfare Begins
The Navies
Confederate High-Water Mark

Perhaps the topic on peace proposals will spur your interest in all peace proposals—that is, how nations end wars and send their troops home safely.

Reference Books

If you do not have access to an electronic database, the printed indexes, such as the *Readers' Guide to Periodical Literature, Bibliographic Index,* and *Humanities Index,* categorize and subdivide topics by alphabetical order. Searching under a keyword or phrase usually leads to a list of critical articles on the subject, and studying the titles might suggest a narrowed topic. For example, looking under the heading "Single Mothers" might produce several possible topics, such as "Welfare Moms," "Single Motherhood," or "Racial Differentials in Child Support."

■■■ **HINT:** Topic selection goes beyond choosing a general category (e.g., "single mothers"). It includes finding a research-provoking issue or question, such as "The foster parent program seems to have replaced the orphanage system. Has it been effective?" That is, you need to take a stand, adopt a belief, or begin asking questions. For more information, see section 2c, "Drafting a Research Proposal."

2b   Writing a Thesis, Enthymeme, or Hypothesis

Usually, one central statement controls an essay's direction and content, so as early as possible, begin thinking in terms of a controlling idea. Each type shown below has a separate mission:

- A **thesis sentence** advances a conclusion the writer will defend: *Contrary to what some philosophers have advanced, human beings have always participated in wars.*
- An **enthymeme** uses a *because* clause to make a claim the writer will defend: *There has never been a "noble savage," as such, because even prehistoric human beings fought frequent wars for numerous reasons.*
- A **hypothesis** is a theory that must be tested in the laboratory, in the literature, and/or by field research to prove its validity: *Human beings are motivated by biological instincts toward the physical overthrow of perceived enemies.*

Each type is discussed next.

Thesis Statement

A thesis sentence expands your topic into a scholarly proposal, one that you will try to prove and defend in your paper. It does not state the obvious, such as "Langston Hughes was a great poet from Harlem." That sentence cannot provoke an academic discussion because readers know that any published poet has talent. The writer must isolate one issue by finding a critical focus, such as this one:

> Langston Hughes used a controversial vernacular language that paved the way for later artists, even today's rap musicians.

This sentence advances an idea that the writer can develop fully and defend with evidence. The writer has made a connection between the subject, Langston Hughes, and the focusing agent, vernacular language. A general thesis might state:

> Certain nutritional foods can prevent disease.

But note how your interest in an academic area can color the thesis:

> **HEALTH:** Nutritional foods may be a promising addition to the diet of people wishing to avoid certain diseases.
>
> **ECONOMICS:** Nutritional foods can become an economic weapon in the battle against rising health care costs.
>
> **HISTORY:** Other civilizations, including primitive tribes, have known about food's nutritional values for centuries. We can learn from their knowledge.

A thesis sets in motion the writer's examination of specific ideas the study will explore and defend. Thus, when confronted by a general topic, such as "television," adjust it to an academic interest, as with "Video replays have improved football officiating but slowed the game" or "Video technology has enhanced arthroscopic surgery."

Your thesis is not your conclusion or your answer to a problem. Rather, it anticipates your conclusion by setting in motion the examination of facts and pointing the reader toward the special idea of your paper, which you save for the conclusion.

Enthymeme

Some of your instructors might want the research paper to develop an argument as expressed in an enthymeme, which consists of two parts: a claim supported with a *because* clause. However, you need to understand that the enthymeme has a structure that depends on one or more unstated assumptions.

> Hyperactive children need medication because ADHD is a medical disorder, not a behavioral problem.

The claim that hyperactive children need medication is supported by the stated reason that the condition is a medical problem, not one of behavior. This writer must address the unstated assumption that medication alone will solve the problem.

> Participating in one of the martial arts, such as Tae Kwan
> Do, is good for children because it promotes self-discipline.

The claim that one organized sporting activity is good for children rests on the value of self-discipline. Unstated is the assumption that one sport, the martial arts, is good for children in other areas of development, such as physical conditioning. The writer might also address other issues, such as aggression or a combat mentality.

Hypothesis

A hypothesis is a theory that must be tested to prove its validity and an assumption advanced for the purpose of argument or investigation. Here's an example:

> Discrimination against girls and young women in the
> classroom, known as <u>shortchanging</u>, harms the chances of
> women to develop fully academically.

This statement could lead to a theoretical study if the student cites literature on the ways in which teachers shortchange students. A professional educator, on the other hand, would probably conduct extensive research in many classroom settings to defend the hypothesis with scientific observation.

Sometimes the hypothesis is *conditional:*

> Our campus has a higher crime rate than other state
> colleges.

This assertion on a conditional state of being could be tested by statistical comparison. At other times the hypothesis is *relational:*

> Class size affects the number of written assignments given
> by writing instructors.

This type of hypothesis claims that as one variable changes, so does another, or that something is more or less than another. It could be tested by examining and correlating class size and assignments.

At other times, the researcher produces a *causal hypothesis:*

> A child's choice of a toy is determined by television
> commercials.

Narrowing a General Subject into a Working Topic

Unlike a general subject, a focused topic should:

- Examine one significant issue, not a broad subject.
- Argue from a thesis sentence, enthymeme, or hypothesis.
- Address a knowledgeable reader and carry that reader to another plateau of knowledge.
- Have a serious purpose, one that demands analysis of the issues, argues from a position, and explains complex details.
- Meet the expectations of the instructor and conform to the course requirements.

This causal hypothesis assumes the mutual occurrence of two factors and asserts that one factor is responsible for the other. The student who is a parent could conduct research to prove or disprove the supposition.

Thus, your paper, motivated by a hypothesis, might be a theoretical examination of the literature or field study on such topics as the diet of migrating geese, the yield of one species of hybrid corn, or the behavior of children as they watch violence on television.

2c Drafting a Research Proposal

A research proposal helps clarify and focus a research project. It comes in two forms: (1) a short paragraph that identifies the project for approval of your instructor, or (2) several pages that give background information, your rationale for conducting the study, a review of the literature, your methods, and the thesis, enthymeme, or hypothesis you plan to defend.

Writing a Short Research Proposal

A short proposal identifies five essential ingredients of your project:

1. The specific topic.
2. The purpose of the paper (explain, analyze, argue).
3. The intended audience (general or specialized).

4. Your position as the writer (informer, interpreter, evaluator, reviewer).
5. The preliminary thesis sentence or opening hypothesis.

One writer developed this brief proposal:

> The world is running out of fresh water while we sip our Evian. However, the bottled water craze signals something— we don't trust our fresh tap water. We have an emerging crisis on our hands, and some authorities forecast world wars over water rights. The issue of water touches almost every facet of our lives, from religious rituals and food supply to disease and political instability. We might frame this hypothesis: Water will soon replace oil as the economic resource most treasured by nations of the world. However, that assertion would prove difficult to defend and may not be true at all. Rather, we need to look elsewhere, at human behavior, and at human responsibility for preserving the environment for our children. Accordingly, this paper will examine (1) the issues with regard to supply and demand, (2) the political power struggles that may emerge, and (3) the ethical implications for those who control the world's scattered supply of fresh water.

Writing a Detailed Research Proposal

A long proposal presents specific details concerning the project. It has more depth and length than the short proposal shown above. The long proposal should include some or all of the following elements:

1. *Cover page* with the title of the project, your name, and the person or agency to whom you are submitting the proposal.
2. An *abstract* that summarizes your project in 50 to 100 words.
3. A *purpose statement* with your *rationale* for the project (see the short proposal above for an example). Use *explanation* to review and itemize factual data. One writer explained how diabetes can be managed. Use *analysis* to classify parts of the subject and to investigate each one in depth (see Melinda Mosier's paper on Shakespeare's soliloquies). Use *persuasion* to question general attitudes about a problem and then to affirm new theories, advance a solution, recommend a course of action, or—in the least—invite the reader into an intellectual dialog.

4. A *statement of qualification* that explains your experience and perhaps the special qualities you bring to the project (i.e., you are the parent of a child with ADHD). If you have no experience with the subject, you can omit the statement of qualification.
5. A *review of the literature* that surveys the articles and books you have examined in your preliminary work.
6. A presentation of your *research methods,* which is a description of the design of the *materials* you will need, your *timetable* for completing the project, and, when applicable, your *budget.* These elements are often a part of a scientific study.

3

Conducting Research

PLANNING AND CONDUCTING RESEARCH   37

FINDING LIBRARY AND DATABASE RESOURCES   42

FINDING WEB AND INTERNET RESOURCES   44

READING AND EVALUATING SOURCES   48

INTEGRATING AND CREDITING SOURCES   54

Voices
from the Community

"Research is formalized curiosity. It is poking and prying with a purpose." —Zora Neale Hurston,
Dust Tracks on a Road

3a Planning and Conducting Research

You may be in the library working on your psychology paper on stress, searching the Web about company-sponsored child care, or surveying neighbors on new city recreation options. Each task raises its own questions and requires different research strategies, sources, and forms for turning inquiry into writing. Each draws on its own narrow research community but addresses a broader audience—academic, work, or public.

Recognizing Research Communities

Successful research writing goes beyond simply conveying information. By blending their own insights with material from print, electronic, or field sources, researchers increase readers' understanding.

37

Writers and readers together ideally form a **research community,** a web of people and texts that (1) share a perspective and focus—a **research topic,** (2) agree on **research questions** worth asking, and (3) use shared terms, **keywords** that form a **research thread** linking topics and resources.

Recognizing Research Topics

Your assignment may launch your inquiry. It may specify the deadlines, format, and sources expected by your teacher, supervisor, or organization.

> **STRATEGY** Begin your inquiry with questions.

- What problem, issue, question, or event piques your curiosity?
- What new, contradictory, or intriguing ideas turn up as you read?
- What ideas do Web surfing, class discussion, or meetings in a work or public setting suggest?
- What would your readers also like to know?

Identifying Keywords

Libraries, search engines, and databases use keywords to categorize and access information. As you consider research topics, note recurring words (*alcohol*), names (*John Glenn*), and phrases (*early childhood*).

> **STRATEGY** Identify and use keywords.

- Write down the keywords that might refer to your topic. Note synonyms (*maturation* for *growth*).

AUDIENCE EXPECTATIONS FOR RESEARCH WRITING			
	ACADEMIC	**WORK**	**PUBLIC**
GOAL	Explain, interpret, analyze, synthesize	Document problems, propose, improve	Support policy or action
READER EXPECTATIONS	Detailed evidence, varied sources	Clear, precise, direct information	Accessible, fair persuasion
TYPICAL QUESTIONS	What does it mean? Why does it happen?	What is the problem? How can we solve it?	How can we improve a policy or situation?
TYPICAL FORMS	Paper to interpret, inform, or argue	Proposal, feasibility study, report	Speech, pamphlet, letter, fact sheet
SAMPLE RESEARCH QUESTION ON COSMETICS	What gender roles do ads reinforce?	How can we develop local packaging?	Are animal tests of cosmetics necessary?

- Refine your list by adding keywords you encounter in print or electronic sources. Drop any you encounter rarely. Use this list to search library catalogs, research databases, and the Web.
- If your keywords produce too many possible sources, look for more precise terms used by people writing about your topic.
- Integrate your keywords into your research questions, thesis, and paper.

Developing Research Questions

Research questions help you focus as you filter information and lead to your **thesis,** the main idea that you explore, support, or illustrate.

Academic

What do experts ask or say about your topic? Do you agree or disagree? What can you add? What ambiguities remain?

Work

What is the problem or situation? What do you propose? Why will it work, work better, or cost less?

Public

What policy or program do you propose? Whom does it benefit? Why? What might its effects be?

Summer Arrigo-Nelson and Jennifer Figliozzi developed these research questions on student drinking for a report on a campus problem.

- Will students with permission to drink at home have different drinking behaviors at college than those without such permission?
- Do students feel that a correlation exists between drinking behaviors at home and at college?

STRATEGY   State your research questions early.

- Aim for two or three direct questions, and embed your keywords.
- Pose questions without clear answers, not with an obvious consensus.
- Design questions that will matter to your audience.

Developing Search Strategies

A **search strategy** is a plan for locating resources to answer research questions and support your thesis. It can include **library sources** (books, articles, databases, media materials), **online sources** (Web sites and discussion groups), and **field sources** (interviews, surveys, and observations).

Primary sources provide information in original (or close-to-original) form: historical and literary texts, letters, videos, survey results, and other data. **Secondary sources** explain, analyze, summarize, or interpret primary sources, telling you what others have said and what issues are debated by scholars and other writers.

STRATEGY Design a search strategy.

- **List resources.** Include the kinds of resources you plan to use—books, scholarly journals, newspapers, Web sites, interviews, and surveys. Explore potential resources under the heading *What about ...?*
- **Identify search tools.** Pay attention to specialized research tools.
  - Indexes of magazine and newspaper articles—*InfoTrac, New York Times Index, Wall Street Journal Index*
  - Indexes of articles in scholarly journals—*Social Sciences Index, MLA International Bibliography, Education Index*
  - Academic and professional databases with built-in search engines—*EBSCOhost, LexisNexis, OCLC First Search*
  - Specialized Web search engines and indexed databases—*Highbeam, AltaVista, Cata List, Dogpile, PAIS*
- **Draw on keywords and research questions.** Use a list of keywords to search indexes, databases, and the Web. Use keywords and your research questions to focus and guide your search.
- **Revise.** Update your research questions, search strategy, and keywords as your research evolves.

Selecting Resources for a Working Bibliography

Build a **working bibliography** of possible sources addressing your research questions. Consult indexes, catalogs, search engines, or databases.

Include
- Items whose titles suggest rich and relevant resources
- Recent and varied sources, from broad surveys to focused studies
- Sources from bibliographies with *annotations* or search engines with *abstracts* that summarize content and utility
- More sources than needed, to allow for any not available or useful

Exclude
- Sources that may be difficult to obtain or that lack credibility
- Sources with a questionable connection to your topic

Keeping Track of Your Sources and Notes

Select a system for recording bibliographic information and taking notes so you can easily document sources. Link your notes to keywords, to research questions, and to page numbers in your sources.

Note Cards

If you prefer cards—easy to group or add—write each bibliography entry on a 3" × 5" and each reading note on a 4" × 6" card.

Research Notebook

In a notebook you can add marginal notes, attach colored dots or flags, or duplicate pages to cut up as you organize.

Electronic Notes

Software files that resemble onscreen cards easily transfer to a reference list or draft paper. Some programs will format entries using the style you select. Be sure to record the following information.

BOOKS	ARTICLES	ELECTRONIC SOURCES
Author(s), editor(s), translator(s)	Author(s)	Name of source
Title: Subtitle	Title: Subtitle	Address/URL/access route/vendor
City: publisher, date	Periodical name	Name of database
Call number and library location	Volume (& issue)	Date of publication or last revision
	Date	Date of access
	Page number(s)	Author or sponsoring group
	Library location	

Pulling Your Research Materials Together

Finding resources is half the challenge; managing the information that you locate is the other half.

- Gather your notes, copies, printouts, files, and other material.
- Sort your resources, and track down missing material.
- Use your research questions as guides to main points and subtopics. Use keywords, color codes, or stacks of material to sort by category.
- If a category contains little information, drop it or do more research. If it contains lots of material, decide whether to break it into subtopics.
- If you need more information, consult a librarian, instructor, or specialist in the field.

3b   Finding Library and Database Resources

Libraries give you access to books and articles (both print and electronic), online research databases, recordings, microforms, and art. Research databases are available on the Web and, increasingly, through college and university libraries.

Finding Library Resources

Visit your library—or its home page—to explore resources for almost all fields of academic, work, or public interest. Start with **ready references,** general encyclopedias, atlases, dictionaries, and statistical abstracts. Then turn to **specialized encyclopedias** and **dictionaries,** as varied as *Current Biography; Encyclopedia of Pop, Rock, and Soul;* and the *McGraw-Hill Encyclopedia of Science and Technology.* Check useful **bibliographies,** listings of resources such as the *MLA International Bibliography* on literature and language or the *International Bibliography of the Social Sciences.*

> **STRATEGY**   Talk to information specialists.
> Reference librarians can help you refine a search strategy, improve keyword searches, and locate materials on campus or on loan.

Periodicals appear regularly with articles by many authors. **Online periodicals** may place past articles in electronic archives; other **Web sites** act like periodicals, adding material as the site is updated. Through your library, the Web, or search engines, you can access **periodical indexes,** some of which supply brief summaries (or abstracts).

Your library will offer access to **general indexes** such as *Academic Index, InfoTrac, OCLC/World Catalog, PAIS (Public Affairs, Information Services),* or *NewsBank.* Academic libraries also supply **specialized indexes** such as *BIZZ (Business Index), Government Documents Catalog Service (GDCS/GPO Index), Current Index to Journals in Education (CIJE), Social Sciences Index,* or *Biological and Agricultural Index.*

PRINT PERIODICALS			
	MAGAZINES	**JOURNALS**	**NEWSPAPERS**
READERS?	General public	Academics, professionals	General public
WRITERS?	Staff, journalists	Scholars, experts	Staff, journalists
HOW OFTEN?	Monthly, weekly	Quarterly, monthly	Daily, weekly
APPEARANCE?	Color, photos, glossy paper, sidebars	Dense text, data, plain paper, little color	Columns, headlines, photos, some color

Using Library Resources

First identify resources, then find them. Start with the library home page or **online catalog.** Search for an *author's name,* the *title* of a work or periodical, or a *keyword.* If you find several items (each listed in a **brief display**), click on one to call up its **full display.** You may also expand a search to related topics, authors, or works or follow related links. Print or record your results, including call numbers and locations.

Government documents include general and technical reports, pamphlets, and regulations issued by Congress, federal agencies, and state or local governments. The *Monthly Catalog of U.S. Government Publications* can help direct your search, as can the *Government Information Sharing Project* <http://govinfo.kerr.orst.edu>, *Library of Congress* <http://www.loc.gov>, and *Thomas Legislative Information* site <http://thomas.loc.gov>.

Special collections house many documents, including those on local history. **Audiovisual collections** contain tapes, films, and recordings. **Microform collections** contain copies of periodicals and documents.

Finding Research Databases

Researchers (student and professional) have come to rely on electronic databases for all kinds of information, especially texts of scholarly articles and general-interest periodical articles. University and public libraries have greatly increased the available number of **online databases.** Most focus on specialized fields and are especially useful for researchers.

You can access research databases at library terminals, through a library's Web site, or through the Web site of a commercial database company such as *Highbeam* or *LexisNexis.* You can generally search a database by author, title, and keyword or by categories appropriate for the materials in a collection. Most databases are updated frequently. Consult library handouts or the information screen of a database to learn what resources it provides and the range of dates for the materials it contains.

Using Research Databases

Databases are of several kinds, varying according to the information and texts they provide.

- **Full-text databases** list articles and other documents and briefly summarize each item. In addition, they provide entire texts of most items indexed. Examples: *Academic Search*

Premier, Academic Universe, ArticleFirst, InfoTrac OneFile, Health Reference Center Academic.

- **Databases containing abstracts** provide brief summaries of a document's content and sometimes full texts of selected items. Some provide electronic links to a library's online subscription to a journal or magazine. Examples: *PsycINFO, Sociological Abstracts, Biological Abstracts, MEDLINE, MLA Bibliography, Historical Abstracts, ERIC.*
- **Indexing or bibliographic databases** provide titles and publication (or access) information for articles and documents in a specialized field. Examples: *Art Index, GEOBASE.*
- **Resource databases** either provide access to information, images, and documents arranged in the form of an electronic reference work, or they offer tools for researchers. Examples: *World-Cat* (library and Internet resources worldwide); *Web of Science* (citation indexes identifying sources used by researchers); *RefWorks* (help with documentation styles in wide range of academic and technical fields).

3c Finding Web and Internet Resources

Many writers conduct significant portions of their research on the Web or through Internet discussion groups. They do so because the available resources are varied, current, and easily accessible. Online texts are often shorter and less detailed than print sources, however, and many are not subjected to the same kinds of review and editorial processes as print texts. Critical evaluation, an important part of all research, is even more important when you review Web and Internet texts.

Developing an Online Search Strategy

In addition to a general search strategy, you should develop an online search strategy to emphasize diversity in the online sources you consult. Diversity provides contrasting perspectives and varied information.

STRATEGY Create a planning list for electronic resources.

Use the following list to help identify varied electronic resources.

- Web sites
- Online versions of printed texts
- Online databases
- Online collections of documents

- Discussion groups and newsgroups
- Visual and audio documents
- Links to Web sites

Finding Web and Internet Resources

You can access Web documents (**pages**) or collections of pages (**sites**) using a **browser,** such as *Internet Explorer* or *Netscape Navigator.* Enter the Web page's address (a **URL** or Uniform Resource Locator), or follow links in an online text. The **Internet** links researchers through email, discussion groups, and Web sites. Materials range from well-researched reports to hasty messages.

Search Engines

To locate sites relevant to your research, use a **search engine** that gathers data about Web sites and discussion groups. **General search engines** typically search for resources according to keywords or phrases you identify. Each search engine typically employs a different principle of selection; as a general rule, use more than one search engine to identify relevant resources.

GENERAL SEARCH ENGINES

Google	<http://www.google.com>
AltaVista	<http://altavista.com>
Yahoo!	<http://www.yahoo.com>
AllTheWeb	<http://alltheweb.com/>
Wisenut	<http://wisenut.com>
Lycos	<http://www.lycos.com>
Teoma	<http://www.teoma.com/>
HotBot	<http://hotbot.com/>

Metasearch sites enable you to conduct your search using several search engines simultaneously—and then to compare the results.

METASEARCH SITES

Dogpile	<http://dogpile.com>
Momma	<http://www.momma.com>
Metacrawler	<http://metacrawler.com>
Profusion	<http://www.profusion.com>

Electronic Messages and Postings

Electronic mail (**email**) allows you to contact people who can answer questions or provide information. Search engines have directory services that can locate email addresses of individuals, and many Web pages let you email the author or sponsor.

Newsgroups and **Web discussion forums** are public sites. Anyone can post messages and read other posts. In contrast, you subscribe to **electronic mailing lists** and then check your email for messages. All these sources are conversational and may or may not supply reliable information.

Searching Efficiently

Select the terms you submit to search engines and indexes carefully. Be ready to revise them.

- Use your research questions and keywords to select search terms.
- Search engines find the exact words you specify. Type—and spell—carefully. Try various word forms and related terms.
- If a database contains items with keywords matching your search terms, the items will appear as your search results.
- Repeat a successful search, looking for other useful keywords and combinations. Use your most effective clusters to search additional databases.

A string of keywords or specific terms is called a **query.** Use your query to narrow a search by grouping terms, specifying those you want to combine, rule out, or treat as alternatives.

STRATEGY   Use advanced search strategies.

If your search produces too many or too few items, try the advanced search strategies for the search engine or index. Many use these markers.

OR (expands): Search for either term
     X OR Y → documents referring to either X or Y
AND (restricts): Search for both terms
     X AND Y → documents referring to both X and Y
NOT (excludes): Search for X unless X includes Y
     X NOT Y → documents referring to X unless they refer to Y

Search engines may automatically combine terms when you enter more than one word (*college drinking policy*) or ask you to use signs (*college + alcohol*) or words (*early childhood education NOT Head Start*).

Using Web Resources

To make effective use of Web resources, you should be able to recognize some important kinds of Web sites and understand their uses.

- **Individual Web sites** are maintained by individuals but are not necessarily *about* these individuals, though they may be *home pages* created to share their lives, interests, or research. Some sites gather accounts of thoughts and actions (**blogs**) in newsworthy settings.

- **Advocacy Web sites** promote an organization's beliefs and policies. Although they favor the organization's position, many explain positions, answer critics, and provide detailed supporting evidence and documentation.

- **Informational Web sites** focus on a subject, such as sleep research, horror movies, or poetry from the 1950s Beat Generation. Their reliability varies, but the best are clearly organized, informative, and trustworthy.

- **Research-oriented Web sites,** sponsored by universities, research institutes, or professional organizations, typically contain (1) full texts of research reports, (2) summaries, (3) downloadable data in tables and graphs, (4) reviews of current research, (5) texts of unpublished papers and presentations, and (6) bibliographies of books, articles, or links.

STRATEGY   Assess your Web and Internet sources.

The readers you address may vary in their response to your sources. Academic readers expect you to find authoritative sites produced by people aware of scholarly discussions. Public readers expect you to use sites with reliable information. Workplace readers expect you to use sites known for accuracy. Ask questions like those below to help decide how authoritative, current, or verifiable your resources are.

- How would you classify this source? Is it an individual, informational, advocacy, or research-oriented site, or something else?
- Does the site name its author or sponsor? Does the sponsor have a reputation for accuracy or expertise?
- If the item is a blog, an email message, or posting, does its author seem to have expertise? Is its argument logical and its evidence reasonable?
- Is the information credible? Does the site provide supporting evidence, alternatives, and complexities?

3d Reading and Evaluating Sources

Research draws on reading in these ways: to gather information and ideas, to synthesize ideas and develop insights, and to evaluate sources.

Summarizing and Paraphrasing

Summarize or paraphrase a source to put its ideas in forms useful for writing. A **summary** presents these ideas in compressed form.

> **STRATEGY** Summarize a source.
> - **Read** carefully, underlining, highlighting, or noting key ideas, supporting evidence, and other information.
> - **Scan** (reread quickly) to decide which ideas and information are most important. Identify the major purpose and sections of the selection.
> - **Sum up** the key ideas of *each section* in *one sentence*.
> - **Capture the main point** of the *entire passage* in *one sentence*.
> - **Combine** your section summaries with your overall summary .
> - **Revise** for clarity. Check against the source for accuracy.
> - **Document** your source using a standard style.

Summer Arrigo-Nelson and Jennifer Figliozzi used summary sentences to introduce a research question, noting sources in APA style.

> First, research has shown that adolescents who have close relationships with parents use alcohol less often than do those with conflictual relationships (Sieving, 1996). For example, a survey of students in grades 7 to 12 reported that about 35% were under parental supervision while drinking (Department of Education, 1993).

A **paraphrase** presents the content of a source in your own words with your own focus and helps you integrate the source with your ideas.

> **STRATEGY** Paraphrase a source.
> - **Read** carefully to understand both the wording and the content.
> - **Write** a draft using your own words in place of the original. You may retain names, proper nouns, and the like from the original.
> - **Revise** for smooth reading and clarity.
> - **Document** your source clearly using a standard style.

Jennifer Figliozzi read this passage in a *Chronicale of Higher Education* article on current alcohol abuse programs at various schools:

The university also now notifies parents when their sons or daughters violate the alcohol policy, or any other aspect of the student code of conduct. "We were hoping that the support of parents would help change students' behavior, and we believe it has," says Timothy H. Brooks, an assistant vice-president and the dean of students.

To integrate this information smoothly, Jennifer combined a paraphrase with a brief quotation and cited it using APA style.

Officials at the University of Delaware thought that letting parents know when students violate regulations on alcohol use would alter students' drinking habits, and one administrator now says, "we believe it has" (Reisberg, 1998, p. A42).

Synthesizing and Questioning

When you synthesize several sources, you explore connections among their conclusions, evidence, and perspectives. When you question and interpret your sources, you go beyond them to develop ideas and insights of your own.

A **synthesis** can identify and relate the ideas in several sources, build links to your research question, or investigate differences among sources.

STRATEGY   Synthesize sources to highlight their relationships.

- **Gather and read** your sources.
- **Focus** on the purpose and role of your synthesis, and draft a sentence summing up your conclusion about the relationship of the sources.
- **Arrange** the order for presenting your sources in the synthesis.
- **Write** a draft synthesis, presenting summaries of sources, offering your conclusion about the relationships, and acknowledging contradictions.
- **Revise** for smooth reading and clear identification of sources.
- **Document** your sources clearly using a standard style.

Kimlee Cunningham used this analytical synthesis to expand her paper's key ideas on the history of women's roles in Disney films. She followed MLA style, citing a one-page article and an online posting.

It is probably an exaggeration to say that a character like Belle in Beauty and the Beast is a lot like a contemporary feminist, as one critic suggests (Showalter). However, we should not simply ignore an interpretation like this. Even if many people view a film like Beauty and the Beast (or Aladdin) as a simple love story (Hoffman), the films nonetheless grow out of the complicated values and roles that shape relationships today. Disney's contemporary portrayal of women characters shows a willingness to change with the times but also a reluctance to abandon traditional values and stereotypes.

As you read, you may raise questions about the ideas and information in a source—questions worth sharing with readers. Consider gathering these questions into a **problem paragraph.**

STRATEGY Create a problem paragraph.

Challenge a source in a **problem paragraph** that notes problems or limitations.

Lily Germaine prepared this note card on bodybuilding.

> Tucker, pp. 389-91   Weight training & self-concept
>
> Tucker uses "although" at least four times when summarizing
> other studies. He's nice on the surface but sets his readers up
> to find fault with other studies that lack objective
> methodology. But he thinks he can be completely objective about
> such a slippery thing as "self-concept." I really question this.

Lily's problem paragraph incorporated her insights.

Does bodybuilding affect self-concept? Before we can answer this question, we need to ask if we can accurately measure such a slippery thing as "self-concept." Some researchers, like Tucker, believe that self-concept can be accurately gauged by mathematical measurements and rigid definitions of terms. For several reasons, however, this assumption is questionable.

As you present the ideas and information in your sources, you should also interpret them and assess their value in answering a research question.

STRATEGY Interpret and assess a source.

- State your source's conclusions accurately.
- State your own viewpoint with supporting evidence.
- Add your interpretations and conclusions.
- Assess the value and accuracy of a source. Look for reasonable judgments supported with examples and for analysis of texts or data.

Evaluating Sources Critically

Bring some healthy skepticism to *all* your print and electronic sources to be sure each is *authoritative* and to figure out any slant, or *bias.*

Evaluating Sources for Credibility

Printed materials can be written by uncredentialed people or can bypass certain review processes (compare the *New York Times* with, say, the *National Enquirer*), yet most published books and articles reflect the efforts of careful reviewers, editors, and publishers. In comparison, on the Internet, *anyone* can present bogus information as if it's reliable, accurate, or based on sound research.

STRATEGY   Evaluate the credibility of your sources.

- Who or what *is* the source? What can you tell about its trustworthiness and authority? Is it located at a reputable site?
- What are the author's credentials or affiliation?
- What processes has the source likely gone through to reach publication? Were there reviewers or an editorial board?
- Does the source meet the standards of your research community?
- Is the source grounded on prior research or credible authorities?
- Does the source document information, quotations, and ideas or clearly attribute them to the author?
- Does the source rely on outdated research or material?

Evaluating Sources for Bias

Scholarly and academic communities pride themselves on objectivity, and materials they produce are checked for balance. Still, every source has its point of view. Some sources that *appear* to be highly academic are sponsored by companies or organizations promoting a product or perspective, and they may knowingly "gear" the material in favor of that purpose.

STRATEGY   Evaluate the bias or possible slant of your sources.

- Does the publisher, publication, or sponsor have a reputation for balance or strong advocacy? Do other sources find the author fair?
- How accurate is the source? Does it use facts? Are its ideas generally consistent with those in other sources? Are they insightful or misleading?
- How does the writer support statements? Do claims exceed the facts?
- Does the source cite experts with political or financial interests? Does it try to hide its viewpoint?

Evaluating Online Sources Critically

These Web pages show how to examine a Web site critically.

"The Good, the Bad and the Ugly: or, Why It's a Good Idea to Evaluate Web Sources," <http://lib.nmsu.edu/instruction/eval.html>
"Thinking Critically about World Wide Web Resources," <http://www.library.ucla.edu/libraries/college/help/critical/index.htm>
"Evaluating Web Resources" <http://www2.widener.edu/Wolfgram-Memorial-Library/webevaluation/webeval.htm>

To evaluate Web sources, ask the questions developed by Paula Mathieu and Ken McAllister for the CRITT (Critical Resources in Teaching with Technology) project at the University of Illinois at Chicago.

- **Who benefits? What difference does that make?** These questions can alert you to the perspective of the source and its effect on accuracy or trustworthiness. The Web pages at <http://www.got-milk.com/better/>, for example, seem dedicated to the reader's health (Figure 3.1). But because this site promotes drinking milk and eating milk products every day, milk processors will also benefit from sales.
- **Who's talking? What difference does that make?** These questions help you assess reliability and the likelihood of bal-

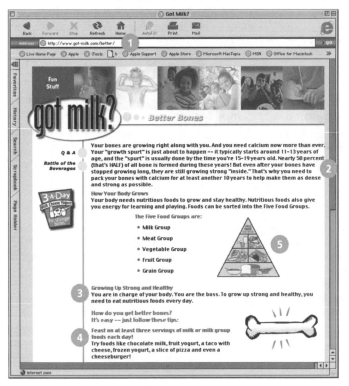

1. Commercial site
2. Links milk and milk products to healthy bones
   Offers diet and exercise advice
4. Advocates drinking milk
5. Uses visuals to convey information

READER'S REACTION: Why are you sharing all this? How do you benefit? How do I know this is accurate, complete information?

FIGURE 3.1
"Got Milk?" Web page

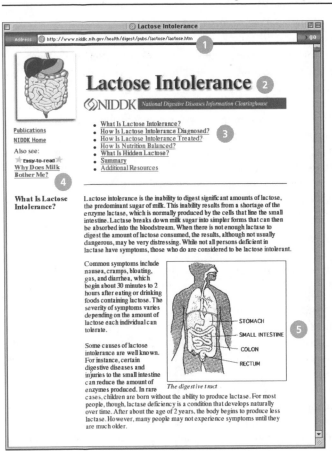

① Government site
② Identifies topic in title
③ Uses questions and answers to explain
④ Supplies link to consumer information
⑤ Adds informative graphics

READER'S REACTION: This explanation is very clear. The sponsor is identified, too.

■■■■ FIGURE 3.2
"Lactose Intolerance" Web page

ance or bias. The "speaker" for the site's positive facts about milk is identified as "us" in the invitation to request more information. The site is linked to another page, however, that identifies the sponsor as MilkPEP (Milk Processor Education Program), sponsored by milk processors. The site is administered by the International Dairy Foods Association. What might be the point of view of these groups? Will all the "facts" appear, especially any that question milk's goodness?

In contrast, the Web page at <http://www.niddk.nih.gov/health/digest/pubs/lactose/lactose.htm> (see Figure 3.2) clearly and impartially answers questions about lactose intolerance, a widespread inability to digest milk sugar. The "speaker" is an authoritative government agency—the National Digestive Diseases Information Clearinghouse, part of the National Institutes of Health.

- **What's missing? What difference does that make?** The *Got Milk* site is a commercial venture promoting cow's milk. Naturally it ignores soy, goat, and other milk (and nonmilk) options. On the other hand, "Lactose Intolerance" does not promote or attack dairy products; instead, its reliable advice ignores commercial and other interests. Each of these Web sites—like every other resource—has a point of view or vested interest that guides its selection and presentation of information.

Turning Inquiry into Writing

After you locate and read useful sources, you're ready to pull your research together and think strategically. Take the following steps.

- Consider what you want your readers to learn, do, or feel.
- Place your research questions in a trial sequence. Refine them.
- State, extend, and modify your rough thesis. Try breaking it into easy-to-read sentences or restating it to help readers follow your reasoning.
- Analyze and respond to your readers' possible reactions.
- Group your materials and arrange them in sequence— beginning, middle, and end. Connect the chunks.
- Try drafting your introduction and conclusion first, focusing on your research questions. Engage readers; keep them thinking.
- Draft the middle so readers can follow your reasoning, see your evidence, and accept your conclusions. Don't just pack in details.
- Ask readers to respond to a draft. Revise, edit, proofread, and design your document. Quote accurately, cite page numbers and authors correctly, and check your documentation form.

3e Integrating and Crediting Sources

By distinguishing your contributions from those of your sources, you'll get credit for your insights and hard work. You'll also avoid inadvertently taking credit for the work of others—a form of theft called **plagiarism.** Carefully citing sources adds to your credibility, substantiates your knowledge, and allows readers to draw on your research.

Documenting Sources for Your Audience

Each community of readers and writers has its own expectations about using sources.

Academic

Academic readers generally expect you to acknowledge prior work, showing how your ideas fit into a research tradition. They look for authoritative evidence and documentation appropriate to the field of research. Try to integrate sources—emphasizing quotations, findings, currency, or other matters—to meet the expectations of readers in a field.

Work

Readers at work expect brief treatment of what they know and extended treatment of what they don't (but need to). They may expect quotations, paraphrases, summaries, or visuals—all documented.

Public

Public readers may appreciate source material but be content with informal citations. But when you advocate a policy or offer controversial interpretations, readers expect fair play and accurate detail.

Using Quotations

Select any quotation carefully, identify your source, retain its exact wording, and integrate it to support your points.

POSSIBLE CONTRIBUTIONS OF QUOTATIONS

- Bolster your conclusions with a recognized authority.
- Convey ideas accurately, stylishly, concisely, or persuasively.
- Provide a jumping-off point, change of pace, or vivid example.

You can quote entire sentences, with proper attribution.

> Celebrities can also play roles in our fantasy lives:"Many people admire, but do not mimic, the audacity of the rebellious rock star" (McVey 32).

Or you can embed a quotation of a few words or lines.

> Many teens were "riveted by Dylan's lyrical cynicism" (Low 124).

Guidelines for Using Quotations

Here are general guidelines.

- Put the exact spoken or written words of your source in quotation marks. Introduce and connect the quotation smoothly, interpreting for readers. Mention the source in your text or a citation.
- Use a colon only after an introductory line that is a complete sentence. Use commas to set off tags such as "*X* said" that introduce or interrupt a quotation. Otherwise, use the context to determine the punctuation.
- Review related conventions: combining marks, capitals, and brackets and ellipses.
- If you use a specific documentation style, check its advice on quotations and in-text citations.

Block Quotations for Prose

When you quote a passage longer than four lines typed (MLA style) or forty words or more (APA style), begin on the line after your introduction. Indent 1" or ten spaces (MLA style) or 1/2" or five spaces (APA style, shown below). Double-space but omit quotation marks (unless they appear in the source).

> Perez (1998) anticipates shifts in staff training:
>
>> The great challenge for most school districts is to earmark sufficient funds for training personnel, not for purchasing or upgrading hardware and software. The technological revolution in the average classroom will depend to a large degree on innovation in professional development.

Begin the first line without further indentation if you quote from one paragraph. Otherwise, indent all paragraphs 1/4" or three spaces (MLA) or any additional paragraph 1/2" or five spaces (APA).

Block Quotations for Poetry

When you quote four or more lines of poetry, begin on the line after your introduction. Indent 1" or ten spaces from the left (MLA style, shown below). Double-space, and don't use quotation marks unless the verse contains them.

> Donald Hall also varies line length and rhythm, as "The Black-Faced Sheep" illustrates.
>
>> My grandfather spent all day searching the valley and edges of Ragged Mountain,

calling "Ke-<u>day</u>!" as if he brought you salt,

"Ke-<u>day</u>! Ke-<u>day</u>!" (lines 9–12)

Integrating Sources into Your Text

Credit your sources, and weave their points or details into your own line of reasoning. To make your writing more sophisticated, quote selectively. Paraphrase, summarize, or synthesize instead.

EMBEDDING SOURCE MATERIAL

- Select sound evidence that supports your purpose and thesis.
- Alternate striking short quotations with paraphrase and summary to avoid long, tedious quotations.
- Draw facts, details, and statistics from your sources as well as ideas and expressions. Credit these, too.
- Don't just tack sources together assuming readers will figure out how to interpret or connect them. Integrate sources so your interpretation and reasoning shape the discussion.

Drawings, photos, tables, graphs, and charts can consolidate or explore data. If you copy or download a visual, you'll need to cite its source and may need permission to use it.

STRATEGY   Integrate visuals for readers.

- Put the visual close to the relevant text without disrupting the discussion. Make sure that it explains or extends your point.
- Use clear, readable visuals in an appropriate size.
- Add labels (MLA: Table 1, Fig. 1; APA: *Figure 1*).

Avoiding Plagiarism

As you quote, paraphrase, or summarize, you *must* cite sources.

- Enclose someone's exact words in quotation marks.
- Paraphrase and summarize in your own words.
- Cite the source of whatever you integrate.

Without quotation marks, the following paraphrase is too close to the original and would be seen as plagiarized.

ORIGINAL PASSAGE

Malnutrition was a widespread and increasingly severe problem throughout the least developed parts of the world in the 1970s, and would continue to be serious, occasionally reaching famine conditions, as the millennium approached. Among the cells of the human body most dependent upon a steady source of nutrients are those of the immune system, most of which live, even under ideal conditions, for only days at a time. (From Laurie Garrett, *The Coming Plague*, New York: Penguin, 1994, p. 199.)

PLAGIARIZED VERSION

In her book about emerging global diseases, Garrett points out that malnutrition can give microbes an advantage as they spread through the population. Malnutrition continues to be a **severe problem throughout the least developed parts of the world.** The human immune system contains cells that are **dependent upon a steady source of nutrients.** These cells may **live, even under ideal conditions, for only days at a time.**

The writer of the plagiarized version made only minor changes in some phrases and "lifted" others verbatim.

APPROPRIATE PARAPHRASE

In her book about emerging global diseases, Garrett points out that malnutrition can give microbes an advantage as they spread through the population. The human body contains immune cells that help to fight off various diseases. When the body is deprived of nutrients, these immune cells will weaken (Garrett 199).

For a paper on the general threat of global disease, the passage could simply be summarized.

APPROPRIATE SUMMARY

Malnutrition can so weaken people's immune systems that diseases they would otherwise fight off can gain an advantage (Garrett 199).

Deciding What to Document

In general, document words, ideas, and information drawn from another person's work. Add credibility by showing your careful research, acknowledging someone's hard work, and giving others access to your sources. What needs documenting may vary with your readers. General readers may expect sources when you identify subatomic particles; physicists probably would assume this is common knowledge.

You **Must** *Document*
- Word-for-word (direct) quotations from a source
- Paraphrases or summaries of someone else's work, whether published or presented orally or electronically

- Ideas, opinions, and interpretations that others have developed, even those based on common knowledge
- Facts or data someone has gathered or identified, unless the information is considered common knowledge
- Information that is disputed or not widely accepted
- Visuals, recordings, performances, interviews, and the like

But Do Not *Document*
- Ideas, opinions, and interpretations that are your own
- Widely known information available in common reference works or generally seen as common knowledge
- Commonly used quotations ("To be, or not to be")

Presenting Sources

In a traditional research paper or report you present information and ideas from your sources as part of your written text: as quotations, summaries, or paraphrases. Writers today have many more choices, however. You may begin by envisioning your paper as a stack of neatly laid out pages emerging from your computer's printer. But this is not your *only* option, nor is it necessarily your best option.

Printed Document with Visuals

A printed document does not have to rely on words alone, and it does not have to be regular (and perhaps unexciting) in appearance. Your word-processing program will enable you to integrate information in the form of charts, graphs, pictures, and clip art. When you incorporate visual material, make sure it adds substantial ideas and information to your work. If you can, place the visual near the relevant part of the written discussion so readers can see the relationship between them.

Presentation programs like *PowerPoint* enable you to arrange information in graphic ways that emphasize relationships and highlight key ideas. They can also incorporate action sequences like arrows linking statements or fades from one piece of text (or a visual) to another. Because *PowerPoint* and similar programs do not allow for the extensive presentation of text, they work best when incorporated within word-processed documents (see Figure 3.3).

Webbed Document

A webbed document, a Web page or a file written in HTML, allows readers to move around at will within a document. You can include electronic links to online texts of research articles you have summarized or paraphrased, giving readers a chance to test the accuracy of

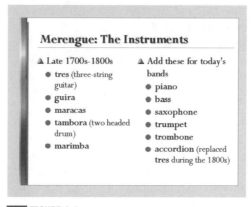

FIGURE 3.3
PowerPoint presentation within a document

your work. Or you can include links to Web sites that provide additional supporting evidence or arguments. If you plan to create such a document, write each section so that it can be understood more or less on its own because Web documents are rarely read in a conventionally linear way.

4

Field Research: Collecting Data outside the Library

The human species is distinguished by its ability to examine the world systematically and create pioneers for the millennium, such as computer technicians, microsurgeons, and nuclear engineers. You may become one of them. Each discipline has different expectations in its methods of inquiry and presentation. This chapter introduces you to types of field research and the results you might expect.

4a Conducting Research within a Discipline

Some disciplines, more than others, require you to work in the laboratory or the field, not just the library. Attitudes and methods differ among the social, physical, and applied sciences, and those three differ in many ways from the attitudes and methods of humanists.

The Social Scientists

Social scientists work from the assumption that behavior can be observed, tested, and catalogued by observation and experimental testing. Professionals perform thousands of experiments every month. They research stress in the workplace, study the effects of birth order on the youngest child, and develop testing mechanisms, such as the Scholastic Aptitude Test (SAT). As a student in the social sciences, you are asked to perform similar but less exhaustive studies, such as the typing mannerisms of students composing on a computer. If your topic examines any aspect of human behavior (for example, road rage on campus streets), prepare to go into the field for some aspects of your research.

The Physical Scientists

Physical scientists wish to discover, define, and explain the natural world. They operate under the assumption that we can know precise data on flora and fauna, geological formations, the various species of animals, and so forth. You may be asked to join a field expedition to catalog one type of fern, to test the water conditions at a local lake, or to locate sinkholes in a confined area. Laboratory experimentation is also a regular activity of scientists, so any experiments you conduct should be recorded in a lab notebook and may become significant to your written reports. If your topic examines the natural world in some way—for example, the growing deer population in the Governor Oaks subdivision—field research may be useful.

The Applied Scientists

Applied scientists *apply* scientific knowledge to make life more efficient, enduring, and comfortable. By means of mathematical formulas and cutting-edge technology, they launch spaceships to encircle the globe, find new ways to repair broken bones, and discover better methods of movie animation. You, too, can participate in such experiments by designing access facilities for students with wheelchairs (for example, should doors open out or open in?), investigating systems to measure the force of lightning strikes, or examining ways to increase the weight of beef cattle. It is not unusual today for undergraduate students to apply computer knowledge to the creation of new programs, even new software and hardware. If your research involves application of scientific information, researching in the field may help you formulate your ideas.

The Humanists

Humanists in the fine arts, literature, history, religion, and philosophy have a distinctive approach to knowledge. While scientists usually investigate a small piece of data and its meaning, humanists examine an entire work of art (Verdi's opera *Rigoletto*), a period of history (the Great Depression), or a philosophical theory (existentialism). Humanists usually accept a poem or painting as a valid entity and search it subjectively for what it means to human experience. However, that does not preclude humanists from conducting field research. For example, a student might go to England to retrace the route of late medieval pilgrims to Canterbury, as such a trip might shed new light on Chaucer's poetry. In another instance, a student's field trip to Jackson, Mississippi, might enlighten the scholar on the fiction of Eudora Welty. Conducting archival research on manuscript materials could take you into unknown territory. Your work with a writer living in your locality may prompt you to seek a personal interview, and correspondence with writers and historians is standard fare in humanist research. Thus, if your research in history, religion, or the arts offers the opportunity for field research, add it to your research program.

4b   Investigating Local Sources

Interviewing Knowledgeable People

Talk to persons who have experience with your subject. Personal interviews can elicit valuable in-depth information. They provide information that few others have. Look to organizations for experienced persons. For example, a student writing on a folklore topic might contact the county historian, a senior citizens organization, or a local historical society. If necessary, the student could post a notice soliciting help: "I am writing a study of local folklore. Wanted: People who have a knowledge of regional tales." Another way to accomplish this task is to request information from an e-mail discussion group, which will bring responses from several persons.

Follow a few general guidelines. Set up your appointments in advance. Consult with persons knowledgeable about your topic. If possible, talk to several people to get a fair assessment. A telephone interview is acceptable, as is e-mail correspondence. Be courteous and on time for interviews. Be prepared with a set of focused, relevant questions. For accuracy and if permitted by the person being interviewed, record the session on audiotape or videotape. Double-check direct quotations with the interviewee or the tape. Get permission before citing a person by name or quoting the person's exact words. Handle private and public papers with great care, and send participants a copy of your report along with a thank-you note. Make a bibliography entry just as you would for a book:

Thornbright, Mattie Sue. Personal interview. 15 Jan. 2004.

Writing Letters and Corresponding by E-mail

Correspondence provides a written record for research. Write a letter asking pointed questions that will elicit relevant responses. Tell the person who you are, what you are attempting to do, and why you are writing to him or her.

Gena Messersmith
12 Morningside Road
Clarksville, TN

Ms. Rachel G. Warren, Principal
Sango High School
Clarksville, TN

Dear Ms. Warren:
I am a college student conducting research into methods for
handling hyperactive children in the public school setting. I am
surveying each elementary school principal in the county. I have
contacted the central office also, but I wished to have perspectives from those of you on the front lines. I have a child with
ADHD, so I have a personal as well as a scholarly reason for this
research. I could ask specific questions on policy, but I have got-
ten that from the central office. What I would like from you is
a brief paragraph that describes your policy and procedure
when one of your teachers reports a hyperactive child. In particular, do you endorse the use of medication for calming the
child with ADHD? May I quote you in my report? I will honor
any request to withhold your name.
     I have enclosed a self-addressed, stamped envelope for your
convenience. You may e-mail me at messersmithg@apsu.edu.
     Sincerely,
     Gena Messersmith

This letter makes a fairly specific request for a minimum amount of
information. It does not require an expansive reply. If Gena Messersmith
uses a quotation from the reply and if she has permission from the interviewee, she can provide a bibliography entry on her Works Cited page.

Warren, Rachel G. Principal of Sango High School,
     Clarksville, TN. E-mail to the author. 5 Apr. 2004.

If Messersmith decides to build a table or graph from replies
received, she must document the survey.

Reading Personal Papers

     Search for letters, diaries, manuscripts, family histories, and other
personal materials that might contribute to your study. The city library
may house private collections, and the public librarian might help
you contact the county historian and other private citizens who have
important documents. Obviously, handling private papers must be
done with the utmost decorum and care. Make a bibliography entry
for such materials.

Joplin, Lester. "Notes on Robert Penn Warren." Unpublished
     paper. Nashville, 1997.

Attending Lectures and Public Addresses

Watch bulletin boards and the newspaper for a public speaker who may contribute to your research. At the lecture, take careful notes, and if the speaker makes one available, secure a copy of the lecture or speech. If you want to use your equipment to make an audiotape or videotape of a speech, courtesy demands that you seek permission. Remember, too, that many lectures, reproduced on video, are available in the library or in departmental files. Always make a bibliography entry for any words or ideas you use.

> Petty-Rathbone, Virginia. "Edgar Allan Poe and the Image of
> Ulalume." Lecture. Heard Library, Vanderbilt U., 2000.

Investigating Government Documents

Documents are available at four levels of government: city, county, state, and federal. As a constituent, you are entitled to examine a wide assortment of records on file at various agencies. If your topic demands it, you may contact the mayor's office, attend and take notes at a meeting of the county commissioners, or search for documents in the archives of the state or federal government.

City and County Government

Visit the courthouse or county clerk's office to find facts on elections, censuses, marriages, births, and deaths as well as census data. These archives include wills, tax rolls, military assignments, deeds to property, and much more. A trip to the local courthouse can help you trace the history of the land and its people.

State Government

Contact a state office that relates to your research, such as Consumer Affairs (which provides general information), Public Service Commission (which regulates public utilities such as the telephone company), or the Department of Human Services (which administers social and welfare services). The names of these agencies may vary from state to state. Each state has an archival storehouse and makes its records available for public review.

Federal Government

Your United States senator or representative can send you booklets printed by the Government Printing Office (GPO). A list of these materials, many of which are free, appears on the GPO Web site www.GPOAccess.gov. In addition, you can gain access to the National Archives Building in Washington, DC, or to one of the regional branches in Atlanta, Boston, Chicago, Denver, Fort Worth, Kansas City, Los Angeles, New York, Philadelphia, or Seattle. Their archives contain court records and government documents that you can review in two books: *Guide to the National Archives of the United States* and *Select List of Publications of the National Archives and Record Service.* You can view some documents on microfilm if you consult the *Catalog of National Archives Microfilm Publications.*

4c   Examining Audiovisual Materials, Television, and Radio

Important data can be found in audiovisual materials. You can find these both on and off campus. Consult such guides as *Educators Guide* (film, film strips, and tapes), *Media Review Digest* (nonprint materials), *Video Source Book* (video catalog), *The Film File,* or *International Index to Recorded Poetry.* Television, with its many channels, such as The History Channel, offers invaluable data. With a VCR, you can record a program for detailed examination. The Internet houses articles on almost every conceivable topic. As for other sources, write bibliography entries for any materials that have merit and contribute to your paper.

"Nutrition and AIDS." Narr. Carolyn O'Neil. CNN.

12 Jan. 1997.

When using media sources, watch closely the opening and closing credits to capture the necessary data for your bibliography entry. As with the personal interview, be scrupulously accurate in taking notes. Citations may refer to a performer, director, or narrator, depending on the focus of your study. It is best to write direct quotations because paraphrases of television commentary can unintentionally be distorted by bias. Always scrutinize material taken from an Internet site.

4d   Conducting a Survey with a Questionnaire

Questionnaires can produce current, firsthand data that you can tabulate and analyze. To achieve meaningful results, you must survey randomly with regard to age, sex, race, education, income, residence, and other factors. Bias can creep into the questionnaire unless you remain objective. Use a formal survey only if you are experienced with tests and measurements and statistical analysis or when you have an instructor who will help you with the instrument. Be advised that most schools have a Human Subjects Committee that sets guidelines, draws up consent forms, and requires anonymity of participants for information-gathering that might be intrusive. An informal survey gathered in the hallways of campus buildings lacks credibility in the research paper.

Surveys usually depend on *quantitative* methodologies, which produce numerical data. That is, the questionnaire results are tallied to reflect campus crime rates, parking slots for students, or the shifts in student population in off-campus housing. In some cases a survey depends on *qualitative* methodologies; these assess answers to questions on social issues, such as the number of biased words in a history text, the reasons for marijuana use, or levels of hyperactivity in a test group of children.

Label your survey in the bibliography entry:

> Mason, Valerie, and Sarah Mossman. "Child Care
>   Arrangements of Parents Who Attend College."
>   Questionnaire. Knoxville: U of Tennessee, 2004.

Keep the questionnaire short, clear, and focused on your topic. Questions must be unbiased. Ask your professor to review the instrument before using it. Design your questionnaire for a quick response to a scale ("Choose A, B, or C"), a ranking (first choice, second choice, and so on), or fill-in blanks. You should also arrange for an easy return of the questionnaire by providing a self-addressed stamped envelope or by allowing respondents to send in their completed questionnaires by e-mail.

Tabulate the responses objectively. Present the results—positive or negative—as well as a sample questionnaire in the appendix to your paper. While results that deny your hypothesis may not support the outcome you desire, they still have value.

4e   Conducting Experiments, Tests, and Observation

Empirical research, performed in a laboratory or in the field, can determine why and how things exist, function, or interact with one another. Your paper will explain your methods and findings in pursuit of a hypothesis or theory. An experiment thereby becomes primary evidence for your paper.

Observation occurs generally in the field, which might be a child care center, a movie theater, a parking lot, or the counter of a McDonald's restaurant. The field is anywhere you can observe, count, and record behavior, patterns, and systems. It can be testing the water in a stream or observing the nesting patterns of deer. Retail merchandisers conduct studies to observe buying habits. A basketball coach might gather and analyze data on shot selections by members of his team. Gathering data is a way of life for television executives, politicians, and thousands of marketing professionals.

A *case study* is a formal report based on your observation of a human subject. For example, you might examine patterns of behavior to build a profile, or you can base your case study on biographical data, interviews, tests, and observation. You might observe and interview an older person with dementia; that would be a case study and evidence for your research paper. Each discipline has its own standards for properly conducting a case study. You should not examine any subject without the guidance and approval of your instructor.

Most experiments and observations begin with a *hypothesis,* which is similar to a thesis sentence. The hypothesis is a statement assumed to be true for the purpose of investigation. *Hummingbirds live as extended families governed by a patriarch* is a hypothesis for which data are needed to prove its validity. *The majority of people will not correct the poor grammar of a speaker* is a hypothesis for which testing and observation must be conducted to prove its validity.

You can begin observation without a hypothesis and let the results lead you to the implications. Shown below is one student's double-entry format used to record observation on the left and commentary on the right. This is a limited example of field notes.

Record:	*Response:*
Day 1	
10-minute session at window, 3 hummingbirds fighting over the feeder	Is the male chasing away the female, or is the female the aggressor?
Day 2	
10-minute session at window, saw 8 single hummingbirds at feeder #1 and 1 guarding feeder #2 by chasing others away.	I did some research, and the red-throated male is the one that's aggressive.

Generally, a report on an experiment or observation follows a format that provides four distinct parts: introduction, method, results, and discussion.

CHECKLIST

Conducting an Experiment or Observation

- Express clearly your hypothesis in the introduction.
- Provide a review of the literature if necessary for establishing an academic background for the work.
- Explain your design for the study—lab experiment, observation, or the collection of raw data in the field.
- Design the work for maximum respect to your subjects. In that regard, you may find it necessary to get approval for your research from a governing board.
- For the results section, maintain careful records and accurate data. Don't let your expectations influence the results.
- In your conclusion, discuss your findings and any implications to be drawn.

5

Understanding and Avoiding Plagiarism

This chapter defines plagiarism, explores the ethical standards for writing in an academic environment, and provides examples of the worst and best of citations. Plus, we must face the newest problem: The Internet makes it easy to copy and download material and paste it into a paper—which in itself is not a problem *unless* you fail to acknowledge the source.

Intellectual property has value. If you write a song, you have a right to protect your interests. Thus, the purpose of this chapter is to explore with you the ethics of research writing, especially about these matters:

- Using sources to enhance your credibility
- Using sources to place a citation in its proper context
- Honoring property rights
- Avoiding plagiarism
- Honoring and crediting sources in online course work

5a Using Sources to Enhance Your Credibility

What some students fail to realize is that citing a source in their papers, even the short ones, signals something special and positive to readers—that the student has researched the topic, explored the literature about it, and has the expertise to share it. By announcing clearly the name of a source, the writer reveals the scope of his or her critical reading in the literature, as shown in these notes by one student:

Sandra Postel says water is "a living system that drives the workings of a natural world we depend on" (19). Postel declares: "A new water era has begun" (24). She indicates that the great prairies of the world will dry up, including

71

America's. Hey, when folks in America notice the drought,
then maybe something will happen. Let's watch what
happens when Texas goes dry as a bone.

These notes give clear evidence of the writer's investigation into the subject, and they enhance the student's image as a researcher. This student will receive credit for naming and quoting the source. The opposite, *plagiarism,* might get the student into trouble, as we discuss in section 5d.

5b   Identifying Bias in a Source

You show integrity in your use of sources by identifying any bias expressed by a writer or implied by the political stance of a magazine. For example, if you are writing about federal aid to farmers, you will find different opinions in a farmer's magazine and a journal that promotes itself as a watchdog to federal spending. One is an advocate and the other a vocal opponent. You may quote these sources, but only if you identify them carefully. Let us examine the problem faced by one student. Student Jamie Johnston, in researching articles on savagery in prehistoric wars, found articles of interest and positioned them in his paper with a description of the sources, as shown in this passage that carefully identifies exactly what the authority claims. Notice especially the final sentence by Johnston.

> The evidence offers several assertions. Ben Harder has
> reported on the work of one forensic anthropologist, John
> Verano, who had investigated a series of "grisly executions"
> in the valley of Peru during the Moche civilization (cited in
> Harder). Victims "were apparently skinned alive. Others were
> drained of blood, decapitated, or bound tightly and left to be
> eaten by vultures" (cited in Harder). Verano has the proof of
> the executions, but not the reason, although his speculations
> center on religious ceremonies.

You owe your readers this favor: Examine articles, especially those in magazines and on the Internet, for special interests, opinionated speculation, or an absence of credentials by the writer. Be wary of Web sites without an academic or government sponsor.

5c   Honoring Property Rights

If you invent a new piece of equipment or a child's toy, you can get a patent that protects your invention. You now own it. If you own a company, you can register a symbol that serves as a trademark for the products produced. You own the trademark. In like manner, if you write a set of poems and publish them in a chapbook, you own the poems. Others must seek your permission before they can reproduce the poems, just as others must buy your trademark or pay to produce your toy.

The principle behind the copyright law is relatively simple. Copyright begins at the time a creative work is recorded in some tangible form—a written document, a drawing, a tape recording. It does not depend on a legal registration with the copyright office in Washington, DC, although published works are usually registered. The moment you express yourself creatively on paper, in a song, on a canvas, that expression is your intellectual property. You have a vested interest in any profits made from the distribution of your work. For that reason, songwriters, cartoonists, fiction writers, and other artists guard their work and do not want it disseminated without compensation.

Scholarly work rarely involves direct compensation, but recognition is certainly an important need. We provide recognition by means of in-text citations and bibliography entries. As a student, you may use copyrighted material in your research paper under a doctrine of *fair use* as described in the U.S. Code, which says:

> The fair use of a copyrighted work . . . for purposes such as criticism, comment, news reporting, teaching (including multiple copies for classroom use), scholarship, or research is not an infringement of copyright.

Thus, as long as you borrow for educational purposes, such as a paper to be read by your instructor, you should not be concerned about violating the copyright law, as long as you provide documentation. However, if you decide to *publish* your research paper on a Web site, then new considerations come into play and you should seek the advice of your instructor.

5d   Avoiding Plagiarism

Write most of the paper yourself. First, develop personal notes full of your own ideas on a topic. Discover how you feel about the issue. Then, rather than copying sources one after another, express your own ideas at the beginning of paragraphs and then synthesize the ideas of others by using summary, paraphrase, and quotation. Rethink and reconsider ideas you gathered in your reading, make meaningful connections, and, when you refer to a specific source—as you inevitably will—give it credit.

Plagiarism is offering the words or ideas of another person as one's own. Major violations, which can bring failure in the course or expulsion from school, are:

- The use of another student's work
- The purchase of a canned research paper
- Copying passages into your paper without documentation
- Copying a key, well-worded phrase without documentation
- Placing specific ideas of others in your own words without documentation

These instances represent deliberate attempts to deceive. Closely related, but not technically plagiarism, is the fabrication of information—that is, making information up. Some newspaper reporters have lost their jobs because of such fabrication.

A gray area in plagiarism is simply student carelessness—for example, failure to enclose quoted material within quotation marks even though you provide an in-text citation, or a paraphrase that never quite becomes paraphrase because too much of the original is left intact. In this area, instructors might step in and help the beginning researcher, for although these cases are not flagrant instances of plagiarism, such errors can mar an otherwise fine piece of research.

There is one safety net: Express clearly the name of your sources to let readers know the scope of your reading on the subject, as in this note in CMS footnote style:

> Commenting on the role that music has in our everyday lives, editor Marc Smirnoff makes this observation in <u>Oxford American:</u> "The music that human beings rely on is essential to them. We know which tunes to listen to when we need an all-important lift (or when the party does) or when we want to wallow in our sadness."[7]

Citations like the one above help establish your credibility because they make clear whom you have read and how your ideas blend with the source.

Scholarly documentation differs from field to field. The style of literary papers is different than that of scientific papers. In the social sci-

CHECKLIST

Documenting Your Sources

- Let a reader know when you begin borrowing from a source by introducing a quotation or paraphrase with the name of the authority.

- Enclose within quotation marks all quoted materials—keywords, phrases, sentences, paragraphs.

- Make certain that paraphrased material is rewritten in your own style and language. The simple rearrangement of sentence patterns is unacceptable.

- Provide specific in-text documentation for each borrowed item, but keep in mind that styles differ for MLA, APA, CSE, and CMS standards. These styles are explained in later chapters.

- Provide a bibliography entry on the Works Cited page for every source cited in the paper.

ences, a paraphrase does not require a page number. In the applied sciences, a number replaces the authority's name, the year, and even the page number. So you will find that standards shift considerably as you move from class to class and from discipline to discipline. The good writer learns to adapt to the changes in the academic standards. Accordingly, this book devotes separate chapters to Modern Language Association (MLA), American Psychological Association (APA), Council of Science Editors (CSE), and *Chicago Manual of Style* (CMS) styles.

Common Knowledge Exceptions

Common knowledge exceptions exist because you and your reader share some perspectives on a subject. For example, if you attend the University of Delaware, you need not cite the fact that Wilmington is the state's largest city, or that Dover is the capital city. Information of this sort requires *no* in-text citation because your local audience will be knowledgeable.

The extended shoreline of Delaware provides one of the most extensive series of national wildlife refuges in the eastern United States. The state stretches from its northern border with Philadelphia to form a 100-mile border with Maryland to its west and south. Its political center is Dover, in the center of the state, but its commercial center is Wilmington, a great industrial city situated on Delaware Bay just below Philadelphia.

However, a writer in another place and time might need to cite the source of this information. Most writers would probably want to document this next passage.

Early Indian tribes on the plains called themselves *Illiniwek* (which meant "strong men"), and French settlers pronounced the name *Illinois* (Angle 44).

Borrowing from a Source Correctly

The next examples in MLA style demonstrate the differences between the accurate use of a source and the dark shades of plagiarism. First is the original reference material; it is followed by several student versions, with discussions of their merits.

Original Material

Imagine your brain as a house filled with lights. Now imagine someone turning off the lights one by one. That's what Alzheimer's disease does. It turns off the lights so that the flow of ideas, emotions and memories from one room to the next slows and eventually ceases. And sadly—as anyone who has ever watched a parent, a sibling, a spouse succumb to the spreading darkness knows—there is no way to stop the lights from turning off, no way to switch them back on once they've grown dim. At least not yet.

But sooner than one might have dared hope, predicts Harvard University neurologist Dr. Dennis Selkoe, Alzheimer's disease will shed the veneer of invincibility that today makes it such a terrifying affliction. Medical practitioners, he believes, will shortly have on hand not one but several drugs capable of slowing—and perhaps even halting—the progression of the disease. Best of all, a better understanding of genetic and environmental risk factors will lead to much earlier diagnosis, so that patients will receive treatment long before their brains start to fade.

From J. Madeleine Nash, "The New Science of Alzheimer's," *Time* 17 July 2000: 51.

Student Version A (Needs Revision)

Alzheimer's disease is like having a brain that's similar to a house filled with lights, but somebody goes through the house and turns out the lights one by one until the brain, like the house, is dark.

This sentence sounds good, and the reader will probably think so also. However, the writer has borrowed the analogy and much of the wording from the original source, so it's not the student's work. In addition, the writer has provided no documentation whatsoever, nor has the writer named the authority. In truth, the writer implies to the reader that these sentences are an original creation when, actually, nothing belongs to the writer.

Student Version B (Needs Revision)

Alzheimer's is a terrifying disease, for both victim and relatives. However, sooner than we might expect, medical scientists will have available several drugs capable of slowing—and perhaps even halting—the progress of the disease. In addition, earlier diagnosis will mean patients can receive treatment before their brains start to go dark.

This version borrows keywords from the original without the use of quotation marks and without a citation. The next version provides a citation, but it too has errors.

Student Version C (Needs Minor Revision)

Alzheimer's is a terrifying disease, but help is on the way. Dr. Dennis Selkoe, a neurologist at Harvard University, predicts that medical practitioners will shortly have on hand several drugs that will slow or stop the progression of the disease (Nash 51).

This version is better. It provides a reference to Dr. Selkoe, who has been cited by Nash. But readers cannot know that the paraphrase contains far too much of Nash's language—words that should be enclosed within quotation marks. Also, the citation to Nash is ambiguous. The next version handles these matters in a better fashion.

Student Version D (Acceptable)

Alzheimer's is a terrifying disease, but help is on the way. In a recent report in *Time,* medical reporter Madeleine Nash cites Dr. Dennis Selkoe, a neurologist at Harvard University, who believes that "medical practitioners . . . will shortly have on hand not one but several drugs capable of slowing—and perhaps even halting—the progression of the disease" (Nash 51).

This version represents a satisfactory handling of the source material. The writer is acknowledged at the outset of the borrowing,

Required Instances for Citing a Source

Examples are in MLA style.

1. An original idea derived from a source, whether quoted or paraphrased.

> Genetic engineering, by which a child's body shape and intellectual ability is predetermined, raised for one source "memories of Nazi attempts in eugenics" (Riddell 19).

2. Your summary of original ideas by a source.

> Genetic engineering has been described as the rearrangement of the genetic structure in animals or in plants, which is a technique that takes a section of DNA and reattaches it to another section (Rosenthal 19–20).

3. Factual information that is not common knowledge within the context of the course.

> Madigan has shown that genetic engineering has its risks: a nonpathogenic organism might be converted into a pathogenic one or an undesirable trait might develop as a result of a mistake (15).

4. Any exact wording copied from a source.

> Woodward asserted that genetic engineering is "a high-stakes moral rumble that involves billions of dollars and affects the future" (68).

the neurologist is given credit for his ideas, and a key section is quoted. A correct page citation closes the material. Let's suppose, however, that the writer does not wish to quote directly at all. The following example shows a paraphrased version:

Student Version E (Acceptable)

> Alzheimer's is a terrifying disease, but help is on the way. In a recent report in *Time*, medical reporter Madeleine Nash

cites Dr. Dennis Selkoe, a neurologist at Harvard University, who believes that the scientific community is knocking on the door of a cure or maybe even a set of cures. The goal, according to Nash, is to halt the disease or at least slow its insidious stalking of some of our best and brightest, such as former President Ronald Reagan (Nash 51).

This version also represents a satisfactory handling of the source material. In this case, no direct quotation is employed, the author and the authority are acknowledged and credited, and the entire paragraph is paraphrased in the student's own language. *Note:* the reference to the former president is not mentioned in the original passage, but such usage is a prime example of common knowledge.

5e Seeking Permission to Publish Material on Your Web Site

You may wish to post your research papers on your personal Web site, if you have one. However, the moment you do so, you are *publishing* the work and putting it into the public domain. That act carries responsibilities. In particular, the *fair use* doctrine of the U.S. Code refers to the personal educational purposes of your usage. When you load borrowed images, text, music, or artwork onto the Internet, you are making that intellectual property available to everybody all over the world.

Short quotations, a few graphics, and a small quantity of illustrations to support your argument are examples of fair use. Permission is needed, however, if the amount you borrow is substantial. The borrowing cannot affect the market for the original work, and you cannot misrepresent it in any way. The courts are still refining the law. For example, would your use of three *Doonesbury* comic strips be substantial? Yes, if you reproduce them in full. Would it affect the market for the comic strip? Perhaps. Follow these guidelines:

- Seek permission to include copyrighted material you publish within your Web article. Most authors grant permission at no charge. The problem is tracking down the copyright holder.
- If you attempt to get permission and if your motive for using the material is *not for profit,* it's unlikely you will have any problem with the copyright owner. The owner would have to prove that your use of the image or text caused him or her financial harm.

- You may publish without permission works that are in the public domain, such as a section of Hawthorne's *The Scarlet Letter* or a speech by the President from the White House. In general, creative works enter the public domain after about seventy-five years (the laws keep changing). Government papers are public domain.
- Document any and all sources you feature on your Web site.
- You may need permission to provide hypertext links to other sites. However, right now the Internet rules on access are being freely interpreted.
- Be prepared for other persons to visit your Web site and even borrow from it. Decide beforehand how you will handle requests for use of your work, especially if it includes your creative efforts in poetry, art, music, or graphic design.

HINT: For information on the Fair Use Laws, visit http://fairuse.stanford.edu/.

6

Finding and Reading the Best Sources

Finding sources worthy of citation in your paper can be a challenge. This chapter cuts to the heart of the matter: How do you find the best, most appropriate sources? Should you read all or just part of a source? How do you respond to it? Also, in this age of electronic publications, you must constantly review and verify to your own satisfaction the words of your sources. It is wise to consider every article on the Internet as suspect unless you access it through your library's databases.

6a Understanding the Assignment

A general search for sources on the Internet may serve your needs for writing a short paper, but the research paper requires you to compose from books, scholarly journals, and academic articles. Also, a specific academic discipline usually controls your research. For example, an assignment to examine the recreational programs at selected day care centers requires research in the literature of the social sciences found at your library's electronic catalogs rather than the Internet.

In addition, you need a mix of primary and secondary sources. *Primary sources* include novels, speeches, eyewitness accounts, interviews, letters, autobiographies, observation during field research, and the written results of empirical research. You should feel free to quote often from a primary source that has direct relevance to your discussion. For example, if you present a poem by Dylan Thomas, you should quote the poem. *Secondary sources* are writings about the primary sources, about an author, or about somebody's accomplishments. Secondary sources include a report on a presidential speech, a review of new scientific findings, analysis of a poem, or a biography of a notable person. These evaluations, analyses, and interpretations provide ways of looking at original, primary sources. Here's a guide to sources for the major disciplines.

Guide to Academic Sources
Humanities

Primary sources in literature and the fine arts are novels, poems, and plays as well as films, paintings, music, and sculpture. Your task is to examine, interpret, and evaluate these original works. Researchers in history must look at speeches, documents written by historic figures, and some government documents.

Secondary sources in the humanities are evaluations in journal articles and books, critical reviews, biographies, and history books.

Field research in the humanities comprises interviews with an artist or government official, letters, e-mail surveys, online discussion groups, and the archival study of manuscripts.

Social Sciences

Primary sources in education, political science, psychology, and other fields include speeches, writings by presidents and others, documents recorded in the *Congressional Record,* reports and statistics of government agencies and departments, and papers at your state's archival library.

Field research is most important in the social sciences and consists of case studies, findings from surveys and questionnaires, tests and test data, interviews, and observation. In business reports, field research consists of market testing, drawings and designs, industrial research, letters, and interviews.

Secondary sources include books and articles on social, political, and psychological issues, analyses and evaluations in journal articles, discussions of the business world in newspapers, magazines, and journals, and—in general—anything written about key personalities, events, products, and primary documents.

Sciences

Primary sources in the sciences consist of the words and theories of scientists discussing natural phenomena or offering their views on scientific issues, such as the words of Charles Darwin or Stephen Hawking. At the same time, journal articles that report on empirical research are considered primary material because they are original in their testing of a hypothesis.

Secondary sources in the sciences are not abundant. They appear generally as review articles that discuss testing and experiments by several scientists—for example, the review of four or five articles on gene mutation.

Field research and laboratory testing are crucial to the sciences and provide the results of experiments, discoveries, tests, and observations.

6b   Identifying the Best Source Materials

Let's look at an inverted pyramid that shows you a progression from excellent sources to less reliable ones. The chart does not ask you to ignore or dismiss items at the bottom, such as magazines and e-mail discussion groups, but it lets you know when to feel confident and when to be on guard about the validity of the source.

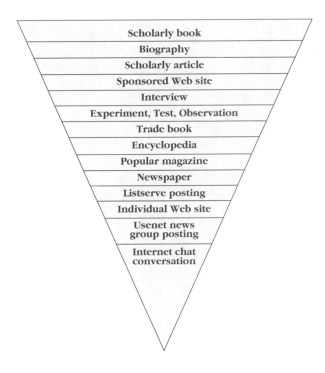

Scholarly book
Biography
Scholarly article
Sponsored Web site
Interview
Experiment, Test, Observation
Trade book
Encyclopedia
Popular magazine
Newspaper
Listserve posting
Individual Web site
Usenet news group posting
Internet chat conversation

Scholarly Book

Scholarly books, including textbooks, treat academic topics with in-depth discussions and careful documentation of the evidence. A college library is a repository for scholarly books—technical and scientific works, doctoral dissertations, publications of the university presses, and many textbooks. Scholarly books are subjected to careful review before publication, and they are published because they give the very best treatment of a subject. However, in the sciences, books grow out of date quickly, so depend on monthly journals to keep your research current.

Biography

The library's electronic catalog can help you find an appropriate biography from among the thousands available; representative databases include *Contemporary Authors* and *Dictionary of American Negro Biography.* You can also learn about a notable person on the Internet by searching for the name of the person and carefully scanning the sites that are returned. Notable persons are likely to have a Web site devoted to them. A *critical biography* is a book devoted not only to the life of the subject but also to his or her life's work; an excellent example is Richard Ellmann's *Oscar Wilde,* a critical study of Wilde's writings as well as his life.

You may need a biography for several reasons:

- To verify the standing and reputation of somebody you want to paraphrase or quote in your paper.
- To provide biographical details in your introduction. For example, the primary topic may be Carl Jung's psychological theories of the unconscious, but information about Jung's career might also be appropriate in the paper.
- To discuss a creative writer's life in relation to his or her work—that is, details of Joyce Carol Oates's personal life may illuminate your reading of her stories and novels.

Scholarly Article

Scholarly articles are best found through one of the library's databases. The academic database takes you to journal articles or articles at academically sponsored Web sites. You can feel confident about the authenticity of journal articles because the authors write for academic honor, they document all sources, and they publish through university presses and academic organizations. Thus, a journal article about child abuse found in *Journal of Marriage and the Family* or found through the PsyINFO database may be considered reliable. Nevertheless, some popular magazines are noted for their quality, such as *Atlantic Monthly, Scientific Review,* and *Discover.* The major newspapers—*New York Times, Atlanta Constitution,* and *Wall Street Journal*—often hire the best writers and columnists, so valuable articles can be found in both printed and online newspapers.

Sponsored Web Site

The Internet supplies both excellent and dubious information. You must be careful when evaluating Web materials. You should ask yourself a few questions about any Web site information:

- Is it appropriate to my work?
- Does it reveal a serious and scholarly emphasis?
- Is it sponsored by a professional institution or organization?

Interview

Interviews with knowledgeable people provide excellent information for a research paper. Whether conducted in person, by telephone, or by e-mail, the interview brings a personal, expert perspective to your work. The key element, of course, is the experience of the person.

Experiment, Test, or Observation

Gathering your own data for research is a staple in many fields, especially the sciences. An experiment brings primary evidence into your paper as you explain your hypothesis, give the test results, and discuss the implications of your findings.

Trade Book

How to Launch a Small Business and *Landscaping with Rocks* are typical titles of nonfiction trade books found in bookstores rather than college libraries (although public libraries often have trade book holdings). Designed for commercial consumption, trade books seldom treat a scholarly subject in depth. Unlike scholarly books and textbooks, manuscripts for trade books do not go through the rigors of peer review. For example, if your topic is dieting, with a focus on fad diets, you will find plenty of diet books at the local bookstore and numerous articles on commercial Web sites. However, serious discussions backed by careful research are found in the journals or at sponsored Web sites.

Encyclopedia

An encyclopedia, by design, contains brief surveys of every well-known person, event, place, and accomplishment. It can support your preliminary investigation for a topic, but most instructors prefer that you go beyond encyclopedias to cite from scholarly books and journal articles. However, specialized encyclopedias often have in-depth articles by noted scholars.

Popular Magazine

Like a trade book, a magazine article seldom offers in-depth information and does not face the critical review of a panel of experts. Thus, you must exercise caution when using it as a source. In general, college libraries house the better magazines—those that have merit in the quality of writing—so depend on the library's list of academic databases. For example, if your paper concerns sports medicine, citing an article from the *Atlantic Monthly* or *Scientific Review* will gain you far higher marks than one from *Sports Illustrated, Sport,* or *NBA Basketball.*

Newspaper

Newspaper reporters write under the pressure of deadlines. They do not have as much time to do careful research as do writers of journal articles. On occasion, a newspaper assigns reporters to a series of articles on a complex topic, and such in-depth analyses have merit. As noted above, the major newspapers—*New York Times, Atlanta Constitution,* and *Wall Street Journal*—often hire highly qualified writers and columnists, so valuable articles can be found in both the printed and online versions of these papers. You must remember, however, that newspaper articles, like those in magazines and on the Internet, must receive cautionary and critical evaluation.

E-mail Discussion Group

E-mail information via a forum established by the instructor for a course deserves consideration when it focuses on academic issues such as British Romantic literature or, more specifically, Shelley's poetry. In some cases, they originate for students in an online course, providing a venue for sharing ideas. However, rather than search for quotable material from e-mail forums, use them as a sounding board to generate ideas and test them with other participants.

Individual Web Site

Anyone can set up a Web site regardless of his or her credentials. You cannot avoid unreliable sites because they pop up on search engines, but you can approach them with caution. For example, a student investigating the topic *fad diets* searched the Web but found mostly home pages that described personal battles with weight loss or commercial sites that were blatant in their attempts to sell. Caution is vital.

Internet Chat Conversations

Real-time Internet conversations have almost no value for academic research and are not legitimate sources for your paper. Seldom do you know the participants beyond their usernames, and the conversations seldom focus on scholarly issues.

6c Evaluating a Source

Confronted by several books and articles, many writers have trouble determining the value of material and the contribution it can make to the research paper. To save time, you must be selective in your reading. To serve your reader, you must cite carefully selected material that is pertinent to the argument. Avoid dumping huge blocks of quotation into the paper because the paper will lack your style and tone of voice. You must be concerned about the relevance, authority, accuracy, and currency of all sources you cite in your paper.

Relevance

To determine how well an article or book fits the demands of your research, skim it. For a periodical or Internet article, examine the title, the abstract or introduction, and both the opening and closing paragraphs.

Authority

To test the authority of a source, examine the credentials of the author (usually found in a brief biographical profile or note of professional affiliation) and the sponsoring institution—usually the publisher of a journal, such as the American Sociological Association, or the sponsor of a Web site, such as http://www.ucla.edu. Look at the bibliography at the end of the article, for it signals the scholarly nature of the work and also points you toward other material on the subject. Study the home page of an Internet article, if there is one. Prefer sites sponsored by universities and professional organizations. Note hypertext links to other sites whose quality may be determined by the domain tags, such as .edu, .org, and .gov. Be wary of .com sites.

Note: The definitive edition of a work is the most reliable version of a play, novel, or collection of poems; it is definitive because it is the one the author supervised through the press. The way an author wanted the work presented can be found only in a definitive edition.

Thus, electronic versions usually do not display the original author's page and type design, unless they are photocopies of the original, as at the JSTOR site.

Accuracy

In the sciences, scholars talk about the verification of an article, which means they can, if necessary, replicate the research and the findings. A scientific report must carefully detail the design of the work, the methods, subjects, and procedures. A lab experiment, for example, should repeat previous findings to demonstrate accuracy. The writer should reveal the details of a control group, an experimental group, and the testing procedures. Any scientific report that does not establish research methods should not be cited.

Currency

Use recent sources for research in the sciences and social sciences. A psychology book may look valuable, but if its copyright date is 1955 the content has probably been replaced by recent research and current developments. When reading a source, be certain at least one date is listed. Electronic publications sometimes show the site has been updated or refreshed, but the article itself may carry an older date. On the Internet, check the date of print publication; it may be different than that of the Web publication. As a general rule, use the most recent date for an article on the Internet, which means you could list as many as three dates—the year of the print publication, the most recent year of the Internet publication, and the date you accessed the material.

7

Organizing Ideas and Setting Goals

Initially, research is haphazard, and your workspace will be cluttered with bits of information on notes and photocopied sheets. After investigating and gathering sufficient sources for your project, you must organize the information to serve specific needs. The structure of your project will become clear only when you organize your research materials into a proposal, a list of ideas, a set of questions, or a rough outline. In most cases, the design of your study should match an appropriate organizational model, sometimes called a *paradigm,* which means "an example that serves as a pattern or model." The organizational models in this chapter will help you organize your notes, photocopies, and downloaded files. Research assignments demand different kinds of papers in a variety of formats. By following an academic model, you can be assured the design of your research project will meet the demands of the assignment.

7a Using the Correct Academic Model (Paradigm)

A traditional outline, because it is content-specific, is useful for one paper only, while an academic pattern, like those shown below, governs all papers within a certain design. For example, a general, all-purpose model gives a plan for almost any research topic.

A General, All-Purpose Model

If you are uncertain about your assignment, start with this basic model and expand it with your own material to develop a detailed outline. Readers, including your instructor, are accustomed to this sequence for research papers. It offers plenty of leeway.

- Identify the subject in the *introduction.* Explain the problem, provide background information, and give a clear thesis statement.

- Analyze the subject in the *body* of the paper. You can compare, analyze, give evidence, trace historical events, and handle other matters.
- Discuss your findings in the *conclusion*. You can challenge an assumption, interpret the findings, provide solutions, or reaffirm your thesis.

The specific design of any model is based on the nature of the assignment and the discipline for which you are writing. Each of the following forms is explained below.

Academic Pattern for the Interpretation of Literature and Other Creative Works

If you plan to interpret a musical, artistic, or literary work, such as an opera, a group of paintings, or a novel, adjust this model to your subject and purpose and build it, with your factual data, into a working outline.

Introduction
  Identify the work.
  Give a brief summary in one sentence.
  Provide background information that relates to the thesis.
  Offer biographical facts about the artist that relate to the specific issues.
  Quote and paraphrase authorities to establish the scholarly traditions.
  Write a thesis sentence that establishes your particular views of the literary work.
Body
  Provide evaluative analysis divided by imagery, theme, design, use of color, character development, structure, symbolism, narration, language, musical themes, and so forth.
Conclusion
  Focus on the artist, not just the elements of analysis as explained in the body.
  Explore the contributions of the artist in accordance with your thesis sentence.

Academic Pattern for the Analysis of History

If you are writing a history or political science paper that analyzes events and their causes and consequences, your paper should conform, in general, to the following plan. Flesh it out with the notes in your research journal to make it a working outline for drafting your paper.

Introduction
   Identify the event.
   Provide the background leading up to the event.
   Offer quotations and paraphrases from experts.
   Give the thesis sentence.
Body
   Analyze the background leading up to the event.
   Trace events from one historic episode to another.
   Offer a chronological sequence that explains how one event
      relates directly to the next.
   Cite authorities who have also investigated this event.
Conclusion
   Reaffirm your thesis.
   Discuss the consequences of this event.

Academic Pattern for Advancing Philosophical and Religious Ideas

If the assignment is to defend or analyze a topic from the history
of ideas, use this next design, adjusting it as necessary. Make it your
working outline by writing sentences and even paragraphs for each
item in the model.

Introduction
   Establish the idea or question.
   Trace its history.
   Discuss its significance.
   Introduce experts who have addressed the idea.
   Provide a thesis sentence that presents your approach to the
      issue(s)—from a fresh perspective, if at all possible.
Body
   Evaluate the issues surrounding the concept.
   Develop a past-to-present examination of theories.
   Compare and analyze the details and minor issues.
   Cite experts who have addressed this idea.
Conclusion
   Advance and defend your thesis as it grows out of evidence
      about the idea.
   Close with an effective quotation from a noted person.

Academic Pattern for the Review of a Performance

If the assignment is to review a musical, artistic, or literary
performance, such as an opera, a set of paintings, a reading, a drama,
or theatrical performance, adjust this paradigm to your subject and

purpose. *Note:* The review differs from the interpretation by its focus on evaluation rather than analysis.

Introduction
Identify the work.
Give a brief summary in one sentence.
Provide background information or history of the work.
Offer biographical facts about the artist that relate to the specific issues.
Quote and paraphrase authorities to establish the scholarly traditions that relate to this work and the performance.
Write a thesis sentence that establishes your judgment of the performance.
Body
Offer an evaluation based on a predetermined set of criteria. Judge a drama by its staging and acting, music by its quality of voice and instruments, art by its design, literature by its themes, and so forth.
Conclusion
Focus on the performance, the performers, and the artist.
Offer a judgment based on the criteria given in the body.

Academic Pattern for Advancing Your Ideas and Theories

If you want to advance a social or legal theory in your paper, use this design, adjusting it to eliminate unnecessary items and adding new elements as appropriate. Build this model into a working outline by assigning your notes, photocopies, and downloaded files to a specific line of the model.

Introduction
Establish the theory, problem, or question.
Discuss its significance.
Provide the necessary background information.
Introduce experts who have addressed the problem.
Provide a thesis sentence that relates the problem to a fresh perspective.
Body
Evaluate the issues involved in the problem.
Develop a chronological examination.
Compare and analyze the details and minor issues.
Cite experts who have addressed the same problem.
Conclusion
Advance and defend your theory.

Discuss the implications of your findings.

Offer directives or a plan of action.

Suggest additional research that might be appropriate.

Academic Pattern for Argument and Persuasion Papers

If you write persuasively or argue from a set position, your paper should conform, in general, to this paradigm. Select the elements that fit your design, begin to elaborate on them, and gradually build a frame for your paper.

Introduction
Establish clearly the problem or controversy that your paper will examine.
Summarize the issues.
Define key terminology.
Make concessions on some points of the argument.
Use quotations and paraphrases to explore the controversy.
Provide background information.
Write a thesis to establish your position.
Body
Develop arguments to defend one side of the subject.
Analyze the issues, both pro and con.
Give evidence from the sources, including quotations from the scholarship as appropriate.
Conclusion
Expand your thesis into a conclusion to demonstrate that your position was formulated logically through careful analysis and discussion of the issues.

Academic Model for a Comparative Study

A comparative study requires that you examine two schools of thought, two issues, two works, or the positions taken by two persons. It explores similarities and differences, generally using one of three arrangements for the body of the paper. As you embellish the model you will gradually build your working outline.

Introduction
Establish A.
Establish B.
Briefly compare the two.
Introduce the central issues.
Cite source materials on the subjects.
Present your thesis.

Body (choose one)

Examine A.	Compare A and B.	Issue 1: Discuss A and B.
Examine B.	Contrast A and B.	Issue 2: Discuss A and B.
Compare and contrast A and B.	Discuss the central issues.	Issue 3: Discuss A and B.

Conclusion

Discuss the significant issues.

Rank one of the subjects over the other, or rate the respective genius of each.

Academic Pattern for a Laboratory Investigation or Field Report

This model has little flexibility. Instructors will expect your report to remain tightly focused on each of these items.

Introduction

Provide the title, the experiment number, and the date.

Describe the experiment.

List any literature consulted.

Objectively describe what you hope to accomplish.

Method

Explain the procedures used to reproduce the experiment.

Explain the design of the test.

Identify any tools or apparatus used.

Identify any variables that affected your research (weather conditions, temperatures, and so on).

Results

Give your findings, including statistical data.

Discussion

Provide your interpretation of the data.

Discuss implications to be drawn from the research.

Comment on what you learned by the experiment (optional).

Academic Pattern for Scientific Analysis

In this situation, you are working with the literature on a scientific issue, so you have more flexibility than with a report on a lab experiment.

Introduction

Identify the scientific issue or problem and state your hypothesis.

Explore the history of the topic.

Cite the literature that pertains to the topic.

Explain the purpose of the examination and its possible implications.

Body

Classify the issues.

Analyze, define, and compare each aspect of the topic.

Offer cause-effect explanations.

Make a detailed inquiry into all relevant issues.

Conclusion

Explain the current findings of scientific studies related to your topic.

Advance your reasons for continued research.

Suggest possible findings.

Discuss the implications of your analysis.

Academic Pattern for a Report of Empirical Research

This pattern is similar to the one for a laboratory investigation, so follow it closely to fill all the required items.

Introduction

Present the point of your study.

State the hypothesis and how it relates to the problem.

Provide the theoretical implications.

Explain the manner in which your study relates to previously published work.

Method

Describe the subject (what was tested, who participated— whether human or animal—and where the field work was accomplished).

Describe your equipment and how you used it.

Summarize the procedure and the execution of each stage of your work.

Results

Summarize the data you collected.

Provide statistical treatment of your findings with tables, graphs, and charts.

Include findings that conflict with your hypothesis.

Discussion

Discuss the implications of your work.

Evaluate the data and its relevance to the hypothesis.

Interpret the findings as necessary.

Discuss the implications of the findings.

Qualify the results and limit them to your specific study.

Make inferences from the results.

Suggest areas worthy of additional research.

7b Using Your Thesis to Control the Outline

After you have selected an academic pattern appropriate to your assignment, you should use your thesis sentence (or hypothesis) to set the tone and direction of your paper. Notice below how variations in the thesis can affect the arrangement of the paper.

Argument

THESIS: Misunderstandings about organ donation distort reality and set serious limits on the availability of organs to persons who need an eye, a liver, or a healthy heart.

Argument 1. Many myths mislead people into believing that donation is unethical.

Argument 2. Some fear that as a patient they might be put down early.

Argument 3. Religious views sometimes get in the way of donation.

This preliminary outline gives this writer three categories for an analysis of the issues.

Cause and Effect

THESIS: Television can have positive effects on a child's language development.

Consequence 1. Television introduces new words.

Consequence 2. Television reinforces word usage and proper syntax.

Consequence 3. Literary classics come alive on television.

Consequence 4. Television exposes children to the subtle rhythms and musical effects of accomplished speakers.

Notice that the thesis on television's educational values points the way to four issues worthy of investigation.

Evaluation

THESIS: The architectural drawing for the university's new student center is not friendly to people who are handicapped.

Evaluation 1.   The common areas seem cramped and
                 narrow, with few open areas in which
                 students can cluster.
Evaluation 2.   Steps and stairs seem all too common in
                 the design.
Evaluation 3.   Only one elevator appears in the plans
                 when three would be fair and equitable.
Evaluation 4.   Only the first-floor rest rooms offer
                 universal access.
Evaluation 5.   The parking spaces designated for people
                 with physical handicaps are located at an
                 entrance with steps, not a ramp.

This outline evolves from a thesis sentence that invites evaluation of an architectural plan.

Comparison

THESIS: Discipline often involves punishment, but child
             abuse adds another element: the gratification of
             the adult.

Comparison 1.   A spanking has the interest of the child
                 at heart, but a beating or a caning has no
                 redeeming value.
Comparison 2.   Time-outs remind the child that
                 relationships are important and to be
                 cherished, but lockouts in a closet only
                 promote hysteria and fear.
Comparison 3.   The parent's ego and selfish interests
                 often take precedence over the welfare of
                 the child or children.

This thesis sentence motivates a pattern of comparison by which to judge the relative differences between punishment of a child and child abuse.

7c   Writing an Outline

Not all papers require a complete, formal outline, nor do all researchers need one. A short research paper can be created from keywords, a list of issues, a rough outline, and a first draft. However, an outline sometimes is important, for it fleshes out the academic pattern you have selected (see section 7a) by classifying the issues of your study into clear, logical categories with main headings and one or more levels of subheadings.

A formal outline is not rigid and inflexible; you may, and should, modify it while writing and revising. In every case, treat an outline or organizational chart as a tool. Like an architect's blueprint, it should contribute to, not inhibit, the construction of a finished product. You may wish to experiment with the Outline feature of your software, which allows you to view the paper at various levels of detail and to highlight and drop the essay into a different organization.

Topic Outline

Build a topic outline of balanced phrases. You can use noun phrases ("the rods of the retina"), gerund phrases ("sensing dim light with retina rods"), or infinitive phrases ("to sense dim light with retina rods"). No matter which grammatical format you choose, follow it consistently throughout the outline. One student used noun phrases to outline her scientific analysis:

I. Diabetes defined
   A. A disease without control
      1. A disorder of the metabolism
      2. The search for a cure
   B. Types of diabetes
      1. Type 1, juvenile diabetes
      2. Type 2, adult onset diabetes
II. Health complications
   A. The problem of hyperglycemia
      1. Signs and symptoms of the problem
      2. Lack of insulin
   B. The conflict of the kidneys and the liver
      1. Effects of ketoacidosis
      2. Effects of arteriosclerosis
III. Proper care and control
   A. Blood sugar monitoring
      1. Daily monitoring at home
      2. Hemoglobin test at a laboratory
   B. Medication for diabetes
      1. Insulin injections
      2. Hypoglycemia agents

   C. Exercise programs
      1. Walking
      2. Swimming
      3. Aerobic workouts
   D. Diet and meal planning
      1. Exchange plan
      2. Carbohydrate counting
IV. Conclusion: Balance of all the factors

Sentence Outline

Instead of an outline with phrases, you may use full sentences for each heading and subheading. Using sentences has two advantages over the topic outline: (1) Many entries in a sentence outline can serve as topic sentences for paragraphs, thereby accelerating the writing process, and (2) The subject-verb pattern establishes the logical direction of your thinking (for example, the phrase *Vocabulary development* becomes *Television viewing can improve a child's vocabulary*). Note below a brief portion of one student's sentence outline.

   I. Organ and tissue donation is the gift of life.
      A. Organs that can be successfully transplanted include the heart, lungs, liver, kidneys, and pancreas.
      B. Tissues that can be transplanted successfully include bone, corneas, skin, heart valves, veins, cartilage, and other connective tissues.
      C. The process of becoming a donor is easy.
      D. Many people receive organ and tissue transplants each year, but still many people die because they did not receive the needed transplant.

8

Writing Effective Notes

Notetaking is the heart of research. If you write notes of high quality, they may need only minor editing to fit the appropriate places in your first draft. Prepare yourself to write different types of notes—quotations for well-phrased passages by authorities but also paraphrased or summarized notes to maintain your voice. This chapter explains the following types of notes:

- *Personal notes* that express your own ideas or record field research.
- *Quotation notes* that preserve the distinguished syntax of an authority.
- *Paraphrase notes* that interpret and restate what the authority has said.
- *Summary notes* that capture in capsule form a writer's ideas.
- *Field notes* that record interviews, tabulate questionnaires, and maintain records of laboratory experiments and other types of field research.

Honoring the Conventions of Research Style

Your notetaking will be more effective from the start if you practice the conventions of style for citing a source within your text, as advocated by MLA, APA, CSE, or CMS and as shown briefly below.

MLA: Lawrence Smith states, "The suicidal teen causes severe damage to the psychological condition of peers" (34).

APA: Smith (1997) stated, "The suicidal teen causes severe damage to the psychological condition of peers" (p. 34).

CMS footnote: Lawrence Smith explains, "The suicidal teen causes severe damage to the psychological condition of peers."[3]

C H E C K L I S T

Writing Effective Notes

1. Write each note in a separate, labeled file within one folder, although you can keep several notes in one computer file if each is labeled clearly. Remember, downloaded files from Internet databases must also be labeled clearly.

2. Accompany each file with the name, year, and page of the source to prepare for in-text citations.

3. Label each file (for example, *objectivity on television*).

4. Write a full note in well-developed sentences to speed the writing of your first draft.

5. Keep everything (photocopy, scribbled note) in order to authenticate dates, page numbers, and full names.

6. Label your personal notes with *my idea* or *personal note* to distinguish them from the sources.

CSE number: Smith (4) said, "The suicidal teen causes severe damage to the psychological condition of peers."

The MLA style is the default style displayed throughout this chapter.

8a Writing Personal Notes

The content of a research paper is an expression of your own ideas as supported by the scholarly evidence. It is not a collection of ideas transmitted by experts in books and articles. Readers are primarily interested in *your* thesis sentence, *your* topic sentences, and *your* personal view of the issues. Therefore, during your research, record your thoughts on the issues by writing plenty of personal notes in your research journal and computer files. Personal notes are essential because they allow you to record your discoveries, reflect on the findings, make connections, and identify the prevailing views and patterns of thought. Remember two standards: (1) The idea written into the file is yours, and (2) the file is labeled with *my idea, mine, personal thought* to distinguish it from information borrowed from a source. Here's an example:

Personal thought

For me, organ donation might be a gift of life, so I have signed my donor card. At least a part of me will continue to

live if an accident claims my life. My boyfriend says I'm
gruesome, but I consider it practical. Besides, he might be
the one who benefits, and then what will he say?

8b Writing Direct Quotation Notes

Quotation notes are essential because they allow you to
capture the authoritative voices of the experts on the topic, feature
well-phrased statements, offer conflicting points of view, and
share the literature on the topic with your readers. Follow these
basic conventions.

1. Select material that is important and well-phrased, not something
   trivial or something that is common knowledge. Not "John F.
   Kennedy was a Democrat from Massachusetts" (Rupert 233) but
   this:

   "John F. Kennedy's Peace Corps left a legacy of lasting
   compassion for the downtrodden"(Rupert 233).

2. Use quotation marks around the quoted material in your notes,
   working draft, and final manuscript. Do not copy or download
   the words of a source into your paper in such a way that readers
   will think *you* wrote the material.
3. Use the exact words of the source.
4. Provide an appropriate in-text citation, as in this note:

   Griffiths, Kilman, and Frost suggest that the killing of
   architect Stanford White in 1904 was "the beginning of the
   most bitterly savage century known to mankind" (113).
   Murder, wars, and human atrocities were the "sad vestiges"
   of an era that had great promise.

5. The parenthetical citation goes *outside* the final quotation mark
   but *inside* the period for quotations within your sentence. Block
   quotations require a different setup.
6. Quote key sentences and short passages, not entire paragraphs.
   Find the essential statement and feature it; do not force your
   reader to read a long quoted passage that has only one statement
   relevant to your point. Make the essential idea a part of your sentence, as shown here:

   Many Americans, trying to mend their past eating habits,
   adopt functional foods as an essential step toward a more

health-conscious future. Balthrop says this group of
believers spends "an estimated \$29 billion a year" on
functional foods (6).

7. Quote from both primary sources (the original words of a writer
   or speaker) and secondary sources (comments after the fact
   about original works). The two types are discussed immediately
   below.

Quoting the Primary Sources

Quote from primary sources for four reasons:

- To draw on the wisdom of the original author
- To let readers hear the precise words of the author
- To copy exact lines of poetry and drama
- To reproduce graphs, charts, and statistical data

Cite poetry, fiction, drama, letters, and interviews. In other cases,
you may want to quote liberally from a presidential speech, cite the
words of a business executive, or reproduce original data.

Quoting the Secondary Sources

Quote from secondary sources for three reasons:

- To display excellence in ideas and expression by experts on
  the topic
- To explain complex material
- To set up a statement of your own, especially if it spins off, adds
  to, or takes exception to the source as quoted

The overuse of direct quotation from secondary sources indicates either (1) that you did not have a clear focus and copied verbatim just about everything related to the subject, or (2) that you had
inadequate evidence and used numerous quotations as padding.
Therefore, limit quotations from secondary sources by using only a
phrase or a sentence:

Reginald Herman says the geographical changes in Russia
require "intensive political analysis" (15).

If you quote an entire sentence, make the quotation a direct
object that tells *what* the authority says.

In response to the changes in Russia, one critic notes, "The
American government must exercise caution and conduct
intensive political analysis" (15).

8c Writing Paraphrased Notes

A paraphrase requires you to restate in your own words the thought, meaning, and attitude of someone else. Your interpretation acts as a bridge between the source and the reader as you capture the wisdom of the source in approximately the same number of words. Use paraphrase to maintain your voice or style in the paper, to avoid an endless string of direct quotations, and to interpret the source as you rewrite it. Keep in mind these five rules for paraphrasing a source:

1. Rewrite the original in about the same number of words.
2. Provide an in-text citation to the source (in MLA style, the author and page number).
3. Retain exceptional words and phrases from the original by enclosing them in quotation marks.
4. Preserve the tone of the original by suggesting moods of satire, anger, humor, doubt, and so on. Show the author's attitude with appropriate verbs: "Edward Zigler condemns . . . defends . . . argues . . . explains . . . observes . . . defines."
5. Put the original aside while paraphrasing to avoid copying word for word. Compare the finished paraphrase with the original source to be certain that the paraphrase truly rewrites the original and that it uses quotation marks with any phrasing or key words retained from the original.

HINT: When instructors see an in-text citation but no quotation marks, they will assume that you are paraphrasing, not quoting. Be sure their assumption is correct.

Here are examples that show the differences between a quotation note and a paraphrased one:

Quotation:

Hein explains heredity in this way: "Except for identical twins, each person's heredity is unique" (294).

Paraphrase:

One source explains that heredity is special and distinct for each of us, unless a person is one of identical twins (Hein 294).

Quotation (block indent of four lines or more):

Hein explains the phenomenon in this way:

> Since only half of each parent's chromosomes are transmitted to a child and since this half

represents a chance selection of those the child
could inherit, only twins that develop from a
single fertilized egg that splits in two have
identical chromosomes. (294)

Paraphrase:

Hein specifies that twins have identical chromosomes
because they grow from one egg that divides after it has been
fertilized. He affirms that most brothers and sisters differ
because of the "chance selection" of chromosomes
transmitted by each parent (294).

As shown in the example immediately above, place any key wording of the source within quotation marks.

 ## Writing Summary Notes

A summary of a source serves a specific purpose, so it deserves
a polished style for transfer into the paper. It requires you to capture
in just a few words the ideas of an entire paragraph, section, or chapter. Store it in your folder with its own file name. It may be a rough
sketch of the source or a polished note. Use it for these reasons:

- To review an article or book
- To annotate a bibliography entry
- To provide a plot summary
- To create an abstract

Success with the summary requires the following:

1. Condense the original content with precision and directness.
   Reduce a long paragraph to a sentence, tighten an article into a
   brief paragraph, and summarize a book in a page.
2. Preserve the tone of the original. If the original is serious, suggest
   that tone in the summary. In the same way, retain moods of doubt,
   skepticism, optimism, and so forth.
3. Write the summary in your own language; however, retain exceptional phrases from the original, enclosing them in quotation marks.
4. Provide documentation.

Use the Summary to Review Briefly an Article or Book

Note this example, which reviews two entire articles:

Alec Twobears has two closely related articles on this subject,
and both, one in 2001 and another in 2002, are about the

failure of the United States to follow through with the
treaties it signed with the Indian nations of North America.
He opens both with "No treaty is a good treaty!" He signals
clearly the absence of trust by native Americans toward the
government in Washington, DC.

Use the Summary to Write an Annotated Bibliography

An annotation offers a brief explanation or critical commentary
on an article or book. Thus, an annotated bibliography is one in which
each source is followed immediately by the annotation, as shown here
in MLA style.

"Top Ten Myths about Donation and Transplantation."
> TransWeb Webcast, 2002. 10 Oct. 2003 <http://
> www.transweb.org/news/zhtm>. This site dispels the many
> myths surrounding organ donation, showing that selling
> organs is illegal, that matching donor and recipient is
> highly complicated, and secret back room operations are
> almost impossible.

Use the Summary in a Plot Summary Note

In just a few sentences, a summary can describe a novel, short
story, drama, or similar literary work, as shown by this next note:

> <u>Great Expectations</u> by Dickens describes young Pip, who
> inherits money and can live the life of a gentleman. But he
> discovers that his "great expectations" have come from a
> criminal. With that knowledge his attitude changes from one
> of vanity to one of compassion.

Use the Summary to Create an Abstract

An abstract is a brief description that appears at the beginning
of an article to summarize the contents. Usually, it is written by the
article's author, and it helps readers make decisions about reading the
entire article. You can find entire volumes devoted to abstracts, such
as *Psychological Abstracts* and *Abstracts of English Studies.* An
abstract is required for most papers in the social and natural sciences.
Here's a sample from one student's paper:

Abstract

Functional foods, products that provide benefits beyond basic
nutrition, are adding billions to the nation's economy each

year. Functional foods are suspected to be a form of preventive medicine. Consumers hope that functional foods can calm some of their medical anxieties, while researchers believe that functional foods may lower health care costs. The paper identifies several functional foods, locates the components that make them work, and explains the role that each plays on the body.

8e Writing Notes from Field Research

For some research projects, you will be expected to conduct field research. This work may require different kinds of notes kept on charts, cards, notepads, laboratory notebooks, a research journal, or the computer. Interviews require careful notetaking during the session and dutiful transcription of those notes to your draft. A tape recorder can serve as a backup to your notetaking. A questionnaire produces valuable data for developing notes and graphs and charts for your research paper.

The procedures and findings of experiments, tests, and measurements serve as your notes for the Method and Results sections of the report. Here is an example of one student's laboratory notebook—a passage he might transfer to the Procedures section of his paper:

First, 25.0 ml of a vinegar sample was delivered to a 50-ml volumetric flask, with a 25-ml pipet, and diluted to the mark with distilled water. It was mixed thoroughly and 50.00-ml aliquot were emptied into three 250-ml conical flasks, with a 25-ml pipet, 50 ml of distilled water, and two drops of phenolphthalein were added to each of the flasks. The samples were then titrated with a .345 M NaOH solution until the first permanent pink color.

8f Using Your Notes to Write an Annotated Bibliography

Writing an annotated bibliography may look like busywork, but it helps you evaluate the strength and nature of your sources. The annotated bibliography that follows is written in MLA style. An *annotation* is a summary of the contents of a book or article. A *bibliography* is a list of sources on a selected topic. Thus, an annotated bibliography does two important things: (1) it lists bibliographic data for a selection of sources, and (2) it summarizes the contents of each book or article.

The annotated bibliography that follows summarizes a few sources on the issue of tanning, tanning beds, lotions, and the dangers of skin cancer.

Levenson 1

Norman Levenson
Professor Davidson
English 1020
24 July 2003

Annotated Bibliography

Brown, Edwin W. "Tanning Beds and the 'Safe Tan' Myth." <u>Medical Update</u> 21 (1998): 6. Brown makes the point that there is "no such thing as a 'safe' or 'healthy' tan." He explains that tanning is the skin's reaction to radiation damage, and "tanned skin is damaged skin." He cautions that tans from tanning beds are no different than those produced by the sun. Like others, he encourages the use of SPF 15 or higher.

Cohen, Russell. "Tanning Trouble: Teens Are Using Tanning Beds in Record Numbers." <u>Scholastic Choices</u> 18 (2003): 23–28. Cohen warns that tanning beds "can be just as dangerous as the sun's rays" (23). The writer explains that tanning salons are not

> Each entry gives full bibliographic information on the source—author, title, and publication data—as well as a brief description of the article or book.

Levenson 2

well regulated, so the amount of exposure can be really dangerous. The writer also explains how skin type affects tanning and the dangers of cancer.

Geller, Alan C., et al. "Use of Sunscreen, Sunburning Rates, and Tanning Bed Use among More Than 10,000 U.S. Children and Adolescents." <u>Pediatrics</u> 109 (2002): 1009–15. The objective of this study was to examine the psychosocial variables associated with teens seeking suntans. It collected data from questionnaires submitted by 10,079 boys and girls 12 to 18 years old. It concluded that many children are at risk for skin cancer because of failure to use sunscreen.

Segilia, Amanda. "Sunscreens, Suntans, and Sun Health." American Cancer Society. Interview. 13 June 2000. 4 June 2003 <http://www.intelihealth.com/search>. This site features Harvard Medical School's Consumer Health Information. In this article, Amanda Segilia, a coordinator of Cancer Control Programs for the American Cancer Society, answers questions about tanning, including the use of sunscreen of SPF 15 or higher, use of suntan lotions, the effects of the sun, and the dangers of skin cancer.

"Skin Protection—My Teen Likes to Tan." St. Louis Children's Hospital. 2003. 3 June 2003 <http://www.stlouischildrens.org/articles/article_print.asp?ID=2670>. This site quotes Susan Mallory, the director of dermatology at St. Louis Children's Hospital, and registered nurse Ann Leonard, who both offer warnings against the use of tanning beds. Rather than damaging the skin with sun or tanning beds, the two experts suggest the use of tanning sprays or lotions.

Levenson 3

"Teens and the Sun." Health Watch. The U of Texas
    Southwestern Medical Center at Dallas. 29 July 2002.
    4 June 2003 <http://www3.utsouthwestern.edu/
    library/consumer/teen&sun02.htm>. This article
    warns teenagers against sun worship and skipping
    sunscreen. The experts suggest more public education
    and warnings. For example, teens should know that
    tanning damages the structure of the skin and
    promotes sagging skin and wrinkles in later life.
Zazinski, Janice. "A Legion of Ladies' Lesions." Research
    Briefs. Boston U. 11 Aug. 2000. 4 June 2003 <www.bu.edu/
    news/research/2000/8-11-suntans-chf.htm>. This
    article cites Dr. Marie-France Demierre, a professor
    of dermatology, who laments the use of tanning
    beds by young women. In truth, women are joining
    men in contracting and dying of melanoma, in great
    part because of tanning beds. Demierre and Zazinski
    warn youngsters against addiction to tanning beds
    and sun worship.

8g Using Your Notes to Write a Review of the Literature

The review of literature presents a set of summaries in essay form
for two purposes.

1. It helps you investigate the topic because it forces you to examine and then to record how each source addresses the problem.
2. It organizes and classifies the sources in some reasonable manner for the benefit of the reader.

Thus, you should relate each source to your central subject, and
you should group the sources according to their support of your thesis. For example, the brief review that follows explores the literature
on the subject of gender communication. It classifies the sources

under a progression of headings: the issues, the causes (both environmental and biological), the consequences for both men and women, and possible solutions.

You must also arrange the sources according to your selected categories or to fit your preliminary outline. Sometimes this task might be as simple as grouping those sources that favor a course or action and those that oppose it. In other cases—let's say it's a paper on Fitzgerald's *The Great Gatsby*—you may need to summarize sources by critics who examine Gatsby's character, others who study Daisy, and still others who write about Nick Carraway.

Like Kaci Holz, who wrote the paper below, you may wish to use side heads to identify your sections.

Holz 1

Kaci Holz
Dr. Bekus
April 23, 2003
English 1010

Gender Communication: A Review of the Literature

Several theories exist about different male and female communication styles. These ideas have been categorized below to establish the issues, shows causes for communication failures, the consequences for both men and women, and suggestions for possible solutions.

The review of literature is an essay on the articles and books that address the writer's topic.

The Issues

Deborah Tannen, Ph.D., is a professor of sociolinguistics at Georgetown University. In her book <u>You Just Don't Understand: Men and Women in Conversation</u>, 1990, she claims there are basic gender patterns or stereotypes that can be found.

The writer uses the sources to establish the issues.

Tannen says that men participate in conversations to establish "a hierarchical social order," while women most often participate in conversations to establish "a network of connections" (Tannen, <u>Don't Understand</u> 24–25). She

Holz 2

distinguishes between the way women use "rapport-talk" and the way men use "report-talk" (74).

In similar fashion, Susan Basow and Kimberly Rubenfeld, in "'Troubles Talk': Effects of Gender and Gender Typing," explore in detail the sex roles and how they determine and often control the speech of each gender. They notice that "women may engage in 'troubles talk' to enhance communication; men may avoid such talk to enhance autonomy and dominance" (186).

In addition, Phillip Yancey asserts that men and women "use conversation for quite different purposes" (71). He provides a 'no' answer to the question in his title, "Do Men and Women Speak the Same Language?" He claims that women converse to develop and maintain connections, while men converse to claim their position in the hierarchy they see around them. Yancey asserts that women are less likely to speak publicly than are men because women often perceive such speaking as putting oneself on display. A man, on the other hand, is usually comfortable with speaking publicly because that is how he establishes his status among others (Yancey 71).

Similarly, masculine people are "less likely than androgynous individuals to feel grateful for advice" (Basow and Rubenfeld 186). Julia T. Wood's book Gendered Lives claims that "male communication is characterized by assertion, independence, competitiveness, and confidence [while] female communication is characterized by deference, inclusivity, collaboration, and cooperation" (440). This list of differences describes why men and women have such opposing communication styles.

In another book, Tannen addresses the issue that boys, or men, "are more likely to take an oppositional stance toward other people and the world" and "are more likely to find opposition entertaining—to enjoy watching a good fight, or having one" (Tannen, Argument 166). Girls try to avoid fights.

Holz 3

Causes

Two different theories suggest causes for gender differences—the environment and biology.

<u>Environmental Causes</u>. Tammy James and Bethann Cinelli in 2003 mention, "The way men and women are raised contributes to differences in conversation and communication . . . " (41). Another author, Susan Witt, in "Parental Influence on Children's Socialization to Gender Roles," discusses the various findings that support the idea that parents have a great influence on their children during the development of their self-concept. She states, "Children learn at a very early age what it means to be a boy or a girl in our society" (253). She says that parents "[dress] infants in gender-specific colors, [give] gender-differentiated toys, and [expect] different behavior from boys and girls" (Witt 254).

Yancey notices a cultural gap, defining culture as "shared meaning" (68). He says, "Some problems come about because one spouse enters marriage with a different set of 'shared meanings' than the other" (69). The cultural gap affects the children. Yancey also talks about the "Battle of the Sexes" as seen in conflict between men and women. Reverting back to his 'childhood gender pattern' theory, Yancey claims, "Men, who grew up in a hierarchical environment, are accustomed to conflict. Women, concerned more with relationship and connection, prefer the role of peacemaker" (71).

Like Yancey, Deborah Tannen also addresses the fact that men and women often come from different worlds and different influences. She says, "Even if they grow up in the same neighborhood, on the same block, or in the same house, girls and boys grow up in different worlds of words" (Tannen, <u>Don't Understand</u> 43).

<u>Biological Causes</u>. Though Tannen often addresses the environmental issue in much of her research, she also looks at the biological issue in her book <u>The Argument</u>

The writer now uses the sources to explain the causes for communication failures.

Holz 4

<u>Culture</u>. Tannen states, "Surely a biological component
plays a part in the greater use of antagonism among men,
but cultural influence can override biological inheritance"
(Tannen, <u>Argument</u> 205). She sums up the nature versus
nurture issue by saying, "The patterns that typify women's
and men's styles of opposition and conflict are the result of
both biology and culture" (207).

Lillian Glass, another linguistics researcher, has a
1992 book called <u>He Says, She Says: Closing the
Communication Gap between the Sexes</u>. Glass addresses the
issue that different hormones found in men and women's
bodies make them act differently and therefore
communicate differently. She also discusses how brain
development has been found to relate to sex differences.

Judy Mann says, "Most experts now believe that what
happens to boys and girls is a complex interaction between
slight biological differences and tremendously powerful
social forces that begin to manifest themselves the minute
the parents find out whether they are going to have a boy
or a girl" (qtd. in McCluskey 6).

Consequences of Gender Differences

Now that we have looked at different styles of
gender communication and possible causes of gender
communication, let us look at the possible results. Michelle
Weiner-Davis is a marriage and family therapist who wrote
the best seller <u>Divorce Busting</u>. She says to the point,
"Ignorance about the differences in gender communication
has been a major contributor to divorce" (qtd. in Warren 106).

Through various studies, Tannen has concluded that
men and women have different purposes for engaging in
communication. In the open forum that Deborah Tannen
and Robert Bly gave in New York in 1993, Tannen (on
videotape) explains the different ways men and women
handle communication throughout the day. She explains

The writer now uses the sources to explain the consequence of communication failures on both men and women.

Holz 5

that a man constantly talks during his workday in order to impress those around him and to establish his status in the office. At home he wants peace and quiet. On the other hand, a woman is constantly cautious and guarded about what she says during her workday. Women try hard to avoid confrontation and avoid offending anyone with their language. So when a woman comes home from work she expects to be able to talk freely without having to guard her words. The consequence? The woman expects conversation, but the man is tired of talking.

Solutions

Answers for better gender communication seem elusive. What can be done about this apparent gap in communication between genders? In his article published in <u>Leadership</u>, Jeffrey Arthurs offers the obvious suggestion that women should make an attempt to understand the male model of communication and that men should make an attempt to understand the female model of communication.

However, in his article "Speaking across the Gender Gap," David Cohen mentions that experts didn't think it would be helpful to teach men to communicate more like women and women to communicate more like men. This attempt would prove unproductive because it would go against what men and women have been taught since birth. Rather than change the genders to be more like one another, we could simply try to "understand" each other better.

In addition, Richard Weaver makes this observation: "The idea that women should translate their experiences into the male code in order to express themselves effectively . . . is an outmoded, inconsistent, subservient notion that should no longer be given credibility in modern society" (439). He suggests three things we can change: 1.) Change

The writer now depends on the sources to provide possible solutions.

Holz 6

the norm by which leadership success is judged,
2.) Redefine what we mean by power, and 3.) Become
more sensitive to the places and times when inequity and
inequality occur (Weaver 439). Similarly, Yancey offers
advice to help combat "cross-cultural" fights. He suggests:
1.) Identify your fighting style, 2.) Agree on rules of
engagement, and 3.) Identify the real issue behind the
conflict (Yancey 71).

   McCluskey claims men and women need honest
communication that shows respect, and they must "manage
conflict in a way that maintains the relationship and gets
the job done" (5). She says, "To improve relationships and
interactions between men and women, we must
acknowledge the differences that do exist, understand how
they develop, and discard dogma about what are the 'right'
roles of women and men" (5).

   Obviously, differences exist in the way men and women
communicate, whether caused by biological and/or
environmental factors. We can consider the possible causes,
the consequences, and possible solutions. Using this
knowledge, we should be able to more accurately interpret
communication between the genders.

Holz 7

The separate Works Cited page gives full information on each source cited in the paper.

Works Cited

Arthurs, Jeffrey. "He Said, She Heard: Any Time You Speak to Both Men and Women, You're Facing Cross-Cultural Communication." <u>Leadership</u> 23.1 (2002): 49. Expanded Academic Index. Austin Peay State U., Woodward Lib. 22 Sept 2003 <http://www.galegroup.com/search>.

Basow, Susan A., and Kimberly Rubenfeld. "'Troubles Talk': Effects of Gender and Gender Typing." <u>Sex Roles: A Journal of Research</u> (2003): 183– . Expanded Academic Index. Austin Peay State U., Woodward Lib. 24 Apr. 2003 <http://web5.infotrac.galegroup.com/search>.

Cohen, David. "Speaking across the Gender Gap." <u>New Scientist</u> 131.1783 (1991): 36. Expanded Academic Index. Austin Peay State U., Woodward Lib. 28 Sept 2003.

<u>Deborah Tannen & Robert Bly: Men & Women Talking Together</u>. New York Open Center. Videocassette. Mystic Fire Video, 1993.

Glass, Lillian. <u>He Says, She Says: Closing the Communication Gap between the Sexes</u>. New York: G.P. Putnam's Sons, 1992.

James, Tammy, and Bethann Cinelli. "Exploring Gender-Based Communication Styles." <u>Journal of School Health</u> 73 (2003): 41–42.

McCluskey, Karen Curnow. "Gender at Work." <u>Public Management</u> 79.5 (1997): 5–10.

Tannen, Deborah. <u>The Argument Culture: Moving from Debate to Dialogue</u>. New York: Random House, 1998.

– – –. <u>You Just Don't Understand: Women and Men in Conversation</u>. New York: Ballantine, 1990.

Warren, Andrea. "How to Get Him to Listen." <u>Ladies' Home Journal</u> 113 (Mar. 1996): 106.

Holz 8

Weaver, Richard L. "Leadership for the Future: A New
    Set of Priorities." <u>Vital Speeches of the Day</u> 61
    (1995): 438–41.

Witt, Susan D. "Parental Influence on Children's
    Socialization to Gender Roles." <u>Adolescence</u> 32
    (1997): 253.

Woods, Julia T. <u>Gendered Lives</u>. San Francisco:
    Wadsworth, 2002.

Yancey, Phillip. "Do Men and Women Speak the Same
    Language?" <u>Marriage Partnership</u> 10 (1993): 68–73.

9
Drafting the Paper in an Academic Style

As you draft your paper, you should adopt an academic style that reflects your discipline, as discussed next in section 9a. Present a fair, balanced treatment of the subject. Mentioning opposing viewpoints early in a report gives you something to work against and may strengthen your conclusion. Keep in mind that negative findings have value and should be reported even if they contradict your original hypothesis.

Three principles for drafting may serve your needs:

- *Be practical.* Write portions of the paper when you are ready, skipping over sections of your outline. Leave plenty of space for notes and corrections.
- *Be uninhibited.* Write without fear or delay because initial drafts are attempts to get words on the page rather than to create a polished document.
- *Be conscientious about citations.* Cite the names of the sources in your notes and text, enclose quotations, and preserve page numbers to the sources.

This chapter will help you find the style necessary for your field of study, focus your argument, and build the introduction, body, and conclusion.

9a Writing for Your Field of Study

Each discipline has its own special language, style of expression, and manuscript format. You will, in time, learn fully the style for your college major. Meanwhile, we can identify a few characteristics to guide your writing styles for papers in the humanities, the social sciences, and the physical sciences.

121

Academic Style in the Humanities

Writing in one of the humanities requires you to adopt a certain style, as shown in the following example, which is written in the CMS footnote style.

> Organ and tissue donation is the gift of life. Each year many people confront health problems due to diseases or congenital birth defects. Tom Taddonia explains that tissues such as skin, veins, and valves can be used to correct congenital defects, blindness, visual impairment, trauma, burns, dental defects, arthritis, cancer, vascular and heart disease.[8] Steve Barnill says, "More than 400 people each month receive the gift of sight through yet another type of tissue donation—corneal transplants. In many cases, donors unsuitable for organ donation are eligible for tissue donation."[9] Barnill notes that tissues are now used in orthopedic surgery, cardiovascular surgery, plastic surgery, dentistry, and podiatry.[10] Even so, not enough people are willing to donate organs and tissues.

Writing in the humanities often displays these characteristics:

- Preoccupation with the quality of life, of art, of ideas (as shown in the first sentence and as echoed in the final sentence)
- Personal involvement on ethical standards
- Use of the present tense to indicate that this problem is an enduring one for humans of past ages as well as the present and the future
- Use of the CMS footnote style or the MLA style
- Discussion of theory as supported by the literature

Academic Style in the Social Sciences

Let us look at how a social science student might write the same passage in APA style.

> Organ and tissue donation has been identified as a social as well as medical problem in the United States. On one side, people have confronted serious problems in securing organs and tissue to correct health problems; on the other, people have demonstrated a reluctance to donate their organs. This need has been identified by Taddonia (2001), Barnill (1999), Ruskin (2000), and others. This hypothesis remains: People

are reluctant to sign the donor cards. Consequently, this study will survey a random set of 1,000 persons who have drivers' licenses. The tabulations will indicate reasons for signing or not signing for donation. Further investigation can then be conducted to determine ways of increasing participation by potential donors.

As shown, writing in the social sciences typically displays these characteristics:

- An objective approach to the topic without signs of personal commitment
- A scientific plan for examining a hypothesis
- Preference for the passive voice
- Minimal quotations from the sources, anticipating that readers will examine the literature for themselves
- An indication of the study's purpose and/or a general plan for empirical research
- Use of APA style for documenting the sources
- Use of past tense or the present perfect tense in references to the source material
- Awareness that this research will prompt further study

Academic Style in the Physical and Medical Sciences

Now let us look at how a medical student might write on this same topic in CSE number style:

Taddonia (1) has shown that human tissue can be used to correct many defects. Barnill (2) showed that more than 400 people receive corneal transplants each month. Yet the health profession needs more donors. It has been shown (3–6) that advanced care directives by patients with terminal illnesses would improve the donation of organs and tissue and relieve relatives of making any decision. Patients have been encouraged to complete organ donation cards (7) as well as to sign living wills (5, 8), special powers of attorney (5), and DNR (Do Not Resuscitate) Orders (5, 8). It is encouraged that advanced care directives become standard for the terminally ill.

Scientific or medical writing, like the passage above, typically displays some of these characteristics.

- An objective approach to the topic without signs of personal commitment

- A search for a professional position (i.e., on organ donation)
- A preference for the passive voice and for past tense verbs
- A preference for the CSE number system or, in some cases, the name-year system (see the samples above)
- A reluctance to quote from the sources
- A willingness to let a number represent the literature that will be cited with full documentation on the page of references

9b Focusing Your Argument

Your writing style in the research paper must be factual, but it should also reflect your thinking on the topic. You will be able to draft your paper more quickly if you focus on the central issue(s). Each paragraph should build on and amplify your primary claim.

Persuading, Inquiring, and Negotiating

Establishing a purpose for writing is one way to focus your argument. Do you wish to persuade, inquire, negotiate? Most research papers make an inquiry.

Persuasion means that you wish to convince the reader that your position is valid and, perhaps, to take action. For example:

Research has shown that homeowners and wild animals cannot live together in harmony. Thus, we need to establish green zones in every city of this country to control the sprawl in urban areas and to protect a segment of the natural habitat for the animals.

Inquiry is an exploratory approach to a problem in which you examine the issues without the insistence of persuasion. It is a truth-seeking adventure. You often must examine, test, or observe in order to discuss the implications of the research. For example:

Many suburban home dwellers complain that deer, raccoons, and other wild animals ravage their gardens, flowerbeds, and garbage cans; however, the animals were there first. This study will examine the problem in one subdivision of 142 homes. How have animals been affected by the intrusion of human beings? How have homeowners been harassed by the animals? The research will examine each side of the conflict by interviews with homeowners and observation of the animals.

Negotiation is a search for a solution. It means that you attempt to resolve a conflict by inventing options or a mediated solution. For example:

> Suburban neighbors need to find ways to embrace the wild animals that have been displaced rather than voice anger at the animals or the county government. Research has shown that green zones and wilderness trails would solve some of the problems; however, such a solution would require serious negotiations with real estate developers, who want to use every square foot of every development.

Maintaining a Focus with Ethical and Logical Appeals

As an objective writer, you must examine the problem, make your claim, and provide supporting evidence. Moderation of your voice, even during argument, suggests control of the situation, both emotionally and intellectually. Your voice alerts the audience to your point of view in two ways:

Ethical appeal. If you project the image of one who knows and cares about the topic, the reader will recognize and respect your deep interest in the subject and the way you have carefully crafted your argument. The reader will also appreciate your attention to research conventions.

Logical appeal. For readers to believe in your position, you must provide sufficient evidence in the form of statistical data, paraphrases, and direct quotations from authorities on the subject.

The issue of organ donation, for example, elicits different reactions. Some people argue from the logical position that organs are available and should be used to help people in need. Others argue from the ethical position that organs might be harvested prematurely or that organ donation violates religious principles. As a writer, you must balance your ethical and logical appeals to your readers.

Focusing the Final Thesis Sentence or Hypothesis

Refining your thesis may keep your paper on track. A thesis statement expresses the theory you hope to support with evidence and arguments. A hypothesis is a theory you hope to prove by investigating, testing, or observing. Both the thesis and the hypothesis are propositions you want to maintain, analyze, and prove. A final thesis statement or hypothesis performs three tasks:

1. Establishes a claim to control and focus the entire paper.
2. Provides unity and a sense of direction.
3. Specifies to the reader the point of the research.

For example, one student started with the topic *exorbitant tuition,* narrowed it to the phrase "tuition fees put parents in debt," and ultimately crafted this thesis:

> The exorbitant tuition at America's colleges is forcing out the poor and promoting an elitist class.

This statement focuses the argument on the effects of high fees on enrollment. The student must prove the assertion by gathering and tabulating statistics.

Questions focus the thesis. If you have trouble finding a claim or argument, ask yourself a few questions. One of the answers might serve as the thesis or the hypothesis.

- What is the point of my research?

  HYPOTHESIS: A delicate balance of medicine, diet, and exercise can control diabetes mellitus.

- Can I tell the reader anything new or different?

  HYPOTHESIS: Most well water in Rutherford county is unsafe for drinking.

- Do I have a solution to the problem?

  THESIS: Public support for "safe" houses will provide a haven for children who are abused by their parents.

- Do I have a new slant and new approach to the issue?

  HYPOTHESIS: Poverty, not greed, forces many youngsters into a life of crime.

- Should I take the minority view of this matter?

  THESIS: Give credit where it is due: Custer may have lost the battle at Little Bighorn, but Crazy Horse and his men, with inspiration from Sitting Bull, <u>won</u> the battle.

- Will an enthymeme serve my purpose by making a claim in a *because* clause?

  ENTHYMEME: Sufficient organ and tissue donation, enough to satisfy the demand, remains almost impossible because negative myths and religious concerns dominate the minds of many people.

C H E C K L I S T

Writing the Final Thesis or Hypothesis

You should be able to answer *yes* to each question below:

- Does the thesis or hypothesis express your position in a full, declarative statement that is not a question, not a statement of purpose, and not merely a topic?
- Does it limit the subject to a narrow focus that grows out of research?
- Does it establish an investigation, interpretation, or theoretical presentation?
- Does it point forward to your findings and a discussion of the implications in your conclusion?

Key words focus the thesis or the hypothesis. Use the important words from your notes and rough outline to refine your thesis sentence. For example, during your reading of several novels or short stories by Flannery O'Connor, you might have jotted down certain repetitions of image, theme, or character. The key words might be *death, ironic moments of humor, hysteria and passion, human shortcomings,* or other issues that O'Connor repeatedly explored. These concrete ideas might point you toward a general thesis:

> The tragic endings of Flannery O'Connor's stories depict desperate people coming face to face with their own shortcomings.

Change your thesis but not your hypothesis. Be willing to abandon your preliminary thesis if research leads you to new and different issues. However, a hypothesis *cannot* be adjusted or changed. It will be proved true, partially true, or untrue. Your negative findings have value, for you will have disproved the hypothesis so others need not duplicate your research. For example, the hypothesis might assert: "Industrial pollution is seeping into water tables and traveling many miles into neighboring well water of Thompson county." Your report may prove the truth of the hypothesis, but it may not. It may only establish a probability and the need for additional research.

9c Designing an Academic Title

A clearly expressed title, like a good thesis sentence, focuses your writing and keeps you on course. Although writing a final title may not be feasible until the paper is written, a preliminary title can provide specific words of identification to help you stay focused. For example, one writer began with this title: "Diabetes." Then, to be more specific, the writer added another word: "Diabetes Management." As research developed and she recognized the role of medicine, diet, and exercise for victims, she refined the title even more: "Diabetes Management: A Delicate Balance of Medicine, Diet, and Exercise." Thereby, she and her readers had a clear idea that the paper was about three methods of managing the disease.

Long titles are standard in scholarly writing. Consider the following examples:

1. Subject, colon, and focusing phrase:

   Organ and Tissue Donation and Transplantation: Myths, Ethical Issues, and Lives Saved

2. Subject, focusing prepositional phrase:

   Prayer at School-Related Activities

3. Subject, colon, type of study:

   Black Dialect in Maya Angelou's Poetry: A Language Study

4. Subject, colon, focusing question:

   AIDS: Where Did It Come From?

5. Subject, comparative study:

   Religious Imagery in N. Scott Momaday's <u>The Names</u> and Heronimous Storm's <u>Seven Arrows</u>

9d Drafting the Paper

As you begin drafting your research report, work systematically through a preliminary plan or outline to keep order as your notes expand your research. Use your notes, photocopies, downloaded material, and research journal to transfer materials directly into the text, remembering always to provide citations to borrowed information. Do not quote an entire paragraph unless it is crucial to your discussion and cannot be easily reduced to a summary. In addition, be conscious of basic writing conventions, as described next.

Writing with Unity and Coherence

Unity refers to exploring one topic in depth to give your writing a single vision. With unity, each paragraph carefully expands on a single aspect of the narrowed subject. *Coherence* connects the parts logically by:

- repetition of key words and sentence structures
- the judicious use of pronouns and synonyms
- the effective placement of transitional words and phrases (e.g., *also, furthermore, therefore, in addition,* and *thus*)

Writing in the Proper Tense

Verb tense often distinguishes a paper in the humanities from one in the natural and social sciences. Use the past tense in the social sciences and the physical sciences. Use the present tense in the humanities. Both the MLA style and the CMS footnote style require the present tense to cite an author's work (e.g., "Patel *explains*" or "the work of Scogin and Roberts *shows*"). The ideas and the words of the writers remain in print and continue to be true in the universal present. Therefore, when writing a paper in the humanities, use the historical present tense, as shown here:

> "It was the best of times, it was the worst of times," writes
> Charles Dickens about the eighteenth century.

> Johnson argues that sociologist Norman Wayman has a
> "narrow-minded view of clerics and their role in the
> community" (64).

Using the Language of the Discipline

Every discipline and every topic has its own vocabulary. Therefore, while reading and taking notes, jot down words and phrases relevant to your research study. Get comfortable with them so you can use them effectively. For example, a child abuse topic requires the language of sociology and psychology, thereby demanding an acquaintance with the following terms:

social worker	maltreatment	aggressive behavior
poverty levels	behavioral patterns	incestuous relations
stress	hostility	battered child
formative years	recurrence	guardians

Many writers create a terminology list to strengthen their command of appropriate nouns and verbs for the subject in question.

Using Source Material to Enhance Your Writing

Readers want to see your thoughts and ideas on a subject. For this reason, a paragraph should seldom contain source material only; it must contain a topic sentence to establish a point for the research evidence. Every paragraph should explain, analyze, and support a thesis, not merely string together a set of quotations. The following passage effectively cites two sources.

> Two factors that have played a part in farm land becoming drought prone are "light, sandy soil and soils with high alkalinity" (Boughman 234). In response, Bjornson says that drought resistant plants exist along parts of the Mediterranean Sea. Thus, hybrids of these plants may serve Texas farmers (34).

The short passage weaves the sources effectively into a whole, uses the sources as a natural extension of the discussion, and cites each source separately and appropriately.

Writing in the Third Person

Write your paper with third-person narration that avoids "I believe" or "It is my opinion." Rather than saying, "I think television violence affects children," drop the opening two words and say, "Television violence affects children." Readers will understand that the statement is your thought and one that you will defend with evidence.

Writing with the Passive Voice in an Appropriate Manner

The passive voice is often less forceful than an active verb. However, research writers sometimes need to use the passive voice verb, as shown here:

> Forty-three students of a third-grade class at Barksdale School were observed for two weeks.

This usage of the passive voice is fairly standard in the social sciences and the natural or applied sciences. The passive voice is preferred because it keeps the focus on the subject of the research, not the writer (you would not want to say, "I observed the students").

Placing Graphics Effectively in a Research Essay

Use graphics to support your text. Most computers allow you to create tables, line graphs, and pie charts as well as diagrams, maps, and original designs. You may also import tables and illustrations from your sources. Place these graphics as close as possible to the parts of the text to which they relate. It is acceptable to use full-color art if your printer prints in color; however, use black for the captions and date. Place a full-page graphic on a separate sheet after making a textual reference to it (e.g., "see Table 7"). Place graphics in an appendix when you have several complex items that might distract the reader from your textual message.

Avoiding Sexist and Biased Language

The best writers exercise caution against words that may stereotype any person, regardless of gender, race, nationality, creed, age, or disability. The following are guidelines to help you avoid discriminatory language:

Age. Review the accuracy of your statement. It is appropriate to use *boy* and *girl* for children of high school age and under. *Young man* and *young woman* or *male adolescent* and *female adolescent* can be appropriate, but *teenager* carries a certain bias. Avoid *elderly* as a noun; use *older persons.*

Gender. Gender is a term used culturally to identify men and women within their social groups. *Sex* tends to refer to a biological factor (see below for a discussion of sexual orientation).

- Use plural subjects so that nonspecific, plural pronouns are grammatically correct. For example, you may specify that Judy Jones maintains *her* lab equipment in sterile condition or indicate that technicians, in general, maintain *their* own equipment.
- Reword the sentence so a pronoun is unnecessary, as in *The doctor prepared the necessary surgical equipment without interference.*
- Use pronouns that denote gender only when necessary when gender has been previously established, as in *Mary, as a new laboratory technician, must learn to maintain her equipment in sterile condition.*
- The use of *woman* and *female* as adjectives varies. Use *woman* or *women* in most instances (e.g., *a woman's intuition*) and use *female* for species and statistics, (e.g., *four female subjects*). Avoid the use of *lady,* as in *lady pilot.*
- The first mention of a person requires the full name (e.g., Ernest Hemingway, Joan Didion) and thereafter requires the use of the surname only (e.g., Hemingway, Didion). In

general, avoid formal titles (e.g., Dr., Gen., Mrs., Ms., Lt., Prof.). Avoid their equivalents in other languages (e.g., Mme, Dame, Monsieur).

- Avoid *man and wife* or *7 men and 16 females*. Keep terms parallel by matching *husband and wife* or *man and woman* and *7 male rats and 16 female rats*.

Sexual Orientation. The term *sexual orientation* is preferred to the term *sexual preference*. It is preferable to use *lesbians* and *gay men* rather than *homosexuals*. The terms *heterosexual, homosexual,* and *bisexual* can be used to describe both the identity and the behavior of subjects—that is, as adjectives.

Ethnic and Racial Identity. Some persons prefer the term *Black*, others prefer *African American,* and still others prefer *a person of color.* The terms *Negro* and *Afro-American* are now dated and not appropriate. Use *Black* and *White*, not the lowercase *black* and *white.* In like manner, some individuals may prefer *Hispanic* or *Latino.* Use the term *Asian* or *Asian American* rather than *Oriental. Native American* is a broad term that includes *Samoans, Hawaiians,* and *American Indians.* A good rule of thumb is to use a person's nationality when it is known (*Mexican, Canadian, Comanche,* or *Nigerian*).

Disability. In general, place people first, not their disability. Rather than *disabled person* or *retarded child* say *person who has scoliosis* or *a child with Down syndrome.* Avoid saying *a challenged person* or *a special child* in favor of *a person with* or *a child with.* Remember that a *disability* is a physical quality while a *handicap* is a limitation that might be imposed by external factors, such as stairs or poverty or social attitudes.

9e   Creating an Introduction, Body, and Conclusion

Writing the Introduction

Use the first few paragraphs of your paper to establish the nature of your study.

SUBJECT: Does your introduction identify your specific topic, and then define, limit, and narrow it to one issue?

BACKGROUND: Does your introduction provide relevant historical data or discuss a few key sources that touch on your specific issue?

PROBLEM: Does your introduction identify a problem and explain the complications your research paper will explore or resolve?

THESIS: Does your introduction use your thesis sentence or hypothesis within the first few paragraphs to establish the direction of the study and to point your readers toward your eventual conclusions?

How you work these essential elements into the beginning of your paper depends on your style of writing. They need not appear in this order, nor should you cram all these items into a short, opening paragraph. Feel free to write a long introduction by using more than one of these techniques:

Open with your thesis statement or hypothesis.
Open with a quotation.
Relate your topic to the well known.
Provide background information.
Review the literature.
Provide a brief summary.
Define key terms.
Supply data, statistics, and special evidence.
Take exception to critical views.
Use an anecdote as a hook to draw your reader into the essay.

The following sample of an introduction gives background information, establishes a persuasive position, reviews key literature, takes exception, gives key terms, and offers a thesis.

John Berendt's popular and successful novel <u>Midnight in the Garden of Good and Evil</u> skillfully presents the unpredictable twists and turns of a landmark murder case set under the moss-hung live oaks of Savannah, Georgia. While it is written as a novel, the nonfiction account of this tragic murder case reveals the intriguing and sometimes deranged relationships that thrive in a town where everyone knows everyone else. However, the mystique of the novel does not lie with the murder case but with the collection of unusual and often complex characters, including a voodoo priestess, a young southern gigolo, and a black drag queen (e.g., Bilkin, Miller, and especially Carson, who describes the people of Savannah as "a type of Greek chorus" [14]). Berendt's success lies in his carefully crafted characterization.

Writing the Body of the Research Paper

When writing the body, you should keep in mind three elements:

ANALYSIS: Classify the major issues of the study and provide a careful analysis of each in defense of your thesis.

PRESENTATION: Provide well-reasoned statements at the beginning of your paragraphs and supply evidence of support with proper documentation.

PARAGRAPHS: Offer a variety of paragraphs to compare, show process, narrate the history of the subject, and show causes.

Use these techniques to build substantive paragraphs for your paper:

Relate a time sequence.

Compare or contrast issues, the views of experts, and nature of literary characters.

Develop cause and effect.

Issue a call to action.

Define key terminology.

Show a process.

Ask questions and provide answers.

Cite evidence from source materials.

Explain the methods used and the design of the study.

Present the results of the investigation with data, statistics, and graphics.

The following paragraph in MLA style demonstrates the use of several techniques—an overview of the problem, citing a source, comparing issues, cause and effect, key terms, and process.

To burn or not to burn the natural forests in the national parks is the question. The pyrophobic public voices its protests while environmentalists praise the rejuvenating effects of a good forest fire. It is difficult to convince people that not all fire is bad. The public has visions of Smokey the Bear campaigns and mental images of Bambi and Thumper fleeing the roaring flames. Chris Bolgiano explains that federal policy evolved slowly "from the basic impulse to douse all fires immediately to a sophisticated decision matrix based on the functions of any given unit of land" (23). Bolgiano declares that "timber production, grazing, recreation, and wilderness preservation elicit different fire-management approaches" (23).

Writing the Conclusion of the Paper

The conclusion is not a summary; it is a discussion of beliefs and findings based on your reasoning and on the evidence and results you presented. Select appropriate items from this list.

THESIS: Reaffirm the thesis sentence, the hypothesis, or the central mission of your study. If appropriate, give a statement in support or nonsupport of an original enthymeme or hypothesis.

JUDGMENT: Discuss and interpret the findings. Give answers. Now is the time to draw inferences, emphasize a theory, and find relevance in the results.

DIRECTIVES: Based on the theoretical implications of the study, offer suggestions for action and for new research.

DISCUSSION: Discuss the implications of your findings from testing or observation.

Use these techniques to write the conclusion:

Restate the thesis and reach beyond it.
Close with an effective quotation.
Return the focus of a literary study to the author.
Compare the past to the present.
Offer a directive or a solution.
Give a call to action.
Discuss the implications of your findings.

This next example in CSE style discusses test results of one student's empirical study.

The results of this experiment were similar to expectations, but perhaps the statistical significance, because of the small subject size, was biased toward the delayed conditions of the curve. Barker (14) and Peay (3) have addressed this point. The subjects were not truly representative of the total population because of their prior exposure to test procedures (e.g., see 2, 3, and 7). Another factor that may have affected the curves was the presentation of the data. The images on the screen were available for five seconds, and that amount of time may have enabled the subjects to store each image effectively. If the time period for each image were reduced to one or two seconds, there could be lower recall scores, thereby reducing the differences between the control group and the experimental group.

9f Revising the Rough Draft

Once you have the complete paper in a rough draft, the serious business of editing begins. First, you should revise your paper on a global scale, moving blocks of material around to the best advantage and into the proper format. Second, edit the draft with a line-by-line examination of wording and technical excellence. Third, proofread the final version to assure that your words are spelled correctly and the text is grammatically sound.

Revision can turn a passable paper into an excellent one. Revise the manuscript on a global scale by looking at its overall design. Do the introduction, body, and conclusion have substance? Do the paragraphs maintain the flow of your central proposition? Does the paper fulfill the requirements of the academic model?

Editing before Printing the Final Manuscript

Global revision is complemented by careful editing of paragraphs, sentences, and individual words. Travel through the paper to study your citation of the sources. Confirm that you have properly quoted or paraphrased each cited source. Check spelling with both the computer and your own visual examination. Here are eight additional tasks:

1. Cut phrases and sentences that do not advance your main ideas or that merely repeat what your sources have already stated.
2. Determine that coordinated, balanced ideas are appropriately expressed and that minor ideas are properly subordinated.
3. Change most of your *to be* verbs (is, are, was) to stronger active verbs.
4. Maintain the present tense in most verbs unless you are writing in APA or CSE styles.
5. Convert passive structures to active unless you want to emphasize the subject, not the actor.
6. Confirm that you have introduced paraphrases and quotations so they flow smoothly into your text.
7. Use formal, academic style, and be on guard against clusters of little monosyllabic words that fail to advance ideas.

    Good: Findings by Marshall (2003) and Fields (2004) confirm
    class size as one indicator of student success.

Wordy: In the writings of two authorities, Marshall (2003) and
　　　Fields (2004), the number of students in a classroom
　　　determines the success of the academic performance.
Examine your wording for its effectiveness in the context of your
subject.
8. Examine your paragraphs for transitions that move the reader
effectively from one paragraph to the next.

Using the Computer to Edit Your Text

Some software programs examine your grammar and mechanics,
look for parentheses that you opened but never closed, find unpaired
quotation marks, flag passive verbs, question your spelling, and mark
other items for your correction. Pay attention to the caution flags raised
by this type of program. After a software program examines the style of
your manuscript, you should revise and edit the text to improve stylistic weaknesses. Remember, it is your paper, not the computer's.

Participating in Peer Review

Peer review has two sides. First, it means handing your paper to
a friend or classmate, asking for opinions and suggestions. Second, it
means reviewing a classmate's research paper. You can learn by
reviewing as well as by writing. Your instructor may supply a peer
review sheet, or you can use the accompanying checklist. Criticize
the paper constructively on each point.

C H E C K L I S T

Peer Review

1. Are the subject and the accompanying issues introduced
early?
2. Is the writer's critical approach to the problem stated clearly
in a thesis sentence? Is it placed effectively in the introduction?
3. Do the paragraphs of the body have individual unity—that
is, does each paragraph develop an important idea and only
one idea? Does each paragraph relate to the thesis?
4. Are sources introduced, usually with the name of the expert,
and then cited by a page number in parentheses? Keep in
mind that Internet sources rarely have page numbers.
5. Is it clear where a paraphrase begins and where it ends?
6. Are the sources relevant to the argument?

7. Does the writer weave quotations into the text effectively while avoiding long quotations that look more like filler than substance?

8. Does the conclusion arrive at a resolution about the central issue?

9. Does the title describe clearly what the writer put in the body of the research paper?

Proofreading

Print a hard copy of your manuscript. Proofread this final version with great care.

CHECKLIST

Proofreading

1. Check for errors in sentence structure, spelling, and punctuation.

2. Check for hyphenation and word division. Remember that no words should be hyphenated at the ends of lines.

3. Recheck the accuracy of all direct quotations. Check for opening and closing quotation marks.

4. Double-check in-text citations to be certain each is correct and that each source is listed on your Works Cited page.

5. Double-check the format—the title page, margins, spacing, content notes, and many other elements. These stipulations are explained in the chapter on using MLA and APA styles and in the glossary.

9g   Writing With Style

Overview

This section discusses the use of stylistic techniques to clarify your writing while making it more persuasive. In this section, the following objectives will be met:

1. Discuss the importance of style in a piece of writing.
2. Define style and the role of style in writing.
3. Show how to use the plain style.
4. Show how to use the persuasive style.

Good Style Is a Choice, Not an Accident

Style does more than dress up the content of your writing. It expresses your attitude toward the work. Style also reflects your character by embodying the values, beliefs, and the relationship you want to share with the readers (Laib 1993, 21). In a word, style is about quality. Style is about your commitment to excellence and attention to detail.

All pieces of writing have a style, whether or not that style was consciously developed by the writers. Consequently, when writers do not pay attention to style, a piece of writing typically exhibits an erratic style that annoys or confuses the readers. Have you ever read a text that just didn't feel right? More than likely, you were reacting to the erratic style used in the text.

Good style is a choice you can and should make. This chapter will discuss two types of style that are prevalent in writing. The *plain style* involves writing strong sentences and paragraphs that express your ideas clearly to the readers. The *persuasive* style is used to motivate the readers by appealing to their emotions and values. Both the plain and persuasive styles have their place in any given piece of writing. The challenge is to balance these two styles in ways that will instruct the readers and move them to action.

What Is Style?

If you are like most people, style is a rather murky concept. Some documents just seem to have a good style, while others do not.

From *Writing Proposals: Rhetoric for Managing Change*, by Richard Johnson-Sheehan.

Consequently, you may have come to believe that good style is something some people have from birth. Good style might even seem accidental. You aren't sure how it happened, but your instructors tell you that something you wrote is very readable, even eloquent.

What is style? Style works at a few different levels. On the sentence level, good style might involve choosing the right words or forming sentences that are easy to read. On the paragraph level, style could involve weaving sentences together in ways that emphasize your main points and lead the readers comfortably through your ideas. At the document level, style involves setting an appropriate tone and weaving themes into your work that appeal to your readers' emotions and values. In his book *Technical Writing Style,* Dan Jones defines style the following way:

> Style affects or influences almost all other elements of writing. Style is your choices of words, phrases, clauses, and sentences, and how you connect these sentences. Style is the unity and coherence of your paragraphs and larger segments. Style is your tone—your attitude toward your subject, your audience, and yourself—in what you write. Style is who you are and how you reflect who you are, intentionally or unintentionally, in what you write (3).

Style does more than make the content easier to read and more persuasive. In many ways, it illustrates your clear-headedness, your emphasis on quality, and your willingness to communicate and work with the readers.

Style is not embellishment or ornamentation. Some people mistakenly believe that style is the spice sprinkled over a piece of writing to make the content more palatable to the readers. These writers throw in some extra adjectives and an occasional metaphor to perk up the bland parts of the writing. But, just as spices are most flavorful when they are cooked into food, style needs to be carefully worked into writing. Indeed, a piece of writing that uses stylistic devices to embellish the content is merely hinting to the readers that the writing lacks substance. Style enhances and amplifies content, but it should never be used to artificially embellish or hide a lack of content.

Classical rhetoricians like Cicero and Augustine discussed style in three levels: plain style, middle style, and grand style. The plain style is for instruction and demonstration, allowing the writer to lay out the facts or describe something in simple terms. The middle style is for persuading people to take action. When using the middle style, the writer highlights the benefits of taking action or doing something a particular way. The grand style is for motivating people to do something they already know they should do. For example, Winston Churchill, Martin Luther King, Jr., and John F. Kennedy regularly used the grand style to motivate their listeners to do what was right, even if people were reluctant to do it.

In this section we will concentrate on using the plain and persuasive styles in writing. An essay that properly combines the plain and persuasive style will be both informative and moving for the readers.

Writing Plain Sentences

As a student, you were more than likely advised to "write clearly" or "write in concrete language" as though simply making up your mind to write clearly or concretely was all it took. In reality, writing plainly is a skill that requires practice and concentration. Fortunately, once a few simple guidelines have been learned and mastered, style writing will soon become a natural strength in your writing.

To start, let us consider the parts of a basic sentence. From your grammar classes, you learned that a sentence typically has three main parts: a subject, a verb, and a comment. The subject is what the sentence is about. The verb is what the subject is doing. And, the comment says something about the subject. For example, consider these three variations of the same sentence.

SUBJECT	VERB	COMMENT
The Institute	provides	the government with accurate crime statistics.
The government	is provided	with accurate crime statistics by the Institute.
Crime statistics	were provided	to the government by the Institute.

The content in these sentences has not changed. Nevertheless, the emphasis in each sentence changes as we replace the subject slot with different nouns. Sentence A is *about* the "Institute." Sentence B is *about* the "government." Sentence C is *about* the "crime statistics." By changing the subject of the sentence, we essentially shift the focus of the sentence, drawing our readers' attention to different issues.

This simple understanding of the different parts of a sentence is the basis for eight guidelines that can be used to write plainer

Guideline 1: The subject should be what the sentence is about.

Guideline 2: Make the "doer" the subject. Subject is the "doer."

Guideline 3: State the action in the verb.

Guideline 4: Put the subject early in the sentence.

Guideline 5: Eliminate nominalizations.

Guideline 6: Avoid excessive prepositional phrases.

Guideline 7: Eliminate redundancy.

Guideline 8: Make sentences "breathing length.

FIGURE 9g.1
Sentence Guidelines

sentences in proposals, as shown in Figure 9g.1. We will discuss these sentence guidelines in more detail in the following pages.

Guideline 1: The subject should be what the sentence is about

At a very simple level, weak style often occurs when the readers cannot easily identify the subject of the sentence. Or, the subject of the sentence is not what the sentence is about. For example, what is the subject of the following sentence?

1. Ten months after the Hartford Project began in which a team of our experts conducted close observations of management actions, our final conclusion is that the scarcity of monetary funds is at the basis of the inability of Hartford Industries to appropriate resources to essential projects that have the greatest necessity.

This sentence is difficult to read for a variety of reasons, but the most significant problem is the lack of a clear subject. What is this sentence about? The word *conclusion* is currently in the subject position, but the sentence might also be about the *experts*, the *Hartford Project*, or *scarcity of monetary funds*. Indeed, many other nouns and nounlike words also seem to be competing to be the subject of the sentence, such as *observations, management, structure, conclusion, inability*, and *company*. These nouns and nounlike words bombard the readers with potential subjects, undermining their efforts to identify what the sentence is about.

When the sentence is restructured around *experts* or *scarcity,* most readers will find it easier to understand:

1a. Ten months after the Hartford Project began, our experts have concluded through close observations of management actions that the scarcity of monetary funds is at the basis of the inability of Hartford Industries to appropriate resources to essential projects that have the greatest necessity.

1b. The scarcity of monetary funds, our experts have concluded through close observations of management actions ten months after the Hartford Project began, is at the basis of the inability of Hartford Industries to appropriate resources to essential projects that have the greatest necessity.

Both of these sentences are still rather difficult to read. Nevertheless, they are easier to read than the original because the noun occupying the subject slot is the focus of the sentence—that is, what the sentence is about. We will return to this sentence about Hartford Industries after discussing the other guidelines for plain style.

Guideline 2: Make the "doer" the subject

Guideline 3: State the action in the verb

In your opinion, which revision of sentence 1 above is easier to read? Most people would point to sentence 1a, in which *experts* is in the subject slot. Why? In sentence 1a, the experts are actually doing something. In sentence 1b, *scarcity* is an inactive noun that is not doing anything. Whereas experts take action, scarcity is merely something that happens.

Guidelines 2 and 3 reflect the tendency of readers to focus on who or what is doing something in a sentence. To illustrate, which of these sentences is easier to read?

2a. On Saturday morning, the paperwork was completed in a timely fashion by Jim.

2b. On Saturday morning, Jim completed the paperwork in a timely fashion.

Most people would say sentence 2b is easier to read because Jim, the subject of the sentence, is actually doing something, while the paperwork in sentence 2a is inactive. The active person or thing usually makes the best subject of the sentence.

Similarly, Guideline 3 states that the verb should contain the action in the sentence. Once you have determined who or what is doing something, ask yourself what that person or thing is actually doing. Find the action in the sentence and make it the verb. For example, consider these sentences:

3a. The detective investigated the loss of the payroll.

3b. The detective conducted an investigation into the loss of the payroll.

3c. The detective is the person who is conducting an investigation of the loss of the payroll.

Sentence 3a is easier to understand because the action of the sentence is expressed in the verb. Sentences 3b and 3c are increasingly more difficult to understand, because the action, *investigate,* is further removed from the verb slot of the sentence.

Guideline 4: Put the subject early in the sentence

Subconsciously, readers start every sentence looking for the subject. The subject anchors the sentence, because it tells the reader what the sentence is about. So, if the subject is buried somewhere in the middle of the sentence, the readers will have greater difficulty finding it, and the sentence will be harder to read. To illustrate, consider these two sentences:

4a. If deciduous and evergreen trees experience yet another year of drought like the one observed in 1997, the entire Sandia Mountain ecosystem will be heavily damaged.

4b. The entire Sandia Mountain ecosystem will be heavily damaged if deciduous and evergreen trees experience yet another year of drought like the one observed in 1997.

The problem with sentence 4a is that it forces the readers to hold all those details (i.e., trees, drought, 1997) in short-term memory before the sentence identifies its subject. Readers almost feel a sense of relief when they find the subject, because they cannot figure out what the sentence is about until they locate the subject. Quite differently, sentence 4b tells the readers what the sentence is about up front. With the subject early in the sentence, the readers immediately know how to connect the comment with the subject.

Of course, introductory or transitional phrases do not always signal weak style. But when these phrases are used, they should be short and to the point. Longer introductory phrases should be moved to the end of the sentence.

Guideline 5: Eliminate nominalizations

Nominalizations are perfectly good verbs and adjectives that have been turned into awkward nouns. For example, look at these sentences:

5a. Management has an expectation that the project will meet the deadline.

5b. Management expects the project to meet the deadline.

In sentence 5a *expectation* is a nominalization. Here, the perfectly good verb *expect* is being used as a noun. After turning the nominalization into a verb, sentence 5b is not only shorter than sentence 5a, it also has more energy because the verb *expect* is now an action verb.

Consider these two sentences:

6a. Our discussion about the matter allowed us to make a decision on the acquisition of the new x-ray machine.

6b. We discussed the matter and decided to acquire the new x-ray machine.

Sentence 6a includes three nominalizations *discussion, decision,* and *acquisition,* making the sentence hard to understand. Sentence 6b turns all three of these nominalizations into verbs, making the sentence much easier to understand. An additional benefit to changing nominalizations into verbs is the energy added to the sentence. Nouns tend to feel inert to the readers, while verbs tend to add action and energy.

Why do writers use nominalizations in the first place? We use nominalizations for two reasons. First, humans generally think in nouns, so our first drafts are often filled with nominalizations, which are nouns. While revising, an effective writer will turn those first-draft nominalizations into action verbs. Second, some people mistakenly believe that using nominalizations makes their writing sound more formal or important. In reality, though, nominalizations only make sentences harder to read. The best way to sound important is to write sentences that readers understand.

Guideline 6: Avoid excessive prepositional phrases

Prepositional phrases are necessary in writing, but they are often overused in ways that make writing too long and too tedious. Prepositional phrases follow prepositions (e.g., in, of, by, about, over, under) and they are used to modify nouns. For example in the sentence "Our house by the lake in Minnesota is lovely," the phrases by the lake and *in Minnesota* are both prepositional phrases. They modify the nouns *house* and *lake*.

Prepositional phrases are fine when used in moderation, but they are problematic when used in excess. For example, in sentence 7a the prepositions have been italicized and prepositional phrases underlined. Sentence 7b is the same sentence with fewer prepositional phrases:

7a. The decline *in* the number *of* businesses owned *by* locals in the town of Artesia is a demonstration *of* the increasing hardship faced *in* rural communities in the southwest.

7b. Artesia's declining number of locally owned businesses demonstrates the increased hardship faced by southwestern rural communities.

You should never feel obligated to eliminate all the prepositional phrases in a sentence. Rather, look for places where prepositional phrases are chained together in long sequences. Then, try to condense the sentence by turning some of the prepositional phrases into adjectives. In sentence 7b, for example, the phrase *in the town of Artesia* was reduced to the adjective *Artesia's*. The phrases *in rural communities in the southwest* were reduced to *by southwestern rural communities*. The resulting sentence 7b is much shorter and easier to read.

Guideline 7: Eliminate redundancy

In our efforts to stress our points, we often use redundant phrasing. For example, we might write *unruly mob*, as though some mobs are orderly, or we might talk about *active participants*, as though someone can participate without doing anything. Sometimes buzzwords and jargon lead to redundancies like, "We should collaborate together as a team" or "Empirical observations will provide a new understanding of the subject." In some cases, we might use a synonym to modify a synonym by saying something like, "We suggested important, significant changes."

Redundancies should be eliminated because they use two words to do the work of one. As a result, the readers need to work twice as hard to understand one basic idea.

Guideline 8: Make sentences "breathing length"

A sentence is a statement designed to be spoken in one breath. When a text is read out loud, the period at the end of each sentence is the reader's signal to breathe. Of course, when reading silently, we do not actually breathe when we see a period. Nevertheless, readers do take a mental pause at the end of each sentence. A sentence that runs on and on forces readers to mentally hold their breaths. By the end of an especially long sentence, readers are more concerned about getting through it than deciphering it.

The best way to think about sentence length is to imagine how long it takes to comfortably say a sentence out loud. If the written sentence is too long to say in one breath, it probably needs to be shortened or cut into two sentences. After all, you don't want to asphyxiate your readers. On the other hand, if the sentence is very short, perhaps it needs to be combined with one of its neighbors to make it a more comfortable breathing length. You also want to avoid hyperventilating the readers with a string of short sentences.

A Simple Method for Writing Plainer Sentences

To sum up the eight sentence guidelines, here is a process for writing plainer sentences. First, write out your draft as usual, not paying too much attention to the style. Then, as you revise, identify difficult sentences and apply the six steps shown in Figure 9g.2.[1]

With these six steps in mind, let us revisit sentence 1, the example of weak style offered at the beginning of our discussion of plain style.

Original

1. Ten months after the Hartford Project began in which a team of our experts conducted close observations of management decisions, our final conclusion is that the scarcity of monetary funds is at the basis of the inability of Hartford Industries to appropriate resources to essential projects that have the greatest necessity.

Revision

1a. After completing the ten-month Hartford Project, our experts concluded that the Hartford Industries' budget shortfalls have limited support for priority projects.

In the revision, the subject (our experts) was moved into the subject slot, and then it was moved to an early place in the sentence. Then, the action of the sentence (concluded) was moved into the verb slot. Prepositional phrases like *to appropriate resources to essential projects* were turned into adjectives. Nominalizations like *conclusion* and *necessity* were turned into verbs or adjectives. And finally, the sentence was shortened to breathing length. The resulting sentence still offers the same content to the readers—just more plainly.

---

1 In his book, *Revising Business Prose*, Richard Lanham offers a simpler technique that he calls the "paramedic method." His method is less comprehensive than the one shown here, but it works well also.

1. Identify who or what the sentence is about.
2. Turn that who or what into the subject, and then move the subject to an early place in the sentence.
3. Identify what the subject is doing, and move that action into the verb slot.
4. Eliminate prepositional phrases, where appropriate, by turning them into adjectives.
5. Eliminate unnecessary nominalizations and redundancies.
6. Shorten, lengthen, combine, or divide sentences to make them breathing length.

FIGURE 9g.2
Six Steps to Plainer Writing

Writing Plain Paragraphs

As with sentences, some rather simple methods are available to help you write plainer paragraphs.

The Elements of a Paragraph

Paragraphs tend to include four kinds of sentences: a transition sentence, a topic sentence, a support sentence, and a point sentence. Each of these sentences plays a different role in the paragraph.

Transition Sentence

The purpose of a transition sentence is to make a smooth bridge from the previous paragraph to the present paragraph. For example, a transitional sentence might state "With these facts in mind, let us consider the current opportunity available." The *facts* mentioned were explained in the previous paragraph. By referring back to the previous paragraph, the transition sentence provides a smooth bridge into the new paragraph. Most paragraphs, however, do not need a transition sentence. These kinds of sentences are typically used when the new paragraph handles a significantly different topic than the previous paragraph.

Topic Sentence

The topic sentence is the claim or statement that the rest of the paragraph is going to prove or support. In an essay, topic sentences typically appear in the first or second sentence of each paragraph. They are placed up front in each paragraph for two reasons. First, the topic sentence sets a goal for the paragraph to reach by telling the readers the claim you are trying to prove. Then, the remainder of the paragraph proves that claim with facts, examples, and reasoning. If the topic sentence appears at the end of the paragraph, the readers are forced to rethink all the details in the paragraph now that they know what the paragraph was trying to prove. For most readers, all that mental backtracking is a bit annoying.

The second reason for putting the topic sentence up front is that it is the most important sentence in any given paragraph. Since readers tend to pay the greatest attention to the beginning of a paragraph, placing the topic sentence up front guarantees they will read it closely. Likewise, scanning readers tend to concentrate on the beginning of each paragraph. If the topic sentence is buried in the middle or at the end of the paragraph, they will miss it.

Support Sentences

The support in the body of the paragraph can come in many forms. There are two ways to argue logically (i.e., using reasoning and examples). Sentences that use reasoning tend to make if/then, cause/effect, better/worse, greater/lesser kinds of arguments for the readers. Meanwhile the use of examples illustrates points for the readers by showing them situations or items that support your claim in the topic sentence. For the most part, sentences that contain reasoning and examples will make up the bulk of a paragraph's support sentences. Other support will come in the form of facts, data, definitions, and descriptions. In the end, support sentences are intended to prove the claim made in the paragraph's topic sentence.

Point Sentences

Point sentences usually restate the topic sentence at the end of the paragraph. They are used to reinforce the topic sentence by restating the paragraph's original claim in new words. Point sentences are especially useful in longer paragraphs where the readers may not fully remember the claim stated at the beginning of the paragraph. These sentences often start with transitional devices like *therefore, consequently,* or *in sum* to signal to the readers that the point of the paragraph is being restated. Point sentences are optional in paragraphs, and they should be used only occasionally when a particular claim needs to be reinforced for the readers. Too many point sentences will cause your proposal to sound too repetitious and even condescending to the readers.

Of these kinds of sentences, only the topic sentence and the support sentences are needed for a good paragraph. Transitional sentences and point sentences are useful in situations where bridges need to be made between paragraphs or specific points need to be reinforced.

Here are the four kinds of sentences used in a paragraph:

8a. How can we accomplish these five goals? (transition) Universities need to study their core mission to determine whether distance education is a viable alternative to the traditional classroom (topic sentence). If universities can maintain their current standards while moving their courses online, then distance education may provide a new medium through which nontraditional students can take classes and perhaps earn a degree (support). Utah State, for example, is reporting that students enrolled in their online courses have met or exceeded the expectations of their professors (support). On the other hand, if standards cannot be maintained, we may find ourselves returning to the traditional on-campus model of education (support). In the end, the ability to meet a university's core mission is the litmus test to measure whether distance education will work (point sentence).

8b. Universities need to study their core mission to determine whether distance education is a viable alternative to the traditional classroom (topic sentence). If universities can maintain their current standards while moving their courses online, then distance education may provide a new medium through which nontraditional students can take classes and perhaps earn a degree (support). Utah State, for example, is reporting that students enrolled in their online courses have met or exceeded the expectations of their professors (support). On the other hand, if standards cannot be maintained, we may find ourselves returning to the traditional on-campus model of education (support).

As you can see in paragraph 8b, a paragraph works fine without transition and point sentences. Nevertheless, they can make texts easier to read while amplifying important points.

Aligning Sentence Subjects in a Paragraph

Have you ever needed to stop reading a paragraph because each sentence seems to go off in a new direction? Have you ever run into a paragraph that actually feels bumpy as you read it? More than likely, the problem was a lack of alignment of the paragraph's sentence subjects. To illustrate, consider this paragraph:

9. The lack of technical knowledge about the electronic components in automobiles often leads car owners to be suspi-

cious about the honesty of car mechanics. Although they might be fairly knowledgeable about the mechanical work-ings of their automobiles, <u>car owners</u> rarely understand the nature and scope of the electronic repairs needed in modern automobiles. For instance, the <u>function and importance</u> of a transmission in a car is generally well known to all car owners; but the <u>wire harnesses and printed circuit boards</u> that regulate the fuel consumption and performance of their car are rarely familiar. <u>Repairs</u> for these electronic components can often run over 400 dollars—a large amount for a customer who cannot even visualize what a wire harness or printed circuit board looks like. In contrast, a <u>400-dollar charge</u> for the trans-mission on the family car, though distressing, is more readily understood and accepted.

There is nothing really wrong with this paragraph—it's just hard to read. Why? It is difficult to read because the subjects of the sen-tences change with each new sentence. Notice the underlined sub-jects of the sentences in this paragraph. These subjects are different, causing each sentence to feel like it is striking off in a new direction. As a result, each new sentence forces the readers to shift focus to con-centrate on something new.

To avoid this bumpy, unfocused feeling, line up the subjects so each sentence in the paragraph stresses the same things. To line up subjects, first ask yourself what the paragraph is about. Then, restruc-ture the sentences to align with that subject. Here is a revision of para-graph 9 that focuses on the "car owners" as subjects:

9a. Due to their lack of knowledge about electronics, some <u>car owners</u> are skeptical about the honesty of car mechanics when repairs involve electronic components. Most of our <u>customers</u> are fairly knowledgeable about the mechanical features of their automobiles, but <u>they</u> rarely understand the nature and scope of the electronic repairs needed in modern automobiles. For example, most <u>people</u> recognize the function and importance of a transmission in an automobile; but, the average <u>person</u> knows very little about the wire harnesses and printed circuit boards that regulate the fuel consumption and performance of their car. So, for most of our customers, a <u>400-dollar repair</u> for these electronic components seems like a large amount, especially when <u>these folks</u> cannot even visualize what a wire harness or printed circuit board looks like. In contrast, <u>most car owners</u> think a 400-dollar charge to fix the transmission on the family car, though distressing, is more acceptable.

In this revised paragraph, you should notice two things. First, the words *car owners* are not always the exact words used in the subject slot. Synonyms and pronouns should be used to add variety to the sentences. Second, not all the subjects need to be related to car owners. In the middle of the paragraph, for example, *400-dollar repair* is the subject of a sentence. This deviation from *car owners* is fine as long as the majority of the subjects in the paragraph are similar to each other. In other words, the paragraph will still sound focused, even though an occasional subject is not in alignment with the others.

Of course, the subjects of the paragraph could be aligned differently to stress something else in the paragraph. Here is another revision of paragraph 9 in which the focus of the paragraph is *repairs*.

9b. <u>Repairs</u> to electronic components often lead car owners, who lack knowledge about electronics, to doubt the honesty of car mechanics. The <u>nature and scope of these repairs</u> are usually beyond the understanding of most nonmechanics, unlike the typical mechanical repairs with which customers are more familiar. For instance, the <u>importance of fixing</u> the transmission in a car is readily apparent to most car owners, but adjustments to electronic components like wire harnesses and printed circuit boards are foreign to most customers—even though these electronic parts are crucial in regulating their car's fuel consumption and performance. So, <u>a repair</u> to these electronic components, which can cost 400 dollars, seems excessive, especially when the repair can't even be visualized by the customer. In contrast, a <u>400-dollar replacement</u> of the family car's transmission, though distressing, is more readily accepted.

In this paragraph, the subjects are aligned around words associated with repairs. Even though the subjects have been changed, the paragraph should still seem more focused than the original.

One important item you should notice is that paragraph 9a is easier for most people to read than paragraph 9b. Paragraph 9a is more readable because it has "doers" in the subject slots throughout the paragraph. In paragraph 9a, the car owners are active subjects, while in paragraph 9b the car repairs are inactive subjects. Much like sentences, the best subjects in a paragraph are people or things that are doing something.

The Given/New Method

Another way to write plain paragraphs is to use the *given/new method* to weave sentences together. Developed by Susan Haviland and Herbert Clark in 1974, the given/new method is based on the assumption that readers will always try to fit new information into what they already know. Therefore, every sentence in a paragraph should contain something the readers already know (i.e., the given) and something new that the readers do not know. To illustrate, consider these two paragraphs:

10a. Santa Fe is a beautiful place with surprises around every corner. Some artists choose to strike off into the mountains to paint, while others enjoy working in local studios.

10b. Santa Fe offers many beautiful places for artists to work, with surprises around every corner. Some artists choose to strike off into the mountains to paint, while others enjoy working in local studios.

Both of these examples are readable, but paragraph 10b is easier to read because the word *artists* appears in both sentences. Example 10a is a little harder to read, because there is nothing given that carries over from the first sentence to the second sentence.

Typically, the given information should appear early in the sentence and the new information should appear later in the sentence. Placed early in the sentence, the given information will provide a familiar anchor or context for the readers. Later in the sentence, the new information builds on that familiar ground. Consider this larger paragraph:

11. Recently, an art gallery exhibited the mysterious paintings of Irwin Fleminger, a modernist artist whose vast Mars-like landscapes contain cryptic human artifacts. One of Fleminger's paintings attracted the attention of some young school children who happened to be walking by. At first, the children laughed, pointing out some of the strange artifacts in the painting. Soon, though, the artifacts in the painting drew the students into a critical awareness of the painting, and they began to ask their bewildered teacher what the artifacts meant. Mysterious and beautiful, Fleminger's paintings have this effect on many people, not just school children.

In this paragraph, the beginning of each sentence provides something given, usually an idea, word, or phrase drawn from the previous sentence. Then, the comment of each sentence adds something new to that given information. By chaining together given and new information, the paragraph builds the readers' understanding gradually, adding a little more information with each sentence.

In some cases, however, the previous sentence does not offer a suitable subject for the sentence that follows it. In these cases, transitional phrases can be used to provide the readers given information in the beginning of the sentence. To illustrate,

12. This public relations effort will strengthen Gentec's relationship with leaders of the community. <u>With this new relationship in place</u>, the details of the project can be negotiated with terms that are fair to both parties.

In this sentence, the given information in the second sentence appears in the transitional phrase, not the subject. Transitional phrases are a good place to include given information when the subject cannot be drawn from the previous sentence.

To sum up at this point, there are two primary methods available for developing plain paragraphs: (1) aligning the subjects of the sentences and (2) using the given/new method to weave the sentences together. Both methods are useful in proposal writing and should be used interchangeably. In some cases, both methods can be employed in the same paragraph as the writer uses various techniques to weave the paragraph into a coherent whole.

When Is It Appropriate to Use Passive Voice?

Before discussing the elements of persuasive style, we should expose one important bogie monster as a fraud. Since childhood, you have probably been warned against using passive voice. In fact, you might even remember various people decreeing that passive voice was off-limits, period. It's bad for you, they said, never use it.

Indeed, passive voice can be problematic when it is misused. One problem is that passive voice removes the doer from the sentence. For example, consider this passive sentence and its active counterpart:

13a. The door was closed to ensure privacy. (passive)

13b. Frank Roberts closed the door to ensure privacy. (active)

Written in passive voice, sentence 13a lacks a doer. The subject of the sentence, the door, is being acted upon, but it's not really doing anything. The second reason passive voice can be problematic is the use of an extra *be* verb (i.e., is, was, were, has been). The extra verb might slow the readers down a bit.

Despite dire warnings about passive voice, it does have a place in certain pieces of writing, especially highly technical or scientific writing. Either of these conditions makes a passive sentence appropriate:

- The readers do not need to know who or what is doing something in the sentence.
- The subject of the sentence is what the sentence is about.

For example, in Sentence 13a, the person who closed the door might be unknown or irrelevant to the readers. Is it important that we know that *Frank Roberts* closed the door? Or, do we simply need to know the door was closed? If the door is what the sentence is about and who closed the door is not important, then the passive is fine.

Consider these other examples of passive sentences:

14a. The shuttle bus will be driven to local care facilities to provide seniors with shopping opportunities (passive).

14b. Jane Chavez will drive the shuttle bus to local care facilities to provide seniors with shopping opportunities (active).

15a. The telescope was moved to the Orion system to observe the newly discovered nebula (passive).

15b. Our graduate assistant, Mary Stewart, moved the telescope to the Orion system to observe the newly discovered nebula (active).

In both these sets of sentences, the passive sentence may be more appropriate, unless there is a special reason Jane Chavez or Mary Stewart need to be singled out for special consideration.

When developing a focused paragraph, passive sentences can often help you align the subjects and use given/new strategies. For example, does the use of passive voice in the following paragraph help make the paragraph more readable?

16a. The merger between Brown and Smith will be completed by May 2004. Initially, Smith's key managers will be moved into Brown's headquarters. Then, other Smith employees will be gradually worked into the Brown hierarchy to eliminate any redundancies. During the merger process, employees at both companies will be offered all possible accommodations to help them through the uncertain times created by the merger.

16b. Brown and Smith will complete their merger in May 2004. Initially, Bill's Trucking Service will move the offices of key managers at Smith into Brown's headquarters. Brown's human resources manager will then gradually move Smith's other employees into the Brown hierarchy to eliminate any redundancies. During the merger, vice presidents, human resources agents, and managers at all levels will offer accommodations to employees at both companies to help them through the uncertain times created by the merger.

Most people would find Paragraph 16a more readable because it uses passive voice to put the emphasis on *employees*. Paragraph 16b is harder to read because it includes irrelevant doers, like Bill's Trucking Service, and it keeps changing the subjects of the sentences, causing the paragraph to seem unfocused.

In scientific and technical writing, the passive voice is often the norm because *who* will be doing *what* is not always predictable. For example, in Sentence 15b, we might not be able to predict in our proposal that Mary Stewart will actually be the person adjusting the telescope on a given evening. More than likely, all we can confidently say is that *someone* at the observatory will move the telescope on a particular day. So, the passive is used because *who* moves the telescope is not important. The fact that the telescope will be moved, on the other hand, is important.

Used properly, passive voice can be a helpful tool in your efforts to write plain sentences and paragraphs. Passive voice is misused when the readers are left wondering who or what is doing the action in the sentence. In these cases, the sentence should be restructured to put the doer in the subject slot of the sentence.

Persuasive Style

Persuasive style uses character and emotion to motivate readers to say yes to your ideas. The persuasive style is designed to move them to take action, while the plain style is particularly useful for describing things or instructing the readers.

When used properly, the persuasive style can add emphasis, energy, color, and feeling to your writing. On the other hand, when used improperly, persuasive style can sound excessive to readers. There is a fine line between persuading the readers with powerful imagery and emotion, and turning them off with the "hard sell." Persuasive style is best used at strategic points in a proposal when you are trying to emphasize or amplify specific ideas. As a rule of thumb, this style is best used in areas of the proposal where you expect the readers to make decisions.

There are, of course, many ways to be persuasive or amplify your arguments. In proposals, though, the following four persuasion techniques are helpful toward giving your writing more impact:

- Elevating the tone
- Using similes and analogies
- Using metaphors
- Changing the pace

Let us consider each of these techniques separately.

Elevating the Tone

Tone is essentially the resonance or pitch that the readers will "hear" as they are looking over your piece of writing. Most people read silently to themselves, but all readers have an inner voice that vocalizes the words as they move from sentence to sentence. By paying attention to tone, you can influence the readers' inner voice in ways that persuade them to read the proposal with a specific emotion or attitude. You can also use tone to establish a sense of character that will reassure the readers about your, your team's, or your company's credibility. Tone puts a human face on the text, if only momentarily, to appeal to the readers on an emotional and character level.

Writers will often choose to elevate the tone at strategic places in their writing, like introductions, openings, closings, and conclusions. For the most part, the plain style, which is used in the bulk of the text sets a rather neutral, professional tone. As you near the closing paragraph of larger sections or the conclusion, however, you should gradually "elevate" the tone of your writing to express a particular emotion or character. Effective public speakers use this tone elevation technique all the time. Their speech may start out with a good amount of energy, but it soon settles into a rather plain style. When the speaker nears important transition points or the conclusion, he elevates the tone. Hearing this elevated tone, the listeners know the speaker is nearing an important point, so they listen more closely.

One easy way to elevate tone in written texts is to first decide what feelings of emotion or character you want to heighten at important points in the writing. Then, map out those feelings on a piece of paper. For example, let us say we want to convey a sense of excitement as the readers are looking over the proposal. We would first put the word 'excitement' in the middle of a sheet of paper. Then, as shown in Figure 9g.3, we would map out the feelings associated with that emotion.

To put this tone of excitement in your writing, weave these words into the text at strategic moments. Subconsciously, the readers will detect this elevated tone in your work, and their inner voice will begin reinforcing the sense of excitement you are trying to convey.

Similarly, if you want to add in a particular sense of character, map out the words associated with that character trait. For instance, let us say you want your proposal to convey a sense of 'security.' A map around security might look like the diagram in Figure 9g.4.

If you weave these words associated with *security* into strategic places in the proposals, the readers will perceive the sense of security that you are trying to convey.

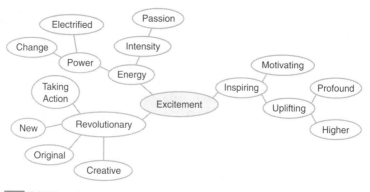

FIGURE 9g.3
Mapping a Tone that Shows Emotion

FIGURE 9g.4
Mapping a Tone that Shows Character

The best places to weave in specific tones are in the introduction and conclusion and the openings and closings of larger sections. These are the places where the readers tend to make decisions about whether or not to accept the argument of the essay.

Of course, writers can overdo the use of a particular tone. To avoid this problem, decide on one emotion and one character for the entire proposal. Multiple emotional or character tones will only confuse and overwhelm the readers. Also, use these words only sparingly. Just like adding spices to food, you want to avoid overseasoning your writing.

Using Similes and Analogies

Similes and analogies are rhetorical devices that help writers define difficult concepts by comparing them to simpler things. For example, let us say an essay we are writing needs to describe a "semiconductor wafer" to people who know almost nothing about semiconductors. A simile could be used to describe the wafer this way: "A semiconductor wafer is like a miniature Manhattan Island crammed on a silicon disk that is only three inches wide." In this case, the simile ("X is like Y") not only clarifies the concept by putting it into familiar terms, it also creates a visual image that helps the readers understand the complexity of the semiconductor wafer.

Analogies are also a good way to help the readers visualize difficult concepts. An analogy follows the structure "A is to B as X is to Y." For example, a medical analogy might be, "Like police keeping order in a city, white blood cells seek to control viruses in the body." In this case, both parts of the analogy are working in parallel. *Police* is equivalent to *white blood cells* and *keeping order in the city* is equivalent to *control viruses in the body*.

Similes and analogies are primarily used to provide the readers with a quick, visual understanding of something unfamiliar by comparing it to something familiar. A good rule of thumb is to reduce the use of similes and analogies when the readers are experts. Use them more often when the readers are less experienced with your subject.

Using Metaphors

Though comparable to similes and analogies, metaphors work at a deeper level in pieces of writing. Specifically, metaphors are used to create or reinforce a particular perspective that you want the readers to adopt toward your subject or ideas. For example, a popular metaphor in Western medicine is the "war on cancer." If we were writing a proposal to request funding on a cancer-related subject, we might weave this metaphor into our proposal. We could talk about *battles with cancer cells, new weapons against cancer,* and the *front line of cancer research.* By employing this metaphor throughout the proposal, we would reinforce a particular perspective about cancer research. A metaphor such as *war on cancer* would add a sense of urgency to our proposal, because it suggests that cancer is an enemy that must be defeated, at almost any cost. Of course, cancer research is not really a war. And yet, we accept this metaphor with little question or dispute.

Metaphors are very powerful tools in writing because they tend to work at a subconscious level. In other words, the use of the *war on cancer* metaphor should not be obvious to the readers. Instead, the metaphor is used in key places to gradually shift the readers' point of view, turning cancer into an enemy in their minds.

But what if a commonly used metaphor, like the *war on cancer*, is not appropriate? In these cases, we can create a new metaphor and use it to invent a new perspective for the readers. For example, perhaps we want our readers to view cancer as something to be managed, not fought. Our new metaphor, *managing cancer* would allow us to talk about *negotiating* with cancer cells or using drugs that *mediate* between cancer cells and regular cells. We might speak of patients as *managers* who set goals and priorities that their body will aim to reach. Doctors might become *consultants* who offer patients advice on managing their illness. This new metaphor, creates a quite different perspective than the *war* metaphor. We can use this new metaphor to shift the readers' perspective, urging them to think differently about how they will handle their illness.

To use metaphors, you should first look for the existing metaphors that are widely used in your field. For example, perhaps you notice that "drugs are a disease in our city" is prevalent in the media. You can then use this metaphor to create a theme. Extending the metaphor, you might say, "Our city needs treatment," or, "We need to control the illness first, then we can begin recovering." By playing off the original metaphor, you can create more metaphorical phrases that reinforce the perspective you want.

In some cases, new metaphors need to be created from scratch. For instance, a piece of writing that is arguing for the construction of a new office building might use a metaphor like, "Harmon Industries needs a new home." This *home* metaphor could then be used to invent a theme in which words associated with homes, like *comfort*, *security*, *garden*, and *family*, are woven into the text. In this case, we could use this *home* metaphor to shift the readers' perspective from "the office building is the workplace" to "the office building is our home."

Changing the Pace

You can also regulate the readers' pace as they work through your piece of writing. Longer sentences tend to slow the reading pace down, while shorter sentences tend to speed up the pace. By paying attention to the length of sentences, you can increase or decrease the intensity of your writing. For instance, let us say you believe a problem is urgent and needs to be handled right away. The best way to increase the intensity in your proposal would be to use short sentences while you describe that problem. As the pace increases, the readers will naturally feel impelled to do something, because they will sense the problem is rapidly growing worse. On the other hand, if you want the readers to be cautious and deliberate, longer sentences will decrease the intensity of the writing, giving the readers the sense that there is no need to rush.

Sentence length is a great way to convey the intensity you want without saying something like "This opportunity is slipping away!" or "We really need to take action now!" Sentence length can also soothe anxious readers by slowing down the pace a bit.

Last Word

After reading through this section, some people may wonder about the ethics of using stylistic devices to influence the readers. Most people would not question the use of plain sentences and paragraphs to help the readers to understand the ideas in a piece of writing. But, the use of persuasive style might sound a bit like manipulating the readers.

To be candid, you *are* manipulating the readers when you are trying to persuade them. That's what writing does. The challenge is to match your piece of writing's style to the readers' needs. Plain style is best for instructing the readers, giving them the facts in a straightforward way. Persuasive style is used to motivate the readers to take action. Motivating people is ethical if you are urging them to do what is best for them. When persuasive style is used properly, it matches tone, choice of words, and pace to the situation that the readers face. It stresses important ideas at important points in the writing.

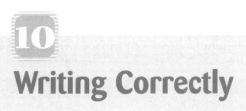

10

Writing Correctly

FRAGMENTS   163

COMMA SPLICES AND FUSED SENTENCES   166

PRONOUN REFERENCE   168

AGREEMENT   170

CORRECT FORMS   174

Voices
from the Community

"All I know about grammar is its infinite power. To shift the structure of a sentence alters the meanings of that sentence, as inflexibly as the position of a camera alters the meanings of the object photographed....
The arrangement of the words matters, and the arrangement you want can be found in the picture in your mind."
—Joan Didion, "Why I Write"

10a Fragments

If you write a group of words that masquerades as a sentence but is incomplete, you may irritate or mislead your readers and undermine your own authority as a writer.

PARTS MISSING   The insurance company processing the claim.
READER'S REACTION: Something is missing. What did it *do*?

EDITED   The insurance company processing the claim **sent** a check.

163

Even with a capital letter at the beginning and a period at the end, a **sentence fragment** is only part of a sentence—it may lack a **subject** (naming the doer) or a **verb** (naming the action or occurrence). It may be a **subordinate clause,** introduced by a word like *because* and mistakenly asked to stand on its own.

Recognizing Sentence Fragments
Subject and Verb

A **complete sentence** must contain both a subject and a complete verb, expressed or implied.

STRATEGY   Ask questions to identify fragments and sentences.

- Test #1: Ask *who* or *what does?* Or *who* or *what is?*

  A word group that doesn't answer "Who?" or "What?" lacks a subject and is a fragment. Especially if it begins with *and* or *but,* it may be detached from a nearby sentence with its subject.

  FRAGMENT   And also needs a counselor.

  READER'S REACTION: I can't tell *who* (or *what*) needs the counselor.

  EDITED   Hope Clinic hired a nurse and also needs a counselor.

  A word group that doesn't answer "Does?" or "Is?" lacks a complete verb and is a fragment.

  FRAGMENT   The new policy to provide coverage on the basis of hours worked.

  READER'S REACTION: I can't tell what the policy *does* or *is.*

  EDITED   The new policy **provides** coverage on the basis of hours worked.

- Test #2: Can you turn a word group into a question that can be answered *yes* or *no?* If you can, it's a sentence.

  Caution: Begin your question with *did.* If you begin with *is, are, has,* or *have,* you may provide a missing verb.

  WORD GROUPS   They signed the petition to recall the mayor. Suspecting his involvement.

  QUESTIONS   Did they sign the petition to recall the mayor? [Yes.] Did suspecting his involvement? [Can't answer.]

  CONCLUSION   The first word group is a sentence, but not the second.

Subordinating Words

Look for a **clause** (a word group with a subject and verb) introduced by a subordinating conjunction (*although, if, because, unless*) or a pronoun (*that, what, which, who*). If this word group is not attached to a main clause that can stand alone, it's a fragment.

STRATEGY   Hunt for a subordinating word.

FRAGMENT   Residents love the mild climate. Which is ideal for outdoor events.

EDITED   Residents love the mild climate, which is ideal for outdoor events.

Editing Sentence Fragments

Complete or attach fragments so that you supply what's missing.

STRATEGY   Attach, rewrite, add, or omit.

- Attach a fragment to a nearby sentence.

  FRAGMENT   Trauma centers give prompt care to heart attack victims. Because **rapid treatment can minimize heart damage.**

  ATTACHED   Trauma centers give prompt care to heart attack victims **because** rapid treatment can minimize heart damage.

- Rewrite to eliminate the fragment.

  FRAGMENT   **Introducing competing varieties of crabs into the same tank.** He did this in order to study aggression.

  REWRITTEN   He **introduced** competing varieties of crabs into the same tank in order to study aggression.

- Drop a subordinating word.

  FRAGMENT   Although **the advisory committee contested the motion.** It still passed by a majority.

  EDITED   The advisory committee contested the motion. It still passed by a majority.

- Supply a missing word.

  FRAGMENT   **The judge allowing adopted children to meet their natural parents.**

  EDITED   The judge **favors** allowing adopted children to meet their natural parents.

Using Partial Sentences

Especially in advertising and creative writing, you'll see *deliberate* fragments used for emphasis or contrast. Use such fragments only when readers will recognize your intention and accept the resulting style. In most academic and professional writing, avoid them.

10b Comma Splices and Fused Sentences

You may confuse or annoy readers if you inappropriately join two or more sentences using either a comma (**comma splice**) or no punctuation at all (**fused sentence**).

COMMA
SPLICE

CBS was founded in 1928 by William S. Paley, his uncle and his father sold him a struggling radio network.

READER'S REACTION: At first I thought that CBS had three founders: Paley, his uncle, and his father.

EDITED

CBS was founded in 1928 by William S. Paley ; his uncle and his father sold him a struggling radio network.

FUSED
SENTENCE

The city had only one swimming pool without an admission fee the pool was in disrepair.

READER'S REACTION: Is there only one pool, or is there only one that's free?

EDITED

The city had only one swimming pool , but without an admission fee, the pool was in disrepair.

A **comma splice** links what could be two sentences with a comma alone. A **fused** (or **run-on**) sentence joins what could be two sentences without any punctuation mark or connecting word at all. Either can confuse a reader about where one part ends and another begins.

Recognizing Comma Splices

Look for sentences with word groups that could stand on their own but are joined by a comma.

STRATEGY   Hunt for commas that string word groups together.

COMMA
SPLICE

The typical Navajo husband is a trustee, the wife and her children own the property.

EDITED

The typical Navajo husband is a trustee , but the wife and her children own the property.

READER'S REACTION: Until you added *but*, I missed your point about the wife's status.

Recognizing Fused Sentences

Though fused sentences may be any length, look for long sentences with little or no internal punctuation.

STRATEGY   Count the statements in a sentence.

If you find several, check the punctuation and connecting words.

FUSED
SENTENCE

The scientists had trouble identifying the fossil it resembled a bird and a lizard.

EDITED   The scientists had trouble identifying the fossil **because** it resembled a bird and a lizard.

READER'S REACTION: Adding *because* separates the two main points and clarifies the sentence.

Editing Comma Splices and Fused Sentences

As you repair sentences, decide how to relate or connect ideas.

STRATEGY   Separate or relate ideas for emphasis.

- Divide into two sentences.
  (_____. _____.)

  FUSED SENTENCE   Football does not cause the most injuries in college gymnastics is more dangerous.

  EDITED   Football does not cause the most injuries in college. Gymnastics is more dangerous.

- Join with a comma plus *and, but, or, for, nor, so,* or *yet.*
  (_____, and _____.)

  FUSED SENTENCE   The clinic is understaffed it still performs well.

  EDITED   The clinic is understaffed, **yet** it still performs well.

- Connect similar or equal ideas with a semicolon.
  (_____; _____.)

  COMMA SPLICE   An autopilot corrects drift, the system senses and reacts to changes in the aircraft's motion.

  EDITED   An autopilot corrects drift; the system senses and reacts to changes in the aircraft's motion.

- Make one part subordinate to relate ideas.
  (Because _____, _____.)

  A subordinator (*because, though, when, unless*) or relative pronoun (*who, which, that*) can show how one idea depends on another.

  COMMA SPLICE   Automobiles are so complex, mechanics may train for years.

  EDITED   **Because** automobiles are so complex, mechanics may train for years.

- Clarify how parts relate with words and a semicolon.
  (_____; therefore, ____.)

  Use words like *however* and *moreover* (conjunctive adverbs) or *for example, consequently,* or *in contrast* plus a semicolon.

  FUSED SENTENCE   Chickens reach market size within months the lobster takes six to eight years.

  EDITED   Chickens reach market size within months; **in contrast,** the lobster takes six to eight years.

Some connecting words may mean the same thing but need different punctuation. The most common pair is *but* and *however*.

Jose likes his job **,** **but** the hours are long.

Jose likes his job **;** **however** **,** the hours are long.

Because introduces a clause with a subject and verb; *because of* introduces a prepositional phrase.

Because the pay is low, Anna wants a new job.

Because of the low pay, Anna wants a new job.

10c Pronoun Reference

When you replace nouns with pronouns, you reduce repetition as you build connections. If readers can't tell which word is replaced, they may be irritated trying to figure out what your sentence means.

AMBIGUOUS REFERENCE
In the circus, Brad's chores included leading the elephants from the cages and hosing **them** down.

READER'S REACTION: What got hosed down? Elephants? Cages? Both?

EDITED
In the circus, Brad's chores included hosing the elephants down after leading **them** from **their** cages.

Most problems occur when an **antecedent**—the word or words to which the pronoun refers—isn't clear. By creating clear pronoun reference, you tie ideas together, clarify relationships, and focus readers' attention.

Recognizing Unclear Pronoun Reference

If readers say they "can't figure out what you're saying," make sure that each pronoun refers clearly to only one possible antecedent that is stated specifically and located close enough to make the connection clear.

STRATEGY   Mark a clear antecedent for each pronoun.

• Can you underline a *single, clear* antecedent?

AMBIGUOUS REFERENCE
Robespierre disagreed with Danton over the path the French Revolution should take. **He** believed that the Revolution was endangered by internal enemies.

READER'S REACTION: I'm lost. Who's *he*? Robespierre or Danton?

EDITED
Robespierre disagreed with Danton over the path the French Revolution should take. **Robespierre** believed that the Revolution was endangered by internal enemies.

- Can you answer,"What does [pronoun *X*] refer to?"

IMPLIED
ANTECEDENT

A hard frost damaged local citrus groves, but **it** has not been determined.

READER'S REACTION: What does *it* mean—the frost? The damage? Or something else?

STATED

A hard frost damaged local citrus groves, but **the extent of the loss** has not been determined.

Editing Pronoun Reference

Focus on the pronoun. If needed, clarify the antecedent or rewrite.

STRATEGY Specify or explain the pronoun.

- Replace the pronoun with the noun to which it refers or with a synonym, or reword.

AMBIGUOUS
REFERENCE

Detaching the measuring probe from the glass cylinder is a delicate job because **it** breaks easily.

READER'S REACTION: Which is so fragile, the probe or the cylinder?

REPLACED
WITH NOUN

Detaching the measuring probe from the glass cylinder is a delicate job because **the probe** breaks easily.

REWORDED

Because the measuring probe breaks easily, detaching it from the glass cylinder is a delicate job.

- Right after *which, this,* or *that,* specify or explain the word to which the pronoun refers.

VAGUE
REFERENCE

Redfish have suffered from oil pollution and the destruction of their swamp habitat. **This** has reduced the redfish population.

READER'S REACTION: Does *this* refer to the destruction of habitat, the pollution, or both?

SPECIFIED

Redfish have suffered from oil pollution and the destruction of their swamp habitat. **This combination** has reduced the redfish population.

Sometimes a pronoun doesn't have to be replaced, just moved—especially to place *who*, *which*, and *that* right after their antecedents.

STRATEGY Move the pronoun close to its antecedent.

CONFUSING

After our dog died, I found an old ball behind **a bush that he loved to chase.**

EDITED

After our dog died, I found behind a bush an **old ball that he loved to chase.**

Especially for many academic readers, a possessive noun used as an antecedent will appear to be an error.

STRATEGY   Eliminate the possessive, and rewrite.

INAPPROPRIATE   In Faulkner's *The Sound and the Fury,* **he** begins from the point of view of a mentally retarded person.

EDITED   In *The Sound and the Fury,* **Faulkner** begins from the point of view of a mentally retarded person.

Remedy problems and guide readers by creating a **reference chain** of pronouns whose antecedent is stated in the first sentence of a passage.

UNCLEAR   Sand paintings were a remarkable form of Pueblo art. An artist would sprinkle dried sand of different colors, ground flower petals, corn pollen, and similar materials onto the floor to create **them.** Encouraging the spirits to send good fortune to humans was **their** purpose.

Because *them* and *their* are buried at the ends of sentences in the middle of the paragraph, readers may lose sight of the topic: sand paintings.

EDITED TO CREATE A REFERENCE CHAIN   Sand paintings were a remarkable form of Pueblo art. To create **them,** the artist would sprinkle dried sand of different colors, ground flower petals, corn pollen, and similar materials onto the floor. **Their** purpose was to encourage the spirits to send good fortune to humans.

STRATEGY   Create a reference chain.

- State the antecedent clearly in the opening sentence.
- Let no other possible antecedents interrupt the chain's links.
- Don't interrupt the chain and try to return to it later.
- Place the pronouns prominently (usually beginning sentences); vary their positions only slightly.

10d Agreement

You give readers mixed signals if you don't coordinate sentence parts.

INCONSISTENT   The city council and the mayor is known for her skillful responses to civic debate.

READER'S REACTION: This sentence opens with two things—the city council and the mayor—but *is* and *her* seem to switch to only the mayor.

EDITED   The city council and the mayor **are** known for **their** skillful responses to civic debate.

Readers expect to see how ideas in a sentence relate to each other grammatically—by showing **agreement** in number, person, and gender.

Recognizing Agreement

A subject and verb in a sentence should agree in number and person. A pronoun (*I, you, she*) should agree with its **antecedent,** the noun or other pronoun to which it refers, in number, person, and gender.

AGREEMENT: NUMBER, PERSON, GENDER

- **Number** shows singular (one) or plural (two or more) items.
  This **community** needs its recreation center.
  These **communities** need to share their facilities.

- **Person** indicates the speaker or subject spoken to or about.
  FIRST PERSON (SPEAKER)   I, we
  SECOND PERSON (SPOKEN TO)   You, you
  THIRD PERSON (SPOKEN ABOUT)   He, she, it, they

- **Gender** refers to masculine (*he, him*), feminine (*she, her*), or neuter (*it*) qualities attributed to a noun or pronoun.

Editing Subject-Verb Agreement

Subjects and verbs should match, both singular or both plural.

STRATEGY   Check the *-s* and *-es* endings.

Add *-s* or *-es* to make nouns plural but present tense verbs singular.

SINGULAR   The dam prevents flooding. [third person]
PLURAL   The dams prevent flooding.

Exceptions

- **Nouns with irregular plurals** (*person/people, child/children*) or with the same form for singular and plural (*moose/moose*)
- **Verbs with irregular forms,** including *be* and *have*

More complicated sentences may lead you to use the wrong verb form.

STRATEGY   Find the *real* subject, and match the verb.

- Mark the subject (not nouns in other word groups). Decide whether it's singular or plural. Edit the verb (or change the subject) to agree.

  DRAFT   The use of new testing **techniques** have increased.
  REAL SUBJECT   The use of new testing **techniques** have increased.
  EDITED   The use of new testing techniques has increased.

- Imagine the core sentence without any intervening expressions. Make the central noun and verb agree.

DRAFT   A regular tune-up, along with frequent oil changes, prolong the life of your car.

IMAGINE: A regular tune-up, ~~along with frequent oil changes,~~ prolong the life of your car.

EDITED   A regular tune-up, along with frequent oil changes, prolongs the life of your car.

ESL ADVICE: Separated Subjects and Verbs

Check for agreement if the subject and verb are separated.

PHRASE   A person **with sensitive eyes** has to wear sunglasses.

CLAUSE   A person **whose eyes are sensitive** has to wear sunglasses.

When the subject is the same in both clauses, the verbs must agree.

SAME SUBJECT   A person who wants to protect her eyes wears sunglasses.

Deciding whether some nouns are singular or plural can be tricky.

STRATEGY   Use a pronoun to test your verb choice.

Decide which pronoun accurately represents a complicated subject: *he, she,* or *it* (singular) or *they* (plural). Read your sentence aloud using this replacement pronoun; edit the verb to agree.

DRAFT   The **news** about the job market [sounds? sound?] good.

PRONOUN TEST: I could replace "The news" with "it" and say "It sounds."

EDITED   The **news** about the job market **sounds** good.

TRICKY SINGULAR AND PLURAL NOUNS

- **Collective noun** naming a unit composed of more than one individual or thing: *staff, flock, audience, tribe*

  SINGULAR   The staff is hardworking. [group as a unit = *it*]

  PLURAL   The staff are caring people. [individual members = *they*]

- Titles of books or names of companies with plural nouns

  SINGULAR   *Hard Times* is a great novel.

  SINGULAR   Burgers to Go is profitable.

- Nouns with plural forms and singular meanings: *politics, mumps*

  SINGULAR   Economics is a popular field of study.

- Compound subjects joined by *and*: the men and women

  PLURAL   Ham and eggs are the main ingredients. [two units]

  SINGULAR   Ham and eggs is my favorite meal. [rarely one unit]

- Alternative subjects joined by *or* (*nor*): *the servers or the cook*
  The verb agrees with the *closer* noun.

    The auditor or the **accountants** review the statement.

    The accountants or the **auditor** reviews the statement.

- Subjects renamed after linking verbs (*is, seems, appears*)
  The verb agrees with the subject (not the words renaming it).

    The chief **obstacle** to change is the mayor and her allies.

Indefinite pronouns do not refer to specific ideas, people, or things. Most (*anyone, each*) require singular verbs, but a few (*both, few*) need plural verbs. Some (*all, most, some*) may take either verb form—singular to refer to something that cannot be counted or plural to refer to two or more items of something that can be counted.

SINGULAR **All** of the food **is** gone.
food = food in general (not countable)

PLURAL **All** of the supplies **are** gone.
supplies = many kinds (countable)

ESL ADVICE: **Quantifiers**

Quantifiers (*each, one, many*) show the amount or quantity of a noun.

EXPRESSIONS FOLLOWED BY PLURAL NOUN + SINGULAR VERB
Each of/Every one of/One of/None of the **students** lives on campus.

EXPRESSIONS FOLLOWED BY PLURAL NOUN + PLURAL VERB
Several of/Many of/Both of   the **students** live off campus.

EXPRESSIONS FOLLOWED BY A SINGULAR OR A PLURAL VERB

noncount noun + singular verb
Some of/Most of/All of/A lot of   the **produce** is fresh.

plural noun + plural verb
Some of/Most of/All of/A lot of   the **vegetables** are fresh.

MUCH AND *MOST* (WITHOUT *OF*)

NONCOUNT NOUN   **Much traffic** occurs during rush hour.

PLURAL NOUN   **Most Americans** live in or near cities.

TRICKY SINGULAR AND PLURAL PRONOUNS

- *Who, which,* and *that* as subjects of clauses
  Match the verb and the word to which the pronoun refers.

    He likes a film that builds suspense but novels that show character.

- *Each* or *every* before a compound subject
  SINGULAR Each clerk and manager checks the log.

- *Each* and *every* after a compound subject
  PLURAL   The clerks and managers each check the log.

Editing Pronoun-Antecedent Agreement

Work with either the pronoun or its **antecedent,** the word to which it refers. Edit to bring the other into agreement.

STRATEGY	Mark the specific word to which a pronoun refers.
INCONSISTENT	**Each** of the samples travels in their own case.
CLEAR	Each of the samples travels in its own case.

When indefinite pronouns are singular, so are other pronouns that refer to them.

> **Somebody** on the team left her racket on the court.

> **Each** of the men has his own equipment.

To avoid sexist language, use plural pronouns and antecedents.

SEXIST	**Everybody** used charts in **his** sales **talk.**
INFORMAL (SPOKEN)	**Everybody** used charts in **their** sales **talks.**
WRITTEN	All presenters used charts in their sales talks.

ESL ADVICE: *This, That, These, Those*

To modify nouns, *this* and *that* are singular; *these* and *those* are plural.

INCONSISTENT	This crystals make snowflakes.
PLURAL	These crystals make snowflakes.
INCONSISTENT	Those experiment takes two days.
SINGULAR	That experiment takes two days.

10e Correct Forms

If you misuse word forms, readers may doubt your ability as a writer and pay more attention to the error than to your point.

DRAFT	By Friday, him and me will submit the report.
	READER'S REACTION: *Him and me* sounds uneducated. Who hired this person?
EDITED	By Friday, he and I will submit the report.

Most readers expect you to edit your writing to use widely accepted forms of verbs, pronouns, adjectives, and adverbs.

Recognizing and Editing Verb Forms

Verbs vary in **tense** as they show past, present, and future time.

Past Tense -ed *Ending for Regular Verbs*

Be sure to write this ending even if you don't hear it pronounced before a -*d* or -*t* sound.

| DRAFT | The company **use** to provide dental benefits. |
| EDITED | The company **used** to provide dental benefits. |

Past Tense Irregular Verbs

Irregular verbs form the past tense in some way other than adding -ed (*run/ran*).

| DRAFT | The movie characters **sweared** constantly. |
| EDITED | The movie characters **swore** constantly. |

Verb Forms in Complex Tenses

Complex tenses have a main verb and a helping verb. The main verb is a **participle, past** (-ed, -en, or irregular form) or **present** (-ing form). The **helping verb** is a form of *be, do,* or *have* or a verb such as *will* or *would.*

	helping verb + main verb (present participle)
-ING FORM	He was **loading** the delivery van.
	helping verb + main verb (past participle)
REGULAR VERB	Mike has **analyzed** the problem.
IRREGULAR VERB	Lynn has **brought** the equipment.

ESL ADVICE: **Common Helping Verbs**

Be: *am, is, are, was, were, be, being, been*
Have: *have, has, had*
Do: *do, does, did*
Modals: *could, should, would, ought to, can, may, might, must, shall, will*

Helping Verbs in Progressive Tenses

These past, present, and future forms show an action in progress using an -ing main verb: *is turning, was turning, will be turning.* In writing, use all the parts of the correct verb even if your spoken dialect omits them.

WORD OMITTED	The interview **starting** now.
EDITED	The interview **is starting** now.
WRONG FORM	The workers **was running** for the door.
EDITED	The workers **were running** for the door.

Past Participles in Perfect Tenses

The present, past, and future perfect tenses combine a helping verb with the past participle (the -ed, -en, or irregular form) to show the order of events. Don't substitute the simple past tense for the past participle.

| MISTAKEN PAST | Pete **had rode** for a year before his injury. |
| EDITED | Pete **had ridden** for a year before his injury. |

Mood

Sentences can be classified by **mood,** the form of the verb that reflects the writer's or speaker's attitude.

- **Indicative:** statements intended as truthful or factual

    Motorcycle helmets **have reduced** injuries.

- **Imperative:** statements acting as commands

    Get a helmet.

- **Subjunctive:** statements expressing uncertainty—a supposition, prediction, possibility, desire, or wish

    If you **were** to crash, the helmet would protect your head.

    Jim's insurance requires that he **wear** a helmet.

The subjunctive appears in formal writing, often in **conditional statements** beginning with *if* and in *that* clauses with verbs such as *ask* or *request*. With *that,* use the basic present form (*wear, be*), even with the third person singular. With *if,* use the basic present, the past (*wore, were* not *was*), or the past perfect (*had worn* not *would have worn, had been*).

ESL ADVICE: Conditional Statements

Conditional statements depend on a condition or are imagined. Each type has an *if* clause and a result clause that combine different verb tenses.

Type I: True in the present

- Generally true in the present as a habit or as a fact

    if + subject + present tense   subject + present tense
    If **I** drive to school every day,   **I** get to class on time.

- True in the future as a one-time event

    if + subject + present tense   subject + future tense
    If **I** drive to school today,   **I** will get to class on time.

- Possibly true in the future as a one-time event

    if + subject + present tense   subject + modal + base form verb
    If **I** drive to school today,   **I** may get to class on time.

Type II: Untrue or contrary to fact in the present

if + subject + past tense   subject + *would/could/might* + base form verb
If **I** drove to school,   **I** would arrive on time.

For Type II, the form of *be* in the *if* clause is always *were*.

Type III: Untrue or contrary to fact in the past

                   subject + *would/could/might* +
if + subject + past perfect tense   *have* + past participle
If **I** had driven to school,   **I** would not have been late.

Lie, Lay, Sit, Set

These forms are confusing for many writers.

VERB	PRESENT	PAST	PAST PARTICIPLE
lie (oneself)	lie	lay	lain
lay (an object)	lay	laid	laid
sit (oneself)	sit	sat	sat
set (an object)	set	set	set

DRAFT   I **laid** down yesterday for a nap. I **have laid** down every afternoon for a week.

EDITED   I **lay** down yesterday for a nap. I **have lain** down every afternoon for a week.

DRAFT   Erica and Steve **sat** the projector on the table.

EDITED   Erica and Steve **set** the projector on the table.

Editing for Clear Tense Sequence

Readers expect you to use one tense or to follow a logical sequence.

STRATEGY   Change tense to relate events in time.

LOGICAL   People **forget** that four candidates **ran** in 1948.

LOGICAL   The accountant **destroyed** the file because **no one had asked** him to save it.

LOGICAL   No one **had recognized** that food from cans sealed with lead solder **is** poisonous.

Recognizing Pronoun Forms

Pronouns change form to fit their roles in a sentence.

SUBJECT   I, you, he, she, it; we, you, they

         I ran out of leaflets, but **he** had plenty.

OBJECT   me, you, him, her, it; us, you, them

         Jamie gave **me** some extras for **them.**

POSSESSIVE   my, mine, your, yours, his, her, hers, its; our, ours, your, yours, their, theirs

         Our client chose **my** leaflet design, not **hers.**

Subject Complement

A pronoun that renames the subject (a **subject complement**) follows *be* (*is, are, was, were*), using the subjective form.

subject   subject complement
The people assigned the report were **Trinh and I.**

STRATEGY Test for pronouns that rename the subject.

Reverse the sentence to make the pronoun the subject.

DRAFT **The last art majors** to get jobs were Becky and **me.**

REVERSED Becky and **me** were the last art majors to get jobs.

REVERSE TEST **Me** was the last art major. [doesn't fit]

EDITED The last art majors to get jobs were Becky and **I.**

Possessive Pronouns

You may be tempted to add an 's to a possessive pronoun just as you do with a noun (**John's** car, the **cat's meow**).

STRATEGY Test your possessive pronouns.

Spell out *it's* as the expression it stands for: *it* + *is*. If the expansion fits, keep the apostrophe. If not, omit it.

DRAFT The food pantry gave away all **it's** tuna.

TEST The food pantry gave away all **it is** tuna.

EDITED The food pantry gave away all **its** tuna.

Editing Pronoun Forms

Compound Subjects and Objects

Use the same form for a pronoun in a compound that you would use if it were by itself.

STRATEGY Try focus-imagine-choose.

• **Focus** on the questionable pronoun.

DRAFT Anna and **me** will develop the video.
FOCUS: *I* or *me*?

• **Imagine** each choice for the pronoun.

Me will develop the video. (no)

I will develop the video. (yes)

• **Choose** the correct form for the compound.

EDITED Anna and **I** will develop the video.

Appositives

When you rename a preceding noun or pronoun in an **appositive**, match the pronoun to the form of the word being renamed.

STRATEGY Test possible replacements.

DRAFT The two illustrators on the panel, **her** and **me,** answered questions.

REPLACEMENT **Her** and **me** answered questions. (no)

REPLACEMENT **She** and **I** answered questions. (yes)

EDITED The two illustrators on the panel, **she and I,** answered questions.

Comparisons with Than or As

When you end a comparison with a pronoun, choose the form based on the information left out.

SUBJECT   I gave her sister more help than **she** [did].

OBJECT   I gave her sister more help than [I gave] **her.**

Who and Whom

Choose *who* and *whoever* as subjects; choose *whom* and *whomever* as objects. When the pronoun is in a clause, make your choice based on its role within the clause, not the sentence as a whole.

SUBJECT   The boy **who wins the race** will get the prize.

SUBJECT   The fine must be paid by **whoever holds the deed.**

SUBJECT   **Who** has the reader's sympathy, Huck or Jim?

OBJECT   Give this task to **whomever you trust.**

OBJECT   **Whom** can Cordelia trust as the scene ends?

Recognizing Adjectives and Adverbs

Adjectives and adverbs **modify** other words, adding to, qualifying, limiting, or extending their meaning.

FEATURES OF ADJECTIVES AND ADVERBS

ADJECTIVES

- Modify nouns and pronouns
- Answer "How many?" "What kind?" "Which one (or ones)?" "What size, color, or shape?"
- Include words like *blue, complicated,* and *good*
- Include words created by adding endings like *-able, -ical, -less, -ful,* and *-ous* to nouns or verbs (*sociological, nervous, seamless*)

ADVERBS

- Modify verbs, adjectives, and other adverbs
- Modify phrases (*almost* over the hill), clauses (*soon after* I added the eggs), and sentences (*Remarkably,* the mechanism was unharmed)
- Answer "When?" "Where?" "How?" "How often?" "Which direction?" "What degree?"
- Include mostly words ending in *-ly* (*quickly*) but also some words that do not end in *-ly* (*fast, very, well, quite, late*)

Editing Adjectives and Adverbs

Because not all adverbs end in *-ly* and some adjectives do (*friendly*), the *-ly* ending won't always help you pick the right form. If you can't tell which to use, ask the questions in the chart above.

DRAFT	Write **careful** so the directions are clear.

QUESTION: Write *how*? It answers an adverb question.

EDITED	Write **carefully** so the directions are clear.

STRATEGY Draw an arrow.

Point to the word that is modified. If it acts as a noun or pronoun, select an adjective; if it acts as a verb, adjective, or adverb, use an adverb.

DRAFT	The insulation underwent **remarkable** quick deterioration.

CONNECTION: *Remarkable* modifies *quick* (and answers the adverb question "How quick?"). (*Quick* in turn modifies *deterioration* and answers the adjective question "What kind of deterioration?") Replace *remarkable* with an adverb.

EDITED	The insulation underwent **remarkably** quick deterioration.

TRICKY ADJECTIVES AND ADVERBS

BAD/BADLY
Use *bad* (adjective) with linking verbs (is, seems, appears).
Use *badly* (adverb) with action verbs.

I feel **bad** that our group argues so much.
The new breathing apparatus works **badly.**

GOOD/WELL
Use *good* (adjective) with linking verbs (is, seems)
Use *well* (adverb) with action verbs unless it refers to health.

The chef's new garlic dressing tastes **good.**
The new pump works **well.**
Nan looks **well.** [health]

REAL/REALLY
Use *really* (adverb), not *real,* to modify an adjective or adverb.

Lu Ming is **really** efficient.
Lu Ming works **really** efficiently.

SURE/SURELY
Use *surely* (adverb) to modify an adjective.

This map is **surely** misleading.

Modifiers with Linking Verbs

Verbs such as *look, feel,* and *prove* can show both states of being (**linking verbs**) and activities (**action verbs**). Use an adjective for a state of being and an adverb for an activity.

ADJECTIVE (BEING)	The metal cover over the motor turned **hot.**
ADVERB (ACTION)	The large wheel turned **quickly.**
ADJECTIVE	The movement grew **rapid.** [The motion became quick.]
ADVERB	The movement grew **rapidly.** [The group spread its ideas.]

Real/Really, Bad/Badly, Good/Well, Sure/Surely

Informal uses of these words may be accepted in speech but not in formal writing.

INFORMAL   I feel **badly** that our group argues so much.

> READER'S REACTION: Someone who *feels badly* has a poor sense of touch.

Double Negatives

Readers are likely to feel that two negatives (*no, none, not, never, hardly, scarcely, don't*) cancel each other out.

DRAFT   The nurses **can't hardly** manage the emergencies.

> READER'S REACTION: This sounds more like a conversation than a report.

EDITED   The nurses **can hardly** manage the emergencies.

ESL ADVICE: Articles and Nouns

The **indefinite articles** are *a* or *an*; the **definite article** is *the*.

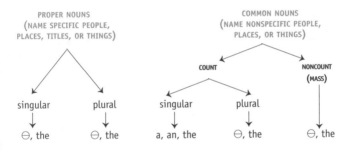

PROPER NOUNS
(NAME SPECIFIC PEOPLE,
PLACES, TITLES, OR THINGS)

COMMON NOUNS
(NAME NONSPECIFIC PEOPLE,
PLACES, OR THINGS)

COUNT   NONCOUNT
(MASS)

singular   plural   singular   plural
⊖, the   ⊖, the   a, an, the   ⊖, the   ⊖, the

⊖ = no article

Singular proper nouns generally use no article, and **plural proper nouns** usually use *the*.

SINGULAR   <u>Rosa Parks</u> helped initiate the civil rights movement.

PLURAL   **The** <u>Everglades</u> have abundant wildlife.

Count nouns name individual items that can be counted: *two chairs, four cups, a hundred beans.*

Singular count nouns cannot stand alone. Use *a* or *an* when you are not referring to any specific person or thing. Use *a* before a consonant sound and *an* before a vowel sound.

I need **a** <u>car</u> to go to work. [unknown, nonspecific, or any car]

Use *the* when you are referring to an exact, known person or thing.

I need **the** <u>car</u> to go to work. [specific, known car]

Plural count nouns use either no article (to show a generalization) or *the* (to refer to something specific).

GENERALIZATION   Books are the best teachers.

SPECIFIC   **The** books on his desk are due Monday.

Noncount nouns (mass nouns) name material or abstractions that cannot be counted: *flour, water, steel.* Noncount (mass) nouns never use *a* or *an.* They may stand alone (when general) or use *the* (when specific).

GENERAL   Laughter is good medicine.

SPECIFIC   **The** laughter of children is good medicine.

Use *the* when a plural count noun or a noncount noun is followed by a modifier, such as an adjective clause or prepositional phrase, that makes the noun specific.

COUNT   **The** airline tickets that you bought are at half price.

NONCOUNT   **The** information on the flight board has changed.

Recognizing and Editing Comparisons

For most modifiers, choose the form based on how many things you compare: **positive** (no others), **comparative** (two things; *-er* or *more*), **superlative** (three or more things; *-est* or *most*).

POSITIVE   The liquid flowed **quickly** into the **large** beaker.

COMPARATIVE   The liquid flowed **more quickly** into the **larger** beaker.

SUPERLATIVE   The liquid flowed **most quickly** into the **largest** beaker.

STRATEGY   Use precise comparative forms.

INACCURATE   Of the four age groups (20–29, 30–44, 45–59, and 60+), those in the older group smoked least.

READER'S REACTION: Did those in the older *groups* or the *oldest group* smoke least?

PRECISE   Of the four age groups (20–29, 30–44, 45–59, and 60+), those in the **oldest group** smoked least.

Most readers won't accept double comparative forms.

DRAFT   Jorge is the **most agilest** athlete.

EDITED   Jorge is the **most agile** athlete.

Illogical Comparisons

Some adjectives and adverbs, such as *unique, impossible, pregnant,* and *dead,* can't logically take comparative forms.

ILLOGICAL   Gottlieb's "Nightscape" is **most unique.**

READER'S REACTION: How can this painting be *more* or *most* if it's *unique*—the only one?

LOGICAL   Gottlieb's "Nightscape" is **unique.**

11

Writing Clearly

CLEAR SENTENCES   183

MIXED STRUCTURES   186

DANGLING AND MISPLACED MODIFIERS   188

UNNECESSARY SHIFTS   190

PARALLELISM   192

COORDINATION AND SUBORDINATION   193

CONCISENESS   196

LANGUAGE CHOICES   198

Voices
from the Community

"The difference between the almost right word and the right word is really a large matter—it's the difference between the lightning bug and the lightning."—Mark Twain, from a letter to George Bainton

11a Clear Sentences

Most readers find murky or tangled sentences hard to read.

INDIRECT OR EVASIVE

It is suggested that employee work cooperation encouragement be used for product quality improvement.

READER'S REACTION: Who is suggesting this? What is "employee work cooperation encouragement"?

CLEAR

We will try to improve our products by encouraging employees to work cooperatively.

183

All communities value clear writing that's easy to read even if it presents complex ideas and reasoning. You can improve foggy sentences by creating clear subjects and verbs and using direct sentence structures.

Recognizing Unclear Sentences

Clear sentences answer the question "Who does what (to whom)?" When a sentence doesn't readily answer this question, try to make its subject and verb easy for readers to identify.

UNCLEAR   One suggestion offered by physicians is that there is a need to be especially observant of a baby's behavior in order to notice any evidence of seizures.

READER'S REACTION: Who's doing the observing?

CLEAR   Physicians suggest that parents watch babies carefully for evidence of seizures.

Editing for Clear Sentences

Readers need to identify subjects (who) and verbs (did what) easily.

STRATEGY   Find your significant subject.

- Ask "Who (or what) am I talking about here?"
- Ask "Is this what I want to emphasize?"

UNFOCUSED   You run the greatest risk if you expose yourself to tanning machines as well as the sun because both can damage the skin.

READER'S REACTION: Isn't the point the danger posed by sunbathing and tanning? Why are they both buried in the middle?

EDITED   Either **the sun or a tanning machine** can damage the skin, and you run the greatest risk from exposure to **both** of them.

Weak Nouns

When you create a noun (*completion*, *happiness*) from another kind of word such as a verb (*complete*) or an adjective (*happy*), you **nominalize** that word. Replace each weak nominalization with a clear and significant subject (or object). Name the action (did what?) in the verb. Avoid weak, lifeless verbs, especially forms of *be*.

In a **noun string,** one noun modifies another or nouns plus adjectives modify other nouns: *jet lag, computer network server.* Turn the key word in a string (usually the last noun) into a verb or a single noun. Then turn other nouns from the string into prepositional phrases.

CONFUSING   The team did a ceramic valve lining design flaw analysis.

EDITED   The team **analyzed** flaws **in** the lining design **for** ceramic valves.

Weak Verbs

Forms of the verb *be* (*is, are, was, were*) show being, not action, and may create dull sentences.

STRATEGY Energize your verbs.

- Use more forceful verbs in place of forms of *be*.

  WEAK   The program **is a money saver.**

  STRONGER   The program **saves money.**

- Turn nouns into verbs to replace general verbs (*do, give, have, get, provide, shape, make*).

  WEAK   We **have done** a study of the project and **will provide** funding for it.

  STRONGER   We **have studied** the project and **will fund** it.

- Drop indirect "there is," "there are," and "it is" patterns.

  DRAFT   **There is** a need for more classrooms at Kenny School.

  EDITED   Kenny School needs more classrooms.

ESL ADVICE: *There* and *It* as Subjects

There and *it* as subjects may not refer to a thing or place (as in *The car is there* or *What did it* [the book, for example] *say?*). *There* may introduce new material, and *it* may refer to weather, time, or distance.

DRAFT   Although there was snowing, it was dancing after dinner.

EDITED   Although **it** was snowing, **there** was dancing after dinner.

Unnecessary Passive Voice

When you turn the doer or actor of a sentence into the receiver of action, you use the **passive voice** instead of the **active.** The passive voice focuses on the action, not the agent; the active voice puts the doer into the first, or subject, position.

STRATEGY Reconsider wordy or evasive passive structures.

PASSIVE   **The people** affected by the toxin were contacted by **the Centers for Disease Control.**

ACTIVE   **The Centers for Disease Control** contacted the people affected by the toxin.

Separated Subject and Verb

Too much distance between a subject and verb can make a sentence difficult to read.

> **STRATEGY**   Keep the verb close to the subject.

CONFUSING   The <u>veterinary association</u>, **in response to the costly guidelines for disposal of medical waste,** <u>has created</u> a low-cost loan program for its members.

EDITED   The veterinary association has created a low-cost loan program for its members **in response to the costly guidelines for disposal of medical waste.**

11b Mixed Structures

When you're reading, you can't ask the writer to explain a confusing shift of topic or a jumbled sentence.

TOPIC SHIFT   One **skill** I envy is **a person** who can meet deadlines.

READER'S REACTION: Does this mean a *skill* is a *person*?

EDITED   One **skill** I envy is **the ability** to meet deadlines.

Mixed sentences shift topics or grammatical structures unexpectedly, throwing the reader off the track. **Incomplete sentences** lack either grammatical or logical completeness. For example, if an advertiser says that X "is better," you expect to hear "than Y."

Recognizing Mixed and Incomplete Sentences

In most sentences, the subject announces a topic, and the **predicate** (the verb and the words that complete it) comments on or renames the topic. With a **topic shift** (**faulty predication**), the second part of the sentence comments on or names a topic different from the one first announced. With a **mixed grammatical pattern,** the sentence shifts from one pattern to another.

> **STRATEGY**   Look for topic and comment.

- Read your sentences aloud for *meaning*, especially how the topic (subject) and comment (predicate) relate.
- Ask "Who does what?" or "What is it?" If the answer is illogical, edit.
- Ask, "What's the topic? How does the rest of the sentence comment on it or rename it?"
- Ask, "Does the sentence clearly tell who does what to whom?"

TOPIC SHIFT   In this factory, **flaws** in the product noticed by any worker **can stop** the assembly line.

READER'S REACTION: Who does what? Flaws can't stop the line.

EDITED   In this factory, **any worker** who notices flaws in the product **can stop** the assembly line.

Editing Mixed and Incomplete Sentences

State your topic; then imagine what readers will expect next.

STRATEGY Rename the subject.

- Keep the topics on each side of *be* equivalent; make sure the second part of the sentence renames the topic in the first part.

TOPIC SHIFT **Irradiation** is **food** that is preserved by radiation.

EDITED Irradiation is a **process** used to preserve food.

- Drop *is when* and *is where*; they create an imbalance on both sides of *be*.

NOT BALANCED **Blocking** is **when** a network schedules a less popular program between two popular ones.

EDITED **Blocking** is the **practice** of scheduling a less popular program between two popular ones.

- Rewrite to eliminate *the reason ... is because*.

Readers expect the subject (topic) to be renamed after *is*. When *because* appears there instead, they find the sentence illogical.

DRAFT The **reason** he took up skating **is because** he wanted winter exercise.

EDITED The reason he took up skating **is that** he wanted winter exercise. [Change *because* to *that*.]

EDITED He took up skating **because** he wanted winter exercise. [Drop *the reason ... is*.]

Inconsistent Sentence Patterns

If you mistake words between the subject and verb for the sentence topic, you may mix up different patterns.

STRATEGY Make the topic for subject and verb the same.

TOPIC SHIFT Programming **decisions** by TV executives consider the need for audience share.

READER'S REACTION: How can decisions think?

EDITED When **making** programming decisions, **TV executives** consider the need for audience share.

Incomplete and Illogical Comparisons

You can sometimes simplify by omitting repeated elements that readers can supply. But if you cut essentials, you may create an **incomplete comparison,** missing words needed for clarity, or an **illogical comparison,** comparing things that aren't comparable.

STRATEGY	Add missing words or a possessive to compare logically.
ILLOGICAL	The fat content in even a small hamburger is more than a skinless chicken breast.
	READER'S REACTION: The fat is more than the chicken breast?
EDITED	The fat content in even a small hamburger is more than **that in** a skinless chicken breast.
EDITED	Even a small **hamburger's** fat content is more than a skinless chicken **breast's.**

11c Dangling and Misplaced Modifiers

Readers generally expect to find related parts of a sentence together.

MISPLACED MODIFIER	The wife believes she sees a living figure behind the wallpaper in the story by Charlotte Perkins Gilman, which adds to her sense of entrapment.
	READER'S REACTION: How could a story add to a feeling of entrapment?
MODIFIER MOVED	The wife **in the story by Charlotte Perkins Gilman** believes she sees a living figure behind the wallpaper, which adds to her sense of entrapment.

Because a **modifier** qualifies, adds to, or limits the meaning of another word or word group, it needs to be positioned logically. Otherwise, readers may find a sentence vague, illogical, or even humorous.

Recognizing Misplaced Modifiers

To recognize a **misplaced modifier,** look for a word or word group that is not positioned closely enough to the word or words it modifies—its **headword**—and instead appears to modify some other word.

MISPLACED	The caterer served food to the clients standing around the room on flimsy paper plates.
	READER'S REACTION: Surely the clients weren't standing on the plates!
MOVED	The caterer served food **on flimsy paper plates** to the clients standing around the room.

Dangling Modifier

To spot a **dangling modifier,** look for a sentence that begins with a modifier but doesn't name the person, idea, or thing modified. Readers will think the modifier refers to the subject of the sentence that follows. If it doesn't, the modifier dangles.

DANGLING	**Looking** for a way to reduce complaints from nonsmokers, **a ventilation fan** was installed.
	READER'S REACTION: How could a fan look for anything?

SUBJECT ADDED   **Looking** for a way to reduce complaints from nonsmokers, **the company** installed a ventilation fan.

Squinting Modifier

To recognize a **squinting modifier,** look for a word that appears to modify both the word before and the word after. Squinting modifiers are often misplaced **limiting modifiers,** words like *only, almost, hardly, just, scarcely,* and *even.* Limiting modifiers can move around in a sentence, generally changing meaning as they do.

SQUINTING   People who abuse alcohol **often** have other problems.

READER'S REACTION: Do they *drink often* or *often have* other problems?

EDITED   People who **often** abuse alcohol tend to have other problems.

Split Infinitives

Some readers find words placed between the parts of an infinitive (*to* plus a verb) irritating. Balance this risk against the directness a split infinitive sometimes offers.

IRRITATING?   The dancers moved **to very rapidly align** themselves.

EDITED   The dancers moved **very rapidly to align** themselves.

Editing Misplaced Modifiers

Make sure modifiers clearly relate to the words they qualify.

STRATEGY   Position and connect modifiers logically.

- Place *who, which,* or *that* close to its headword.

    MISPLACED   The inspectors discovered another tank behind the building that was leaking toxic waste.

    MOVED   **Behind the building,** the inspectors discovered another tank that was leaking toxic waste.

- State the word being modified.

    DANGLING   While shopping, a stuffed alligator caught my eye.

    SUBJECT ADDED   While **I was** shopping, a stuffed alligator caught my eye.

- Ask, "What do I really mean here? Who's doing what?" Then rework the sentence to state that point as directly as possible.

    DANGLING   After debating changes in the regulations for months, the present standards were allowed to continue.

    READER'S REACTION: *Who* is debating? Not the standards!

    REWRITTEN   The commission debated changes in the regulations for months but decided to continue the present standards.

11d Unnecessary Shifts

Especially in formal contexts, readers expect logically consistent writing.

SHIFTED   If **parents** called the school board, **we** could explain why **we** oppose the new policy.

READER'S REACTION: I'm confused. Who should do what?

EDITED   If **parents** called the school board, **they** could explain why **they** oppose the new policy.

Although listeners tolerate shifts during conversation—or ask for clarification—readers are likely to be irritated by illogical shifts.

Recognizing Shifts in Person and Number

A shift in **person** occurs when you switch illogically from one perspective (*I, you, he,* or *she*) to another. A shift in **number** occurs when you illogically switch sentence elements, especially pronouns and **antecedents** (the words to which they refer), between singular and plural.

INCONSISTENT   When **a business executive** is looking for a new job, **they** often consult a placement service.

READER'S REACTION: Who is "they"? The executive?

EDITED   When **business executives are** looking for **new jobs, they** often consult a placement service.

FIRST, SECOND, AND THIRD PERSON IN THREE COMMUNITIES

- **First person singular (*I*).** Use *I* to refer to yourself as the writer or person whose experiences and perceptions are an essay's subject. Readers may find *I* too personal in some formal academic contexts, especially in the sciences.
- **First person plural (*we*).** Use *we* in a collaborative project with several authors. In some academic papers, you may use *we* as you refer to ideas you and your readers share. *We* is common at work and in public when you represent or appeal to your organization.
- **Second person (*you*).** Use *you* to refer directly to the reader ("you, the reader"). In most academic and work writing, readers find *you* inappropriate, but some situations call for *you*, as in a set of instructions or a plain-language contract. In public writing that urges action, *you* can engage the reader in a civic appeal.
- **Third person (*he, she, it, they, one, someone,* and comparable pronouns).** Use these pronouns to refer to the ideas, things, and people you write about, including *people, person,* and names of groups (such as *students*). Avoid sexist use of *he* and *she*. Be alert to exclusionary uses of pronouns, such as inappropriately pitting *we* against *they*.

Editing Shifts in Person and Number

Reflect a consistent perspective in person and number.

STRATEGY   Match references, and edit for consistency.

- Do nouns and pronouns refer to the same person?
- Are they consistently singular or plural?

SINGULAR   If **a person** has some money to invest, **he or she** should
seek financial advice.

PLURAL   If **people** have some money to invest, **they** should seek
financial advice.

Recognizing Shifts in Tense

The **tense** of a verb indicates time as past, present, or future.
When you change tense within a passage, you signal a change in time
and the relationship of events. Illogical shifts can mislead your
readers.

ILLOGICAL SHIFT   Scientists **discovered** nests that **indicated** how some dinosaurs
take care of their young.

LOGICAL   Scientists **discovered** nests that **indicate** how some
dinosaurs **took care** of their young.

ESL ADVICE: **Verb Tense and Expressions of Time**

Use both verb tense and time expressions (*today, soon*) to show changes in
time. Keep these consistent.

INCONSISTENT   I **study** English last year, and now I **worked** for an American
company.

EDITED   I **studied** English last year, and now I **work** for an American
company.

Editing Shifts in Tense

Shift tense because your account or convention requires the
change.

STRATEGY   Match your verbs to your intended time.

INCONSISTENT
SHIFT TO PRESENT   We **had been searching** for a festival site when suddenly
Tonia **yells,** "This is it!"

EDITED   We **had been searching** for a festival site when suddenly
Tonia **yelled,** "This is it!"

Follow convention, and use present tense when you summarize or
analyze events or information from a work such as a novel or film.

INCONSISTENT   As the novel begins, Ishmael **comes** to New Bedford to ship out on a whaler, which he soon **did.**

CONVENTIONAL   As the novel begins, Ishmael **comes** to New Bedford to ship out on a whaler, which he soon **does.**

11e Parallelism

When you use consistent patterns, readers can follow your ideas easily and concentrate on your meaning because they know what to expect.

WEAK   Hal furnished his apartment with what he purchased at flea markets, buying items from want ads, and gifts from friends.
READER'S REACTION: This list seems wordy and jumbled.

PARALLEL   Hal furnished his apartment with **purchases from flea markets,**
items from want ads,
and **gifts from friends.**

Parallelism is the expression of similar or related ideas in similar grammatical form; it creates sentence rhythms and highlights ideas.

Recognizing Faulty Parallelism

Once you begin a parallel pattern, you need to complete it.

MIXED   Swimming is an exercise that **aids** cardiovascular fitness, **develops** overall muscle strength, and **probably without causing** injuries.

PARALLEL   Swimming is an exercise that **aids** cardiovascular fitness, **develops** overall muscle strength, and **causes** few injuries.

Editing for Parallelism

When you place items in a series, pair, or list, make sure they have the same structure even if they differ in length and wording. With the seven coordinating conjunctions (*and, but, or, for, nor, so,* and *yet*), use parallelism to heighten similarities or contrasts.

MIXED   A well-trained scientist keeps a detailed lab notebook and the entries made accurately.

PARALLEL   A well-trained scientist keeps a **detailed and accurate** lab notebook.

Edit each series with the full sentence in mind. If the lead-in word can be the same, don't repeat it. If the lead-in words differ, include them.

INCOMPLETE   The main character in the novel *Tarzan of the Apes* has appeared on television, films, and comic books.
READER'S REACTION: I doubt he appeared *on* films and *on* comic books.

EDITED   The main character in the novel *Tarzan of the Apes* has
          appeared **on** television, **in** films, and **in** comic books.

STRATEGY   Use parallelism to organize meaning.

- Build up to a key point placed last in a series.

    To complete their campaigns, candidates need stamina, courage, and, most
    of all, **ambition.**

- List items in parallel form.

    These trends characterized the early 1960s:

    1. **A growing** civil rights movement
    2. **A developing** anticommunist foreign policy
    3. **An increasing** emphasis on youth in culture and politics

- Emphasize clusters of sentences and paragraphs.

    Each of us probably belongs to groups whose values conflict. **You may
    belong to** a religious organization that **endorses restraint in** alcohol
    use while **you also belong to** a social group that **accepts drinking. You
    may belong to** a sports team **that supports** competing and a club **that
    promotes** cooperation.

- Connect sections of an essay or a report.

    The opening for each paragraph can be a simple parallel element.

    One reason for approving this proposal now is . . .

    A second reason for acting is . . .

    The third, and most important, reason for taking steps is . . .

11f   Coordination and Subordination

Suppose you were editing a report with this passage.

California's farmers ship fresh lettuce, avocados, and other produce to
supermarkets. They never send fresh olives.

READER'S REACTION: These sentences sound choppy. How do they connect?

Using **coordination,** you could give equal emphasis to the
statements.

California's farmers ship fresh lettuce, avocados, and other produce to
supermarkets **, but** they never send fresh olives.

Using **subordination,** you could show the relative weight of ideas.

California's farmers ship fresh lettuce, avocados, and other produce to
supermarkets, **though** they never send fresh olives.

Recognizing Coordination

Use coordination to link words, phrases, or clauses to emphasize their equal weight, balance the structure, or express addition or opposition.

CREATING AND PUNCTUATING COORDINATION

- Use *and, but, or, for, nor, so,* or *yet* (coordinating conjunctions). Precede them with a comma when joining two main clauses, word groups that could stand on their own as sentences.

  cut **and** hemmed   intrigued **yet** suspicious

  The new zoning board met **,** **but** it did not vote.

- Use pairs like *either/or, neither/nor,* and *not only/but also.*

  either music therapy **or** pet therapy

- Use a semicolon.

  Some customers fidgeted **;** others stared at the ceiling.

- Use conjunctive adverbs like *however, moreover, nonetheless, thus,* and *consequently* preceded by a semicolon.

  The managers could speed up the checkout line**s ; however ,** they seldom pay much attention to the problem.

- Use a colon.

  Magazine racks by the checkout counters serve a useful purpose **:** they give customers something to read while waiting.

EXPRESSING RELATIONSHIPS THROUGH COORDINATION

RELATIONSHIP	COORDINATING CONJUNCTION	CONJUNCTIVE ADVERB
addition	, and	; in addition, ; furthermore,
opposition or contrast	, but , yet	; in contrast, ; however, ; nonetheless,
result	, so	; therefore, ; consequently, ; thus,
cause	, for	
choice	, or	; otherwise
negation	, nor	

Recognizing Subordination

Subordination creates sentences with unequal elements: the **main clause** (which could stand alone as a sentence) presents the central idea; at least one **subordinate clause** (which could not stand alone) modifies or comments on it. You signal this unequal relationship by beginning the subordinate clause with a **subordinator** or **relative pronoun,** a word like *while, although,* or *which,* and attaching it to the main clause.

CREATING AND PUNCTUATING SUBORDINATION

- **Use a subordinating conjunction** such as *although* or *because* to create a subordinate clause at the beginning or end of a sentence.

  At the beginning of a sentence: Add a comma *after* an introductory clause that begins with a subordinating conjunction.

  Once she understood the problem, she had no trouble solving it.

  At the end of a sentence: Do not use a comma if the clause is *essential* to the meaning of the main clause (restrictive); use a comma if the clause is *not essential* (nonrestrictive).

ESSENTIAL	Radar tracking of flights began **because several airliners collided in midair.**
NONESSENTIAL	The present air traffic control system works reasonably well, **although accidents still occur.**

- **Use a relative pronoun** (*who, which, that*) to create a relative clause at the end or in the middle of a sentence. A clause containing information *essential* to the meaning of the main clause begins with *that* and should not be set off with commas. Set off nonessential information.

ESSENTIAL (NO COMMA)	The anthropologists discovered the site of a building **that early settlers used as a meetinghouse.**
NONESSENTIAL (COMMA)	At one end of the site they found remains of a smaller building, **which may have been a storage shed.**

EXPRESSING RELATIONSHIPS THROUGH SUBORDINATION

RELATIONSHIP	CONJUNCTION OR OTHER WORD
Time	before, while, until, since, once, whenever, whereupon, after, when
Cause	because, since
Result	in order that, so that, so, that
Concession or contrast	although, though, even though, as if, while
Place	where, wherever
Condition	if, whether, provided, unless, rather than
Comparison	as
Identification	that, which, who

Editing for Coordination and Subordination

How can you tell how much coordination or subordination to use? Read your writing aloud. Watch for short, choppy sentences or long, dense passages. Consider your community: academic readers may accept more subordination than work colleagues who favor conciseness.

STRATEGY	Replace *and, so,* and *but* to vary or specify.
DRAFT	The fresh grapefruit in supermarkets is picked before it matures to avoid spoilage, **and** it can taste bitter, **but** the grapefruit in cans is picked later, **and** it tastes sweeter.
EDITED	The fresh grapefruit in supermarkets is picked before it matures **,** **so** it can taste bitter. The grapefruit in cans is picked later **;** **consequently,** it tastes sweeter.

Help readers see what matters most; put key ideas in a main clause and secondary ideas in a subordinate clause.

STRATEGY	Move a main point to a main clause.
DRAFT	His equipment was inferior, although Jim still set a school record throwing the discus.
	READER'S REACTION: Isn't Jim's achievement the point?
EDITED	**Although** his equipment was inferior, Jim still set a school record throwing the discus.

ESL ADVICE:	Structures for Coordination and Subordination

Use both coordinators and subordinators, but don't mix the two.

MIXED	**Although** frogs can live both on land and in water, **but** they need to breathe oxygen.
CONSISTENT COORDINATION	Frogs can live on land and in water, **but** they need to breathe oxygen.
CONSISTENT SUBORDINATION	**Although** frogs can live on land and in water, they need to breathe oxygen.

11g   Conciseness

When you leave extra words in your writing, you waste the time of readers who value clarity, efficiency, or convincing advocacy.

WORDY	**There is evidence that the use of** pay **as an** incentive **can be a factor** in improvement **of the** quality **of** work.
	READER'S REACTION: Why is this so long-winded?
ABRUPT	Incentive pay improves work quality.
RESHAPED	Incentive pay **often encourages** work **of higher** quality.

Conciseness means using only the words you need—not the fewest possible, but only those that suit your purpose, meaning, and readers.

Recognizing Common Types of Wordiness

Look carefully for both unnecessary and repetitive words.

Wordy Phrases

Shrink wordy phrases to one or two words—or none.

COMMON WORDY PHRASES	
PHRASE	REPLACEMENT
due to the fact that	because
at the present moment	now
has the capability of	can
in a situation in which	when
as a matter of fact	[omit]
in my opinion	[omit]

All-Purpose Words

These sound serious, yet words like *factor, aspect, situation, type, field, kind,* and *nature* are often fillers, as are modifiers like *very, totally, major, great, really, definitely,* and *absolutely.*

WORDY   Young Goodman Brown is so **totally** overwhelmed by **his own** guilt that he becomes **extremely** suspicious of the people **all** around him. [22 words]

CUT   Young Goodman Brown is so overwhelmed by guilt that he becomes suspicious of the people around him. [17 words]

REWRITTEN   Young Goodman Brown's **overwhelming** guilt makes him **suspect everyone**. [9 words]

Redundant Expressions

Redundant pairs (*each and every*) and phrases (*large in size*) say the same thing twice. Eliminate them.

WORDY   Because it was **sophisticated in nature** and **tolerant in style,** Kublai Khan's administration aided China's development in the 1200s.

CUT   Because it was **sophisticated and tolerant,** Kublai Khan's administration aided China's development in the 1200s.

REWRITTEN   Kublai Khan's **adept and tolerant administration** aided China's development in the 1200s.

Editing for Conciseness

Edit expressions and patterns that lead to wordiness.

STRATEGY Vary your cutting and trimming.

- Cut or rewrite what you've already stated or clearly implied.
- Reduce writer's commentary ("In my paper, I will show . . .).
- Compress or delete word groups beginning with *which, who, that,* and *of* by converting clauses to phrases, phrases to words.

CLAUSES Chavez Park, **which is an extensive facility in the center of town,** was named after Cesar Chavez, **who fought for migrant farmers' rights.**

PHRASES Chavez Park, **an extensive facility in the center of town,** was named after Cesar Chavez, **an advocate for migrant farmers.**

WORDS Chavez Park, **a downtown facility,** was named after **migrant advocate** Cesar Chavez.

- Highlight the key points in a passage that interprets or draws conclusions. Combine them as you drop remaining generalities; then add specific supporting detail.

WORDY **Glaciers** were of central importance in the **shaping** of **the North American landscape.** Among the many remnants of glacial activity are **deeply carved valleys** and **immense piles of sand and rock.**

COMBINED Glaciers carved deep valleys and left behind immense piles of sand and rock, shaping much of the North American landscape.

DETAILED Glaciers carved deep valleys and left behind immense piles of sand and rock, shaping much of the North American landscape in the process. **Cape Cod and Long Island are piles of gravel deposited by glaciers.**

11h Language Choices

Every speaker of English uses a particular variety of the language—a **dialect**—shaped by region, culture, and home community.

HOME VARIETY Miss Brill **know** that the lovers **making** fun of her, but she **act** like she **don't** care.

EDITED Miss Brill **knows** that the lovers **are making** fun of her, but she **acts as if** she **doesn't** care.

In the communities where they're used, these varieties seem natural. In academic, work, and public settings, however, such variations are generally seen as "errors."

Recognizing and Editing Language Varieties

A "rule" in one dialect may break a rule in another. In all language, the rules are structures and conventions that people in a group agree, unconsciously, to use. By **code-shifting,** you can substitute "standard edited American English" for your home language variety when you write a college essay, a letter to an official, or a company report.

STRATEGY   Look for "rules" in your home language.

Rule in KY: Rule elsewhere:
The lawn needs mowed.   The lawn needs <u>to be</u> mowed.

Recognizing and Editing Disrespectful Language

Treat others fairly by eliminating sexist and discriminatory language. Avoid using *mankind* or *men* for humankind and words implying men in occupations (*firemen*). To replace *he, his,* or *him* for all people, try a plural construction (e.g., *their* rather than *his and hers* for *his*).

SEXIST   Every trainee brought **his** laptop with **him.**

AWKWARD   Every trainee brought **his or her** laptop with **him or her.**

BETTER   All trainees brought **their** laptops with **them.**

STRATEGY   Watch for stereotyped roles.

STEREOTYPED   The OnCall Pager is **smaller than most doctors' wallets** and **easier to answer than phone calls from their wives.**
              READER'S REACTION: I'm a woman doctor, and I'm insulted. OnCall will never sell a pager in my office!

EDITED   The OnCall Pager **will appeal to doctors because it's small** and easy to operate.

Most readers won't tolerate unfair biases against groups of people.

DEMEANING   My paper focuses on the **weird** courtship rituals of a **barbaric** Aboriginal tribe in southwestern Australia.
              READER'S REACTION: Your paper sounds biased. How can you treat this topic fairly if you don't respect the tribe?

EDITED   My paper focuses on the unique courtship rituals of an Aboriginal tribe in southwestern Australia.

RACIST   The economic problems in border states are compounded by increasing numbers of **wetbacks** from Mexico.
              READER'S REACTION: This derogatory name is offensive. I object to characterizing a group of people this way.

EDITED   The economic problems in border states are compounded by increasing numbers of illegal immigrants from Mexico.

12

Writing with Conventions

COMMAS 202

SEMICOLONS AND COLONS 207

APOSTROPHES 209

QUOTATION MARKS 211

ITALICS AND UNDERLINING 213

CAPITALS 214

ABBREVIATIONS 216

NUMBERS 218

HYPHENS 219

SPELLING 221

OTHER MARKS AND CONVENTIONS 223

Voices
from the Community

"Parenthetical remarks (however relevant) are unnecessary."

—Frank L. Visco, *How to Write Good*

12a   Commas

Because a comma can join, separate, or disrupt, it's easy to misuse.

CONFUSING	During the study interviews were used to gather responses from participants, and to supplement written artifacts. READER'S REACTION: I can't tell where ideas begin and end.
EDITED	During the study **,** interviews were used to gather responses from participants and to supplement written artifacts.

Instead of sprinkling commas at pauses, consider your readers. Public and work communities that favor direct prose may expect the fewest commas, while academic readers are likely to expect formal comma usage.

Recognizing Commas That Join Sentences

When you use *and, but, or, for, nor, so,* or *yet* (**coordinating conjunctions**) to link two word groups that can stand alone as sentences, place a comma *before* the conjunction. (Avoid a comma splice.)

DRAFT	The rain soaked the soil and the mud buried the road.
EDITED	The rain soaked the soil **,** **and** the mud buried the road.

Editing Commas That Join Sentences

Readers react more strongly if you omit a conjunction than a comma, but in formal texts they'll see both as errors. Even to join short main clauses, a comma is always acceptable but might be omitted informally.

> **STRATEGY**   Analyze the pair joined by a conjunction.

If you find main clauses that could stand alone before and after the conjunction, add a comma *before* the conjunction.

Apex tried to ship the order **,** **but** the truck was late.

If you find any other sentence element before or after the conjunction, do *not* separate that pair with a comma.

PAIR SPLIT	We sanded **,** and stained the old table.
EDITED	We **sanded** and **stained** the old table.
PAIR SPLIT	I used stain that was cheap **,** and easy to clean.
EDITED	I used stain that was **cheap** and **easy to clean**.

Recognizing Commas That Set Off Sentence Elements

The simplest sentences need no comma.

noun phrase   verb phrase
The storm   developed quickly.

You may add a layer to the beginning with an **introductory expression** or interrupt a sentence with **parenthetical expressions** or **nonrestrictive modifiers** that add interesting detail. Set these off with commas.

INTRODUCTORY	**For nearly an hour**, the rain drenched Old Town.
TRANSITION	**In addition**, the hail caused damage.
INTERRUPTER	It broke, **I think**, a dozen church windows.
CONJUNCTIVE ADVERB	We hope, **therefore**, that someone starts a repair fund.
TAG QUESTION	We'll contribute, **won't we?**
CONTRAST	The windows' beauty touches all of us, **not just the church members.**
DIRECT ADDRESS	Recall, **friends of beauty**, that every gift helps.
NONRESTRICTIVE MODIFIER	The stained glass, **glowing like exotic jewels**, enriches us all.

Editing Commas That Set Off Sentence Elements

Use two commas to enclose an expression in midsentence; use just one after an opening or before a closing expression.

Introductory Elements

Readers expect a comma to signal where the introduction ends and the main sentence begins.

STRATEGY Set off introductory wording for readability.

CONFUSING	Forgetting to alert the media before the rally Jessica rushed to the park.
EDITED	Forgetting to alert the media before the rally, Jessica rushed to the park.

In general, put a comma after a long introductory element following a subordinating conjunction (*although*, *because*, *when*), a preposition (*during*, *without*, *between*), or a verbal. Also add a comma if a short introductory element might confuse readers.

CONFUSING	By six boats began showing up.
EDITED	By six, boats began showing up.

Parenthetical Expressions

Use commas to help readers identify word groups that interrupt a sentence.

DRAFT	Teams should meet even spontaneously as needed.
EDITED	Teams should meet, even spontaneously, as needed.

Nonessential, Nonrestrictive Modifiers

Midsentence modifiers act as adjectives or adverbs, adding detail that qualifies other words.

> **STRATEGY**   Test whether a modifier is essential.
>
> Drop the modifier, and see whether the essential meaning of the sentence stays the same. If it does, even if it's less informative, the modifier is **nonrestrictive,** adding detail that's interesting or useful but not necessary for meaning. Set it off *with* commas so readers see it as nonessential.
>
> | | |
> |---|---|
> | DRAFT | Their band **which performs in small clubs** has gotten fine reviews. |
> | | TEST: Their band has gotten fine reviews. [The meaning is the same though it's less informative.] |
> | COMMAS ADDED (NONRESTRICTIVE) | Their band, which performs in small clubs, has gotten fine reviews. |

If dropping a modifier eliminates essential information and changes the meaning of the sentence, the modifier is **restrictive.** Add it *without* commas so readers see it as a necessary part of the sentence.

DRAFT	The charts, **drawn by hand,** were hard to read.
	TEST: The charts were hard to read. [This says *all* the charts were hard to read but means that only *some* were.]
COMMAS OMITTED (RESTRICTIVE)	The charts **drawn by hand** were hard to read.

Who, Which, *and* That

Add commas to set off nonrestrictive (nonessential) clauses beginning with *who, which, whom, whose, when,* or *where.* Because *that* can specify, rather than add, use it in restrictive (essential) clauses. *Which* often adds nonessentials but can be used either way.

NONRESTRICTIVE	Preventive dentistry, **which is receiving great emphasis,** may reduce visits to the dentist's office.
RESTRICTIVE	Dentists **who encourage good oral hygiene** often supply helpful advice.
RESTRICTIVE	They also provide sample products **that encourage preventive habits.**

Appositives

An **appositive,** a noun or pronoun that renames a preceding noun, is usually nonrestrictive (nonessential). If so, add commas.

NONRESTRICTIVE   Amy Nguyen **,** **a poet from Vietnam ,** published another collection of verse.

RESTRICTIVE   The well-known executive **Louis Gerstner** went from RJR Nabisco to IBM.

Editing Disruptive Commas

Unless you need to set off an intervening expression, you'll irritate readers if a comma separates subject and predicate.

> **STRATEGY**   Drop extra commas between subject and verb.

SPLIT SUBJECT AND PREDICATE   The painting *Rocks at L'Estaque* **,** is in the Museu de Arte.

EDITED   The **painting** *Rocks at L'Estaque* **is** in the Museu de Arte.

Subordinating conjunctions shouldn't be followed by commas because they introduce entire clauses. Don't mistake them for conjunctive adverbs (such as *however*) or transitional expressions (such as *for example*), which should be set off with commas.

> **STRATEGY**   Omit commas right after words like *because*.

EXTRA COMMA   Although **,** Jewel lost her luggage, she had her laptop.

EDITED   Although Jewel lost her luggage, she had her laptop.

Editing Commas with Words in a Series

Use commas to separate or relate items in a series.

Series of Three or More

To avoid ambiguity, consistently use commas between all items of roughly equal status. If an item has multiple parts, place a comma after the entire unit.

The Human Relations Office has forms for medical benefits **,** dental and vision options **,** **and** retirement contributions.

Although readers in the academic community frequently expect the comma just before *and*, it's often omitted, especially in a short, clear list.

Numbered or Lettered List

Punctuate a list in a sentence like a series; when items contain commas, separate them with semicolons.

You should (a) measure the water's salinity, (b) weigh any waste in the filter, and (c) determine the amount of dissolved oxygen.

Adjectives in Sequence

When you use **coordinate adjectives,** each modifies the noun (or pronoun) on its own. Separate them with commas to show their equal application to the noun. When you use **noncoordinate adjectives,** one modifies the other, and it, in turn, modifies the noun (or pronoun). Don't separate these adjectives with a comma.

STRATEGY Ask questions about adjectives.

If you answer one of these questions with *yes,* the adjectives are coordinate. Separate them with a comma.

- Can you place *and* or *but* between the adjectives?

COORDINATE (EQUAL) Irrigation has turned dry, infertile [*dry and infertile?— yes*] land into orchards.

NOT COORDINATE The funds went to new computer [*new and computer?— no*] equipment.

- Is the sense the same if you reverse the adjectives?

COORDINATE (EQUAL) We left our small, cramped [*cramped small?—yes, the same*] office.

NOT COORDINATE We bought a red brick [*brick red?—no, could mean a color*] building.

COMMA CONVENTIONS

DATES
May 3, 1999   on Monday, June 23,   on July 4, 1776,
5 April 1973   October 2001   fall 2002   June 3

NUMBERS
1,746 sheep (or 1746 sheep) $8,543,234   page 2054

ADDRESSES AND PLACE NAMES IN SENTENCES
in Chicago   in Chicago, Illinois, during May
Fredelle Seed Brokers, Box 389, Holland, MI 30127

PEOPLE'S NAMES AND TITLES
Shamoon, Linda   Cris Burk, A.I.A., was the designer.

OPENINGS AND CLOSINGS OF LETTERS
PERSONAL   Dear Nan,   Dear Soccer Team,   Regards,
BUSINESS OR FORMAL   Dear Ms. Yun: Sincerely,

12b   Semicolons and Colons

Semicolons and colons help readers make connections.

TWO SENTENCES   On April 12, 1861, one of Beauregard's batteries fired on Fort **Sumter** ● **The** Civil War had begun.

> READER'S REACTION: These sentences may present facts or drama, but they don't *necessarily* connect events.

SEMICOLON   On April 12, 1861, one of Beauregard's batteries fired on Fort **Sumter**; **the** Civil War had begun.

> READER'S REACTION: The semicolon encourages me to link the battery firing to the Civil War beginning.

COLON   On April 12, 1861, one of Beauregard's batteries fired on Fort **Sumter**: **the** Civil War had begun.

> READER'S REACTION: Now I see the guns' firing as a dramatic moment: the beginning of the Civil War.

You can use semicolons and colons to relate your ideas and to encourage readers to take different perspectives.

Recognizing Semicolons That Join Sentences

A semicolon can dramatically highlight a close relationship or a contrast as it creates a brief pause.

TWO SENTENCES   Demand for paper is at an all-time high ● Business alone consumes millions of tons each year.

ONE SENTENCE
WITH SEMICOLON   Demand for paper is at an all-time high; business alone consumes millions of tons each year.

Editing Semicolons That Join Sentences

When you use a semicolon alone to link main clauses, you assume readers can figure out how the clauses relate. When you add words, you specify the connection for readers.

Assertion; →   transition, →   assertion
I like apples;   **however,**   I hate pears.

You can choose a **conjunctive adverb** (*thus, moreover*) or a **transitional expression** (*for example, in contrast, on the other hand*). Vary the punctuation depending on where you place such wording.

BETWEEN CLAUSES   Joe survived the flood; **however,** Al was never found.
WITHIN CLAUSE   Joe survived the flood; Al, **however,** was never found.
AT END OF CLAUSE   Joe survived the flood; Al was never found, **however.**

STRATEGY   Test both sides of the semicolon.

A semicolon joins main clauses that could stand on their own as sentences. Sometimes, elements in a second clause can be deleted if they "match" elements in the first clause even though the second couldn't stand alone.

ELEMENTS INCLUDED	In winter, the **hotel guests enjoy** a roaring log fire ; in summer, the **hotel guests enjoy** the patio by the river.
ELEMENTS OMITTED	In winter, the **hotel guests enjoy** a roaring log fire ; in summer, the patio by the river.

Editing Semicolons in a Complex Series

When items in a series contain commas, readers may have trouble deciding which commas separate parts of the series and which belong within items. To avoid confusion, put semicolons between such items.

I met Debbie Rios, the attorney ; Rhonda Marron, the accountant ; and the new financial director.

Recognizing and Editing Colons

A colon effectively joins main clauses when the second clause focuses, sums up, or illustrates the first.

COLON WITH MAIN CLAUSES	The blizzard swept the prairie : the Oregon Trail was closed.

The words *before* the colon generally form a complete sentence while those after—the example, list, or quotation—may or may not.

COLON WITH LIST	The symptoms are as follows : cough, fever, and pain.

When you introduce a list with a word group other than a complete sentence, do not use a colon.

DRAFT	Her pastimes were : walking, volunteering, and cooking.
EDITED	Her pastimes **were walking,** volunteering, and cooking.
EDITED	**She had three pastimes :** walking, volunteering, and cooking.

Whether a quotation is integrated with your words or set off as a block, a sentence must precede a colon. If not, use a comma.

COLON WITH QUOTATION	Dan answered his critics : "Sales are up and costs down."

COLON CONVENTIONS

Web Site Design : *A Beginner's Guide*	John 8 : 21–23
"Diabetes : Are You at Risk?"	http : //www.nytimes.com
10 : 32 a.m. Dear Ms. Will : (business letter)	a ratio of 2 : 3

12c Apostrophes

Like the dot above the *i*, the apostrophe may seem trivial, but without it, readers would stumble over your text.

MISUSED OR LEFT OUT	Though its an 1854 novel, Dickens *Hard Times* remain's an ageless critique of education by fact's.
	READER'S REACTION: I can't tell possessives from contractions and plurals in this sentence.
EDITED	Though it᾽s an 1854 novel, Dickens᾽s *Hard Times* **remains** an ageless critique of education by **facts.**

In all three communities, readers see apostrophes as conventional, not flexible. Check carefully for them.

Recognizing Apostrophes That Mark Possession

Nouns that express ownership are called **possessive nouns.** Mark them to distinguish them from plurals.

APOSTROPHE MISSING The cats meow is becoming fainter.

> **READER'S REACTION:** I expected "The cats meow all night." Do you mean many cats or the meow of one cat?

APOSTROPHE ADDED The **cat**᾽**s** meow is becoming fainter.

STRATEGY Test nouns for possession.

If you can turn a noun into a phrase using *of*, use a possessive form. If not, use a plural.

DRAFT	The officers reports surprised the reporters.
	TEST: The reports *of* the officers? [*yes, possessive*]
	TEST: Surprised *of* the reporters? [*no, plural*]
EDITED	The officers᾽ reports surprised the reporters.

Editing Apostrophes That Mark Possession

Decide what to add: ' + -*s* or just '.

STRATEGY Check the ending of the noun.

- **Does the noun end in a letter other than -*s*? Add ' + s.**

  Ohio᾽s taxes   the dog᾽s collar   women᾽s track

- **Does the noun end in -*s*, and is it plural? Add '.**

  the Solomons᾽ car   buses᾽ routes

- **Does the noun end in -*s*, and is it singular?**

OPTION #1 (PREFERRED)	Add ' + -*s*: Chris᾽s van
OPTION #2	Add ' *after* the final -*s*: Chris᾽ van

- **Does the noun end in *-s* and sound awkward?**

OPTION #1	Hodges ' s (sounds awkward as "Hodges-es")
	Add ' but no *-s:* Hodges ' (shows one *-s* sound)
OPTION #2	Change the construction.
DRAFT	the Adams County Schools ' s policy
EDITED	the policy of the Adams County Schools

Decide whether nouns joined by *and* or *or* act separately or together.

SEPARATE LAWYERS	**Bo ' s and Hal ' s** lawyers are ruthless.
SINGLE LEGAL TEAM	**Bo and Hal ' s** lawyers are ruthless.

Omit unnecessary apostrophes in other words that end in *-s*.

VERB (NOT NOUN)	The staff **orders** supplies early.
PERSONAL PRONOUNS	If **your** car is here, why take **hers**?

> **APOSTROPHE CONVENTIONS**
>
> **Dates**   the ' 90s   the class of ' 05   1980s
>
> **Plural Letters and Numbers**   p ' s and q ' s   size 10 ' s
>
> **Abbreviations**   IQs   TAs
>
> **Dialect**   I'm **a-goin '** for some **o '** them shrimp.
>
> **Hyphenated Noun**   My **father-in-law '** s library is huge.
>
> **Multiword Noun**   The **union leaders '** talks collapsed.

Recognizing Apostrophes That Mark Contractions

Informally, use an apostrophe to mark omitted letters when words are combined in a **contraction** (can't = can + not). In most academic writing, avoid splicing nouns with *is* (Zorr's testing = Zorr is testing).

Editing Apostrophes That Mark Contractions

Some confusing contractions sound like other words.

they're = they + are   there = adverb

who's = who + is   whose = possessive pronoun

STRATEGY	Expand contractions to test the form.
DRAFT	**Its** the best animal shelter in **its** area.
	EXPANSION TEST: *It is* [*yes, a fit*] the best animal shelter in *it is* [*no, not a fit*] area.
EDITED	**It ' s** the best animal shelter in **its** area.

12d   Quotation Marks

Quotation marks set off someone else's spoken or written words.

DRAFT   "Without the navigator," the pilot said, we would have
                    crashed.

                    READER'S REACTION: Without quotation marks, I didn't realize that the pilot
                    said the last part, too.

EDITED   "Without the navigator," the pilot said, "we would have
                    crashed."

Readers in academic, work, and public communities expect you to
position quotation marks to show who said what.

Recognizing Marks That Set Off Quotations

When you quote *directly,* use double quotation marks (" ")
around the exact words quoted. In dialogue, use new marks and
indent when a new person speaks.

DIRECT QUOTATION   "The loon can stay under water for several minutes,"
(SPOKEN)   the ranger told us.

DIRECT QUOTATION   Gross argues that "every generation scorns its off-
(WRITTEN)   spring's culture" (9).

DIRECT QUOTATION   "Every generation," so Gross claims, "scorns its off-
INTERRUPTED   spring's culture" (9).

ESL ADVICE: Quotation Marks

Check for American conventions if your native language uses other marks for
quotations or if you are used to British conventions. Search for these marks
with your computer to spot unconventional usage.

Editing Marks That Set Off Quotations

When one quotation contains another, use single marks (' ') for
the inside quotation and double marks (" ") for the one enclosing it.

QUOTATION INSIDE   De Morga's account described the battle that "caused
QUOTATION   his ship to 'burst asunder'" (Goddio 37).

For *indirect* quotations that paraphrase or sum up someone's
words, omit quotation marks.

PARAPHRASE   The pilot credited the navigator with the safe landing.
(INDIRECT)

SUMMARY   Gross believes that, after just one generation, the social
(INDIRECT)   consequences of a major war nearly vanish (5).

COMBINING MARKS

- Position commas to help readers distinguish your introduction, commentary, or source from the quotation.

  "Our unity," said the mayor, "is our strength."

- If your words end with *that*, don't include a comma.

  Some claimed that "calamity followed Jane." Jane replied that she simply out-ran it.

- Place these marks *inside* concluding single or double quotation marks: commas, periods, and question or exclamation marks that apply to the quoted material. Place these marks *outside:* semicolons, colons, and question or exclamation marks that apply to the whole sentence.

Editing Quotation Marks With Titles of Short Works

Use quotation marks for titles of short works, parts of larger works, and unpublished works.

CONVENTIONS FOR TITLES

ITALICS OR UNDERLINING	QUOTATION MARKS
BOOK, NOVEL, COLLECTION *The Labyrinth of Solitude* *The White Album*	**CHAPTER, ESSAY, SELECTION** "The Day of the Dead" "Once More to the Lake"
PAMPHLET *Guide for Surgery Patients*	**SECTION** "Anesthesia"
LONG POEM *Paradise Lost* *The One Day*	**SHORT POEM, FIRST LINE TITLE** "Richard Cory" "Whoso list to hunt"
RADIO, TV PROGRAM *The West Wing* *Car Talk*	**EPISODE, REPORT** "Gone Quiet" "Daycare Dilemmas"
MUSICAL WORK, ALBUM *Messiah* *Invisible Touch* *Organ Symphony* BUT Symphony no. 3 in C Minor, op. 78	**SECTION, SONG** "All We Like Sheep" "Big Money"
MAGAZINE, NEWSPAPER *Discover* the *Denver Post*	**ARTICLE** "What Can Baby Learn?" "Asbestos Found in Schools"
SCHOLARLY JOURNAL *Composition Review*	**ARTICLE** "Student Revision Practices"

ITALICS OR UNDERLINING	QUOTATION MARKS
PLAY, FILM, ART WORK	UNPUBLISHED WORK, LECTURE
King Lear	"Renaissance Women"
Winged Victory	"Sources of Heroic Ballads"

NO ITALICS, UNDERLINING, OR QUOTATION MARKS

SACRED BOOKS, PUBLIC OR LEGAL DOCUMENTS

Bible, Koran, Talmud, United States Constitution

TITLE OF YOUR OWN PAPER (UNLESS PUBLISHED)

The Theme of the Life Voyage in Crane's "Open Boat"

The Role of Verbal Abuse in The Color Purple

12e Italics and Underlining

Type that slants to the right—italic type—emphasizes words and ideas. In handwritten or typed texts, underlining is its equivalent: The Color Purple = *The Color Purple*.

UNDERLINING   Alice Walker's novel The Color Purple has been praised and criticized since 1982.

READER'S REACTION: I can spot the title right away.

Some readers, including many college teachers, prefer underlining because it's easy to see. Observe your community's conventions.

Recognizing Conventions for Italics (Underlining)

Italicize titles of most long, complete works. Italicize names of specific ships, planes, trains, and spacecraft (*Voyager VI, Orient Express*) but not *types* of vehicles (Boeing 767) or *USS* and *SS* (USS *Corpus Christi*). Italicize uncommon foreign expressions (*omertà*) but not common ones (junta, taco). Italicize scientific names for plants (*Chrodus crispus*) and animals (*Gazella dorcas*) but not common names (seaweed, gazelle).

Editing for Conventions That Show Emphasis

Use italics to focus on a term or a word, letter, or number as itself.

In Boston, *r* is pronounced *ah* so that *car* becomes *cah*.

Set off technical or unusual terms with quotation marks or italics.

In real estate, "FSBO" (pronounced "fizbo") refers to a home that is "for sale by owner."

You can—*sparingly*—use italics for emphasis or contrast or use quotation marks for irony, sarcasm, or distance from a term.

> **STRATEGY** Rewrite to eliminate excessive emphasis.
>
> In personal and informal writing, underlining may add "oral" emphasis.
>
> INFORMAL <u>Hand</u> the receipts to me.
>
> MORE FORMAL Give the receipts to me personally.

12f Capitals

Readers expect capital letters to signal the start of sentences or to identify specific people, places, and things.

CAPITALS MISSING thanks, ahmed, for your file. i'll review it by tuesday.

> READER'S REACTION: Email or not, missing capitals are distracting.

CAPITALS IN PLACE Thanks, Ahmed, for your file. I'll review it by Tuesday.

Follow capitalization conventions to make reading easy.

Recognizing Capitals That Begin Sentences

Capital letters begin both sentences and partial sentences.

Pack for Yellowstone this July. **W**ildlife and wonders galore!

Editing Capitals That Begin Sentences

When capitals are flexible, be consistent within a text.

> **STRATEGY** Adjust your capitals when you quote.
>
> Especially in the academic community, capitalize the first word in a quotation that is a complete sentence or that begins your sentence.
>
> SENTENCE QUOTED According to Galloway, "**T**he novel opens with an unusual chapter" (18).
>
> Don't capitalize part of a quotation integrated into your sentence structure or interrupted by your own words.
>
> INTEGRATED Galloway notes that the book "**o**pens with an unusual chapter" (18).
>
> INTERRUPTED "**T**he novel," claims Galloway, "**o**pens with an unusual chapter" (18).

Sentence in Parentheses

Capitalize the first word of a sentence that stands on its own, but not one placed *inside* another sentence.

FREESTANDING By this time, the Union forces were split into nineteen sections. (**E**ven so, Grant was determined to unite them.)

ENCLOSED Saskatchewan depends on farming (**t**he province produces over half of Canada's wheat), oil, and mining.

First Word in a Line of Poetry

Traditionally, lines of poetry begin with capitals, but follow the poet's practice.

We said goodbye at the barrier,

And she slipped away....

Robert Daseler, "At the Barrier," *Levering Avenue*

Questions in a Series

Capitalize or lowercase the series.

OPTION #1   Do we need posters? **S**igns? **F**lyers?

OPTION #2   Do we need posters? signs? flyers?

Sentence After a Colon

If a *sentence* follows a colon, choose capitals or lowercase. Otherwise, do not use a capital.

OPTION #1   The province is bilingual: **O**ne-third speak French and the rest English.

OPTION #2   The province is bilingual: one-third speak French and the rest English.

Run-In List

When items in a list are not presented on separate lines, don't capitalize word groups or sentences.

NOT CAPITALIZED   Include costs for (a) labs, (b) phones, and (c) supplies.

Vertical List

Capitalize sentences in vertical lists. Choose whether to capitalize word groups in an outline without periods.

OPTION #1   OPTION #2

1. **L**ab facilities   1. lab facilities
2. **E**quipment   2. equipment

Editing Capitals That Begin Words

Capitalize names of specific people, places, and things (**proper nouns**) as well as related **proper adjectives.**

Brazil, Dickens   Brazilian music, Dickensian plot

In titles, capitalize first and last words, and all words between *except* articles (*a, an, the*), prepositions under five letters (*of, to*), and coordinating conjunctions (*and, but*). Capitalize the word after any colon.

The Mill on the Floss   "Civil Rights: What Now?"

Building a Small Business (your own title)

In an APA reference list, capitalize only proper nouns and the first letters of titles and subtitles of full works.

CAPITALIZATION CONVENTIONS

CAPITALS	LOWERCASE
INDIVIDUALS, RELATIVES	
Georgia O'Keeffe, Mother	my cousin, her dad
PEOPLE, LANGUAGES	
Maori, African American	the language, the people
TIME PERIODS, SEASONS	
October, Ramadan	spring, winter, holiday
RELIGIONS, RELATED SUBJECTS	
Talmud, Bible, God	talmudic, biblical, a god
ORGANIZATIONS, INSTITUTIONS, MEMBERS	
U.S. Senate	a senator
Air Line Pilots Association	the union, a union member
PLACES, RESIDENTS, GEOGRAPHIC REGIONS	
Malaysia, the Southwest	the country, southwestern
BUILDINGS, MONUMENTS	
Taj Mahal, Getty Museum	the tower, a bridge
HISTORICAL PERIODS, EVENTS, MOVEMENTS	
Jazz Age, Postmodernism	the movement, a trend
ACADEMIC INSTITUTIONS, COURSES	
Harbor Community College	a university, the college
Sociology 203, Art 101	a philosophy course
COMPANY NAMES, TRADE NAMES, VEHICLES	
Siemens, Kleenex, Voyager	the company, tissues, van
SCIENTIFIC, TECHNICAL, MEDICAL TERMS	
Big Dipper, Earth (planet)	star, earth (ground)

12g Abbreviations

When they are accepted by both writer and reader, abbreviations act as a kind of shorthand, making a sentence easy to write and read.

CONFUSING **Jg. Rich.** Paret was a **U of C** law **prof.**

READER'S REACTION: What is "U of C"—the University of California?

CLEAR Judge Richard Paret was a University of Chicago law professor.

Try to aid readers, not baffle them with inappropriate abbreviations.

Recognizing and Editing Abbreviations

Titles with Proper Names

Abbreviate a title just before or after a person's name. Use one form of a title at a time.

Jack Gill, **Sr.**   **Dr.** Vi McGee   Vi McGee, **D.D.S.**

If titles such as *Dr.* or *Mrs.* do not require periods in your first language as they do in English, proofread carefully.

Spell out the title if it's part of your reference to the person or if it does not appear next to a proper name.

Professor Drew   Prof. Ann Drew   NOT Prof. Drew

Exceptions: Rev. Mills   Dr. Smith

Abbreviated academic titles such as *M.A., Ph.D., B.S.,* and *M.D.* can be used on their own or after a name.

People and Organizations

Readers accept abbreviations that are familiar (IBM), simple (AFL-CIO), or standard in context (FAFSA). Most use capitals without periods.

Organizations	NAACP, AMA, GM, CNN, 3M
Countries	USA (*or* U.S.A.), UK (*or* U.K.)
People	JFK, LBJ, FDR, MLK
Things or Events	FM, TB, AWOL, DUI, TGIF

STRATEGY   Introduce an unfamiliar abbreviation.

Give the full expression when you first use it, and show the abbreviation in parentheses. Then, use just the abbreviation.

The **American Library Association (ALA)** studies policy on information access. The **ALA** also opposes censorship.

Dates and Numbers

Abbreviations ($, no. for number) may be used with *specific* dates, numbers, or amounts.

AD	*anno Domini,* "in the year of Our Lord"
BC	*before Christ*
BCE	*before common era* (alternative for BC)
CE	*Common Era* (alternative for AD)
a.m. or A.M.	*ante meridiem,* "before noon" (A.M. in print)
p.m. or P.M.	*post meridiem,* "after noon" (P.M. in print)

Editing to Use Abbreviations Sparingly

In research, scientific, technical, or specialized contexts, such as documenting sources, you can abbreviate more than in formal text.

> **CONVENTIONS FOR ABBREVIATIONS**
>
> - **In formal writing**
>   Thursday, not Thurs.   Walton Avenue, not Ave.
>   *Exception:* 988 Red Road, Paramus, NJ 07652
>   physical education   quart   mile   kilogram   chapter
>   *Exceptions:* rpm, mph (with or without periods)
> - **In tables or graphs:** @, #, =, −, +, other symbols
> - **In documentation:** ch.   p.   pp.   fig.
> - **In documentation and parentheses (from Latin)**
>   e.g.: for example (*exempli gratia*)   i.e.: that is (*id est*)
>   et al.: and others (*et alii*)   etc.: and so forth (*et cetera*)

12h   Numbers

You can convey numbers with numerals (37, 18.6), words (fifteen, two million), or a combination (7th, 2nd, 25 billion).

GENERAL TEXT   These **fifty-two** chemists represent **thirty** labs.
> READER'S REACTION: In general academic texts, I expect most numbers to be spelled out.

TECHNICAL   These **52** chemists represent **30** labs.
> READER'S REACTION: In technical papers, I expect more figures.

Follow the advice here for numbers in general writing. In technical, business, and scientific contexts, seek advice from a teacher, supervisor, colleague, or style guide about conventional and consistent usage.

> **CONVENTIONS FOR NUMBERS IN GENERAL TEXT**
>
> - **Addresses and Routes**
>   Interstate 6   2450 Ridge Road, Alhambra, CA 91801
> - **Dates**
>   September 7, 1976   1880–1910   from 1955 to 1957
>   1960s   the sixties   the '60s (informal)
>   nineteenth century   AD (or CE) 980   class of '05
> - **Times of Day**
>   10:52   6:17 a.m.   12 p.m. (noon)   12 a.m. (midnight)
>   four in the morning   four o'clock   half past eight

CONVENTIONS FOR NUMBERS IN GENERAL TEXT

- **Parts of a Written Work**

  Chapter 12

  Genesis 1:1–6 or Gen.1.1–6 (MLA style)

  Macbeth 2.4.25–28 (or act II, scene iv, lines 25–28)

- **Measurements, Fractions, Decimals, Statistics**

120 MB	55 mph	6'4"	47 psi
21 ml	7-5/8	27.3	67 percent (or 67%)
7 out of 10	3 to 1	won 5 to 4	a mean of 23

- **Money**

  $7,883 $4.29 $7.2 million (or $7,200,000)

- **Rounded**

  75 million years   three hundred thousand voters

- **Ranges:** Simply supply the last two figures in the second number unless readers will need more to avoid confusion.

  34–45   95–102 (not 95–02)   370–420   1534–620

- **Ranges of Years:** Supply all digits for different centuries.

  1890–1920   1770–86   476–823   42–38 BC

- **Clusters:** items 2, 5, and 8 through 10 (or 8–10)

Recognizing When to Spell or Use Numerals

In general, spell out numbers composed of one or two words, treating hyphenated compounds as a single word.

ten books   **twenty-seven** computers   **306** employees

Editing Numbers in General Text

Treat comparable numbers consistently in a passage, either as numerals (used for all if required for one) or as words.

CONSISTENT   Café Luna's menu soon expanded from **85** to **104** items.

STRATEGY   Spell out opening numbers, or rewrite.

INAPPROPRIATE   **428** houses are finished.

DISTRACTING   **Four hundred twenty-eight** houses are finished.

EASY TO READ   In Talcott, **428** houses are finished.

12i   Hyphens

Readers expect hyphens both to join and divide words.

CONFUSING   The Japanese language proposal is well prepared.

     READER'S REACTION: Is the proposal *in* or *about* the Japanese language?

CLARIFIED   The Japanese-language proposal is well prepared.

Type a hyphen as a *single* line (-) with no space on either side: well-trained engineer, not well - trained engineer.

Recognizing Hyphens That Join Words

A **compound word** is made from two or more words that may be hyphenated (*double-decker*), spelled as one word (*timekeeper*), or treated as separate words (*letter carrier*). Compounds change rapidly; check a current dictionary. Observe accepted practice in work or public contexts.

Editing Hyphens That Join Words
Numbers

In general (not technical) writing, hyphenate numbers between twenty-one and ninety-nine (even if part of a larger one), inclusive numbers, and fractions: *fifty-one thousand, volumes 9–14, two-thirds.*

Prefixes and Suffixes

Hyphenate a prefix before a capital or number and with *ex-, self-, all-, -elect,* and *-odd: pre-1989, self-centered.*

Letters with Words

Hyphenate a letter and a word forming a compound, except in music terms: *A-frame, T-shirt, A minor, G sharp.*

Confusing Words

Use hyphens to help readers distinguish different words with the same spelling *(recreation, re-creation)* or to clarify words with repeated letters *(anti-imperialism, post-traumatic).*

Compound Modifiers

When two or more words work as a single modifier, generally hyphenate them *before* but not *after* a noun.

BEFORE NOUN (-)   Many **nausea-inducing** drugs treat cancer.
AFTER NOUN (NO -)   Many drugs that treat cancer are **nausea inducing**.

Do not hyphenate *-ly* adverbs (highly regarded staff) or comparative forms (more popular products).

STRATEGY   Try suspended hyphens with modifiers.

Reduce repetition with hyphens that signal the suspension of an element until the end of a series of parallel compound modifiers. Leave a space after the hyphen and before *and*, but not before a comma.

The lab uses **oil- and water-based** compounds.

Editing Hyphens That Divide Words

Traditionally you could split a word at the end of a line, marking the break between syllables with a hyphen. Now word processors automatically hyphenate but often create hard-to-read lines or incorrectly split words. As a result, many writers turn off this feature. When you must divide an electronic address, do so after a slash. Don't add a hyphen.

12j Spelling

Readers in all communities expect accurate spelling.

INCORRECT   The city will not **except** any late bids.

> READER'S REACTION: I get annoyed when careless or lazy writers won't correct their spelling!

PROOFREAD   The city will not **accept** any late bids.

Readers may laugh at a newspaper misspelling but harshly judge a writer who misspells in an academic paper or work document.

Using the Computer to Proofread for Spelling

When you use a spelling checker, the computer compares each word in your text with the words in the dictionary in its memory. If it finds a match, it assumes your word is correct. If it does *not* find a match, it asks you if the word is misspelled. What it can't identify are words correctly spelled but used incorrectly such as *lead* for *led.*

Recognizing and Editing Spelling Errors

Correct errors you see; ask readers to help you spot others.

STRATEGY   Go beyond the spelling checker.

- Say the word carefully. Look up possible spellings, even odd ones. If you reach the right area in a dictionary, you may find the word.
- Try a dictionary for poor spellers that lists correct spellings (*phantom*) and likely misspellings (*fantom*).
- Try a thesaurus; the word may be listed as a synonym.
- Ask others for technical terms; verify their advice in a dictionary.
- Check the indexes of books on the word's topic.
- Look for the word in textbooks, company materials, or newspapers.
- Add a tricky word to your own spelling list. Invent a way to remember it (associating the two *z*'s in *quizzes* with boredom—*zzzzzz*).

Try to identify spelling patterns that will help you improve.

COMMON SPELLING PATTERNS

PATTERNS FOR PLURALS

WORD ENDING	CHANGE	EXAMPLES
most nouns	add -s	novels, contracts
consonant + -o	often add -es	potatoes, heroes
	some add -s	cellos, memos
vowel + -o	add -s	stereos, videos
consonant + -y	y to i + -es	gallery → galleries
proper noun + -y	add -s	Kennedy → Kennedys
vowel + -y	add -s	days, journeys, pulleys
-f or -fe	often f to v + -s	life → lives
	or -es	self → selves
	some add -s	beliefs, roofs, turfs
-ch, -s, -ss, -sh, -x, or -z (a hiss sound)	most add -es	benches, buses, foxes, kisses, buzzes
one-syllable ending in -s or -z	many double final consonant	quiz → quizzes
foreign roots	follow original language	datum → data, criterion → criteria
irregular nouns		foot → feet
compound	last word	basketballs
	first word if most important	sister-in-law → sisters-in-law

PATTERNS FOR BEGINNINGS (PREFIXES)

Prefixes do not change the spelling of the root word that follows: *precut, post-traumatic, misspell, unendurable.*

PREFIX FOR *NOT*	COMBINATION	EXAMPLES
im-	with b, m, p	impatient, imbalance
in-	with others	incorrect, inadequate

PATTERNS FOR ENDINGS (SUFFIXES)

Suffixes may change the root word or pose other problems.

SUFFIX	CHANGE	EXAMPLES
starts with consonant	keep silent -e	fateful, gentleness
	exceptions	judgment, truly, argument, ninth
starts with vowel	drop silent -e	imaginary, generation, decreasing, definable
	exceptions	noticeable, changeable

SUFFIX	COMBINATION	EXAMPLES
-ery	4 common words	stationery (paper), cemetery, monastery, millinery
-ary	most others	stationary (fixed in place), secretary, primary, military
"-seed" sound	most use -cede	precede, recede
	several use -ceed	proceed, succeed, exceed
	one uses -sede	supersede

SUFFIX	COMBINATION	EXAMPLES
-able	add if root stands on own	charit**able**, advis**able**
with -ee root	keep -e	agree**able**
-ible	add if root can't stand on own	cred**ible**, irreduc**ible**

PATTERNS FOR SEQUENCES OF LETTERS WITHIN WORDS

LETTER GROUP	SEQUENCE	EXAMPLES
ie	i before e except after c, or sounding like a as in n**ei**ghbor and w**ei**gh.	bel**ie**ve, gr**ie**f, fr**ie**nd rec**ei**ve, dec**ei**t
	exceptions	anc**ie**nt w**ei**rd, s**ei**ze, for**ei**gn, h**ei**ght, th**ei**r, **ei**ther, n**ei**ther, l**ei**sure

The Glossary also lists **homophones,** different words that sound alike.

COMMONLY CONFUSED WORD PAIRS

WORD	MEANING	WORD	MEANING
all ready	prepared	already	by this time
its	possessive of it	it's	it is
than	compared with	then	next
their	possessive of they	there	in that place
whose	possessive of who	who's	who is
your	possessive of you	you're	you are

12k   Other Marks and Conventions

You can use punctuation marks to change the style and sense of your prose and adjust its effects on readers.

DASHES   The boy —**clutching his allowance**— came to the store.

READER'S REACTION: Dashes show strong emphasis; I can tell how hard the boy worked to save his money.

PARENTHESES   The boy (**clutching his allowance**) came to the store.

READER'S REACTION: Parentheses deemphasize his savings, thus giving his arrival more significance.

COMMAS   The boy, **clutching his allowance,** came to the store.

READER'S REACTION: This direct account doesn't emphasize either the savings or the arrival.

Punctuation marks set boundaries, guide readers, and add emphasis.

Recognizing and Editing Parentheses

Parentheses *enclose*: you can't use just one, and readers will interpret whatever falls between the pair as an aside.

When you sign up for Telepick (including Internet access), you will receive an hour of free calls.

When parentheses *inside a sentence* come at the end, punctuate *after* the closing mark. When you enclose a *freestanding sentence*, punctuate *inside* the closing mark.

INSIDE SENTENCE   People on your list get discounts (once they sign up).

SEPARATE SENTENCE   Try Telepick now. (This offer excludes international calls.)

You can use parentheses to mark numbered or lettered lists.

NUMBERED LIST   Fax Harry's Bookstore (555-0934) to (1) order books, (2) inquire about items, or (3) sign up for events.

Recognizing and Editing Dashes

Too many may strike academic readers as informal, but dashes can add flair to work and public appeals, ads, or brochures. Type a dash as two unspaced hyphens, without space before or after: --. A print dash appears as a single line: —. Use one dash with an idea or series that opens or ends a sentence; use a pair to enclose words in the middle.

OPENING LIST   **Extended visiting hours, better meals, and more exercise**—these were the inmates' demands.

PAIR IN THE MIDDLE   For her service to two groups—**Kids First and Food Basket**—Olivia was voted Volunteer of the Year.

STRATEGY   Convert excessive dashes to other marks.

Circle dashes that seem truly valuable—maybe marking a key point. Replace others with commas, parentheses, colons, or emphatic wording.

Recognizing and Editing Brackets

Academic readers expect you to use brackets scrupulously (though other readers may find them pretentious). When you add your words to a quotation for clarity or background, bracket this **interpolation**. Also bracket *sic* (Latin for "thus") after a source error to confirm your accuracy.

INTERPOLATION   As Walz notes, "When Catholic Europe adopted the new Gregorian calendar in 1582, Protestant England still followed October 4 by October 5 [Julian calendar]" (4).

Recognizing and Editing Ellipses

The **ellipsis** uses three *spaced* periods to mark where something has been left out. Academic readers expect ellipses to mark omissions of irrelevant material from quotations; other readers may prefer full quotations.

CONVENTIONS FOR ELLIPSIS MARKS

- Use three spaced periods . . . for ellipses in a sentence or within a line of poetry.
- Use a period before an ellipsis ending a sentence. . . .
- Leave a space before the first period . . . and after the last unless the ellipsis is bracketed.
- Omit ellipses when you begin quotations (unless needed for clarity) or use clearly incomplete words or phrases.
- Retain another punctuation mark before omitted words if needed for the sentence structure; . . . omit it otherwise.
- Supply a series of spaced periods (MLA style) to show an omitted line (or more) of poetry in a block quotation.
- When quoting a text that uses ellipses, bracket your ellipses [. . .] in MLA style.

When you drop *part* of a sentence, maintain normal sentence structure so readers can follow the passage.

INTERVIEW NOTES   Museum Director: "We expect the Inca pottery in our special exhibit to attract historians from as far away as Chicago, while the vivid jewelry draws the public."

CONFUSING DRAFT   The museum director hopes "the Inca pottery . . . historians . . . vivid jewelry . . . public."

EDITED   The museum director "expect[s] the Inca pottery . . . to attract historians . . . while the vivid jewelry draws the public."

In narrative, ellipses can show a pause or ongoing action.

FOR SUSPENSE   Large paw prints led to the tent. . . .

Recognizing and Editing Slashes

You can use a slash to mark alternatives (the **on/off** switch), especially in technical documents, but readers may find it informal or imprecise (preferring *or* instead). When you quote poetry *within* your text, separate lines of verse with a slash, typing a space before and after.

The speaker in Sidney's sonnet hails the moon: "O Moon, thou climb'st the skies! / How silently ..." (lines 1–2).

Recognizing and Editing End Marks

Speakers change pitch or pause to mark sentence boundaries. Writers use symbols—period, question mark, exclamation point.

LESS FORMAL	And why do we need you? You help our lovable pups find new families!
	READER'S REACTION: This bouncy style is great for the volunteer brochure but not the annual report.
MORE FORMAL	The League's volunteers remain our most valuable asset, matching abandoned animals with suitable homes.

Readers in all communities expect periods to end sentences. Some readers may accept informal use of question marks and exclamation points.

Periods

All sentences that are *statements* end with periods—even if they contain embedded clauses that report, rather than ask, questions. Periods also mark decimal points (5.75) and abbreviations (Dr., Ms., pp., etc., a.m.) though many abbreviations, pronounced as words or by letter, don't require them (NASA, GOP, OH).

Question Marks

End a direct question with a question mark, but use a period to end an **indirect question**—a sentence with an embedded clause that asks a question.

DIRECT	When is the train leaving?
DIRECT: QUOTED	Lu asked, "Why is it so hot?"
DIRECT: TWO CLAUSES	Considering that the tax break has been widely publicized, why have so few people filed for a refund?
INDIRECT	Jose asked if we needed help.

Exclamation Points

These marks end emphatic statements such as commands or warnings but are rarely used in academic or work writing.

EMPHATIC	Get the campers off the cliff!

STRATEGY	Use draft punctuation to guide your editing.

Like question marks, exclamation points can be used informally, expressing dismay, shock, or strong interest. Edit for strong words to emphasize.

DRAFT	Rescuers spent hours (!) trying to reach the child.
EDITED	Rescuers spent **agonizing** hours trying to reach the child.

Recognizing and Editing Electronic Addresses

When you cite an electronic address, record its characters exactly—including slashes, @ ("at") signs, underscores, colons, and periods.

http://www.access.gpo.gov/su_docs

Combining Marks

- **Always use marks that enclose in pairs**.

  ( )   [ ]   " "   ' '

  Use commas and dashes in pairs to enclose midsentence elements. Type a dash as a pair——of hyphens.

- **Use multiple marks when each mark plays its own role**. If an abbreviation with a period falls in the *middle* of a sentence, the period may be followed by another mark, such as a comma, dash, colon, or semicolon.

  Experts spoke until 10 **p.m.,** and we left at 11 **p.m.**

- **Eliminate multiple marks when their roles overlap**. When an abbreviation with a period concludes a sentence, that one period will also end the sentence. Omit a comma *before* midsentence parentheses; *after* the parentheses, use whatever mark would otherwise occur.

- **Avoid confusing duplicates**. If items listed in a sentence include commas, separate them with semicolons, not more commas.

  ___,___,___; ___,___,___; and ___.

  If one parenthetical element falls within another, use brackets to enclose the unit inside the parentheses.

  _____ (__ [___] ___).

  Use one pair of dashes at a time, not dashes within dashes.

Grammar at a Glance

How can you recognize a sentence? 229

How do words work in sentences? 230

How do sentence patterns work? 230

What are the principal parts of verbs? 231

What are the tenses of verbs in the active voice? 231

How can you recognize active and passive verbs? 233

What are verbal phrases? 233

What are the forms of some common irregular verbs? 234

What do pronouns do? 234

What are the forms of comparatives and superlatives? 235

How do you choose a preposition? 236

How Can You Recognize a Sentence?

A **sentence**—also called a **main (or independent) clause**—is a word group that can stand alone. It has a subject and a predicate (a verb and any words that complete it).

SENTENCE   **Hungry bears** were hunting food.

SENTENCE   Because spring snows had damaged many plants, **hungry bears** were hunting food in urban areas.

A **subordinate (or dependent) clause** has a subject and a predicate, yet it cannot stand on its own because it begins with a subordinating word like *because, although, which*, or *that*.

FRAGMENT   Because **spring snows** had damaged many plants

A **phrase** is a word group that lacks a subject, a predicate, or both. It cannot stand alone.

FRAGMENT   were hunting   in urban areas   the hungry bears

For further help in recognizing sentences, refer to Chapter 10.

HOW DO WORDS WORK IN SENTENCES?	
You can recognize	By looking for words that do this
nouns	name a person, a place, an idea, or a thing (Jed, cafeteria, doubt, chair)
pronouns	take the place of a noun (them, she, his)
verbs	express action (jump, write), occurrence (become, happen), and being (be, seem)
adverbs	modify or qualify verbs, adjectives, and other adverbs telling when, where, how, how often, which direction, or what degree (now, very, quite, too, quickly)
adjectives	modify or qualify nouns and pronouns, telling how many, what kind, which one, what size, what color, or what shape (five, many, attractive, blue, young)
prepositions	add information by linking the noun or pronoun following to the rest of the sentence (after, at, in, by, on, near, with)
conjunctions	join other words, signaling their relationships (and, but, because, though)
interjections	convey a strong reaction or emotion (Oh, no! Hey!)

How Do Sentence Patterns Work?
Five Basic Predicate Structures

1. Subject + intransitive verb

The bus crashed.

2. Subject + transitive verb + direct object

A passenger called the police.

3. Subject + transitive verb + indirect object + direct object

The paramedic gave everyone a blanket.

4. Subject + transitive verb + direct object + object complement

Officials found the driver negligent.

5. Subject + linking verb + subject complement

The quick-thinking passenger was a hero.

Four Sentence Structures

1. A **simple sentence** has one main (independent) clause and no subordinate (dependent) clauses.

The mayor proposed an expansion of city hall.

2. A **compound sentence** has two or more main (independent) clauses and no subordinate (dependent) clauses.

main clause   main clause

Most people praised the plan, yet **some found it** dull.

3. A **complex sentence** has one main (independent) clause and one or more subordinate (dependent) clauses.

subordinate clause   main clause

Because people objected, **the architect revised the plans.**

4. A **compound-complex sentence** has two or more main (independent) clauses and one or more subordinate (dependent) clauses.

subordinate clause   subordinate clause

Because he wanted to make sure that the expansion did not damage

main clause

the existing building, **the architect examined the older**

main clause

structure, and **he asked the contractor to test the soil stability.**

Four Sentence Purposes

A **declarative sentence** makes a statement: The motor is making a rattling noise. An **interrogative sentence** poses a question: Have you checked it for overheating? An **imperative sentence** requests or commands: Check it again. An **exclamatory sentence** exclaims: It's on fire!

What Are the Principal Parts of Verbs?

BASE FORM	PAST	PRESENT PARTICIPLE	PAST PARTICIPLE
REGULAR VERBS			
live	lived	living	lived
IRREGULAR VERBS			
eat	ate	eating	eaten
run	ran	running	run

What Are the Tenses of Verbs in the Active Voice?

Decide when actions or events occur; then use this chart to help you select the tense you need for a regular (*examine*) or irregular (*begin*) verb.

Present, Past, and Future (Showing Simple Actions)

Present: action taking place now, including habits and facts occurring all the time

I/you/we/they	examine/begin
he/she/it	examines/begins

Past: action that has already taken place at an earlier time

I/you/he/she/it/we/they	examined/began

Future: action that will take place at an upcoming time

I/you/he/she/it/we/they	will examine/begin

Present, Past, and Future Perfect (Showing Order of Events)

Present Perfect: action that has recurred or has continued from the past to the present

I/you/we/they	have examined/begun
he/she/it	has examined/begun

Past Perfect: action that had already taken place before something else happened

I/you/he/she/it/we/they	had examined/begun

Future Perfect: action that will have taken place by the time something else happens

I/you/he/she/it/we/they	will have examined/begun

Present, Past, and Future Progressive (Showing Action in Progress)

Present Progressive: action that is in progress now, at this moment

I	am examining/beginning
you/we/they	are examining/beginning
he/she/it	is examining/beginning

Past Progressive: action that was in progress at an earlier time

I/he/she/it	was examining/beginning
you/we/they	were examining/beginning

Future Progressive: action that will be in progress at an upcoming time

I/you/he/she/it/we/they	will be examining/beginning

Present, Past, and Future Perfect Progressive (Showing the Duration of Action in Progress)

Present Perfect Progressive: action that has been in progress up to now

| I/you/we/they | have been examining/beginning |
| he/she/it | has been examining/beginning |

Past Perfect Progressive: action that had already been in progress before something else happened

| I/you/he/she/it/we/they | had been examining/beginning |

Future Perfect Progressive: action that will have been in progress by the time something else happens

| I/you/he/she/it/we/they | will have been examining/beginning |

How Can You Recognize Active and Passive Verbs?

Verbs in the **active voice** appear in sentences in which the doer (or agent) of an action is the subject of the sentence.

	DOER (SUBJECT)	ACTION (VERB)	GOAL (OBJECT)
ACTIVE	The car	**hit**	the lamppost.
ACTIVE	Dana	**distributed**	the flyers.

A verb in the **passive voice** adds a form of *be* as a helping verb to the past participle form. The subject (or doer) may appear as an object after the word *by* in an optional prepositional phrase.

	GOAL (SUBJECT)	ACTION (VERB)	[DOER: PREPOSITIONAL PHRASE]
PASSIVE	The lamppost	**was hit**	[by the car].
PASSIVE	The flyers	**were distributed**	[by Dana].

What Are Verbal Phrases?

Three verb parts—participles, gerunds, and infinitives—are known as **verbals.** They can function as nouns, adjectives, or adverbs, but they can never stand alone as verbs.

1. Build **participial phrases** with *-ing* (present participle) or *-ed/-en* (past participle) forms, using them as adjectives.

   Few neighbors **attending the meeting** owned dogs.
   They signed a petition **addressed to the mayor.**

2. Build a **gerund phrase** around the *-ing* form (present participle) used as a noun.

   Closing the landfill may keep it from **polluting the stream.**

3. Build an **infinitive phrase** around the *to* form, using it as an adjective, adverb, or noun.

   He used organic methods **to raise his garden.**
   To live in the mountains was his goal.

What Are the Forms of Some Common Irregular Verbs?

PRESENT	PAST	PAST PARTICIPLE
arise	arose	arisen
be	was/were	been
begin	began	begun
bite	bit	bitten/bit
bring	brought	brought
come	came	come
do	did	done
drink	drank	drunk
eat	ate	eaten
fly	flew	flown
go	went	gone
lay	laid	laid
lie	lay	lain
ride	rode	ridden
run	ran	run
see	saw	seen
set	set	set
sing	sang	sung
sit	sat	sat
take	took	taken
write	wrote	written

What Do Pronouns Do?

- **Personal pronouns:** Designate persons or things using a form reflecting the pronoun's role in the sentence.

  SINGULAR   *I, me, you, he, him, she, her, it*
  PLURAL   *we, us, you, they, them*

- **Possessive pronouns:** Show ownership (see Chapter 12 on apostrophes).

  SINGULAR   *my, mine, your, yours, her, hers, his, its*
  PLURAL   *our, ours, your, yours, their, theirs*

- **Relative pronouns:** Introduce subordinate clauses that act as adjectives and answer the questions "What kind of?" and "Which one?"

  who, whom, whose, which, that

- **Interrogative pronouns:** Introduce questions.

  who, which, what

- **Reflexive pronouns:** End in -self or -selves and enable the subject or doer also to be the receiver of an action.

- **Intensive pronouns:** End in -self or -selves and add emphasis.

  SINGULAR   *myself, yourself, herself, himself, itself*
  PLURAL   *ourselves, yourselves, themselves*

- **Demonstrative pronouns:** Point out or highlight an antecedent, refer to a noun or a pronoun, or sum up an entire phrase or clause.

  this, that, these, those

- **Reciprocal pronouns:** Refer to individual parts of a plural antecedent.

  one another, each other

- **Indefinite pronouns:** Refer to people, things, and ideas in general rather than to a specific antecedent (e.g., *anyone, both, each, few, none*).

What Are the Forms of Comparatives and Superlatives?

Adjectives

One syllable: Most add -*er* and -*est* (*pink, pinker, pinkest*).
Two syllables: Many add -*er* and -*est*; some add either -*er* and -*est* or *more* and *most* (*foggy, foggier, foggiest; more foggy, most foggy*).
Three (or more) syllables: Add *more* and *most* (*plentiful, more plentiful, most plentiful*).

Adverbs

One syllable: Most add -*er* and -*est* (*quick, quicker, quickest*).
Two (or more) syllables: Most add *more* and *most* (*carefully, more carefully, most carefully*).

Negative Comparisons (Adjectives and Adverbs)

Use *less* and *least* (*less full, least full; less slowly, least slowly*).

Irregular Forms

ADJECTIVE	COMPARATIVE	SUPERLATIVE
bad	worse	worst
good, well (healthy)	better	best
ill (harsh, unlucky)	worse	worst
a little	less	least
many, much, some	more	most
badly, ill (badly)	worse	worst
well (satisfactorily)	better	best

ESL ADVICE: How Do You Choose a Preposition?

Prepositions of time: *at*, *on*, and *in*

- Use *at* for a specific time. Use *on* for days and dates. Use *in* for non-specific times during a day, month, season, or year.

  Brandon was born **at** 11:11 a.m. **on** a Monday **in** 1996.

Prepositions of place: *at*, *on*, and *in*

- Use *at* for specific addresses. Use *on* for names of streets, avenues, and boulevards. Use *in* for areas of land—states, countries, continents.

  She lives **on** Town Avenue but works **at** 99 Low Street **in** Dayton.

  Arrange prepositional phrases in this order: place, then time.

  The runners will start **in the park** on Saturday.

***To* or no preposition to express going to a place**

- When you express the idea of going to a place, use the preposition *to*.

  I am going **to** work.   I am going **to** the office.

- In some cases, use no preposition: I am going home.

***For* and *since* in time expressions**

- Use *for* with an amount of time (minutes, hours, days, months, years) and *since* with a specific date or time.

  The housing program has operated **for** many years, **since** 1971.

Prepositions with nouns, verbs, and adjectives

- Nouns, verbs, and adjectives may appear with certain prepositions.

  NOUN + PREPOSITION   He has an <u>understanding</u> **of** global politics.

  VERB + PREPOSITION   Managers <u>worry</u> **about** many things.

Quick Tips for Writers, Readers, and Speakers

Tips for Academic Writers

Who Are Your Academic Readers?

- Are they classmates, your teacher, or others?
- What do your readers already know?
- What do they want to find out?
- What do they want you to demonstrate?

What Do Academic Readers Expect You to Do?

- Analyze or interpret a text or an event.
- Review and cite related theory and research.
- Reason logically and critically about a question.
- Bring fresh insights, and draw your own conclusions.

What Might You Try to Do in Your Writing?

- State your thesis and main points clearly.
- Use pertinent detail to support your views.
- Write clearly and logically, even on a complex topic.
- Acknowledge other views as you explore a topic.

What Form Should You Use?

- Analyze the criteria explained in your assignment.
- Ask about the form of writing required; review examples of essays, arguments, reports, reviews, lab reports, or other required forms.
- Ask advice from other students; look over comments from peers or instructors on previous papers of the same type.

Taking It Online

- Reading and writing across the disciplines
  http://writing.colostate.edu/references/documents.cfm

237

Tips for Workplace Writers

Who Are Your Workplace Readers?

- Are they co-workers, supervisors, clients, customers, government agencies, work groups, or others?
- What do your readers already know?
- What do they expect you to provide?
- Do they need to decide, implement, or understand?

What Might These Readers Expect You to Do?

- Provide or request information.
- Analyze problems.
- Recommend actions or solutions.
- Identify and evaluate alternatives.

What Might You Try to Do in Your Writing?

- Focus on the task, problem, or goal.
- Present the issue clearly and accurately.
- Organize efficiently, and summarize for busy readers.
- Use concise, clear, direct prose.

What Form Should You Use?

- Ask your supervisor or colleagues what form of writing (or oral presentation) your audience expects.
- Review examples of memos, letters, charts, reports, manuals, evaluations, or other expected forms.
- Follow the approach and pattern generally used in this form and in models prepared at your workplace.

Taking It Online

- Résumés
  http://owl.english.purdue.edu/workshops/hypertext/
  ResumeW/index.html
  http://jobstar.org/tools/resume/
- *Plain Language Action Network*
  http://www.plainlanguage.gov/main.htm

Tips for Public Writers

Who Are Your Readers?

- Are they members of your organization, possible supporters of your cause, public officials, community activists, local residents, or others?
- What do your readers value? What concerns them?

- What do readers want to accomplish?
- What do you have in common? Where do you differ?

What Might These Readers Expect You to Do?

- Provide issue-oriented information, especially local background, data, and evidence.
- Encourage civic involvement and decision making.
- Persuade others to support a cause or issue.

What Might You Try to Do in Your Writing?

- Persuade, enlighten, alert, or energize readers to act.
- Recommend policies, actions, or solutions.
- Be an advocate for your cause.
- Present relevant evidence to support your position.
- Recognize the interests and goals of others.

What Form Should You Use?

- Work collaboratively with others who have experience preparing flyers, newsletters, brochures, fact sheets, committee reports, public comments, letters, or other forms.
- Review similar materials prepared by your group or by other civic or special-interest groups.

Taking It Online

- Press releases
  http://www.stetson.edu/~rhansen/prguide.html
- Grant proposals
  http://www.hfsp.org/how/grantsmanship.html
  http://www.fdncenter.org/learn/shortcourse/prop1.html

Tips for Readers

Preread Before You Read

- Review any abstract, table of contents, menu, or headings.
- Note the author's credentials, publication date, and similar information on the title or home page.
- Scan for unfamiliar key words and concepts.
- Turn to an introductory text or encyclopedia article for background or definitions of complex terms.
- Predict what you expect based on similar texts.

Respond as You Read

- Pause and assess as you reach logical breaks.
- Note what you've learned and what's confusing.

- Skim each section after you have read it, reviewing major points and their connections.
- Summarize chunks, briefly noting a section's main point.
- Highlight or make notes during your second reading—not your first—so you know what's really important.
- Share insights with classmates or work colleagues, comparing reactions to content and language.

Follow up After You Read

- Write your interpretations, questions, objections, evaluations, or applications (to class, work, service learning, or civic activities) in the margins if the text is yours.
- Respond in a journal or on note cards, noting what you think and what the author says.
- Reread difficult material, skimming to trace its logic and studying or reading aloud key passages.

Taking It Online

- Evaluating reading
  http://www2.widener.edu/Wolfgram-Memorial-Library/
  webevaluation/examples.htm

Tips for Speakers

Plan Ahead

- Review criteria for an academic assignment.
- Identify audience expectations and time limits.
- Gather accurate, persuasive resources.
- Group your information, or outline your remarks.
- Write out "talking points"—main points, transitions, key sentences, and reminders to yourself.
- Prepare visuals—and backups—so they are clear, large enough to read, and relevant to your talk.
- Prepare any handouts to supplement your talk.

Rehearse

- Practice aloud, and time your presentation.
- Ask others for suggestions on content or delivery.
- Practice more if you stumble, lose your place, or forget key ideas; refine your talking points.
- Try videotaping or tape recording to spot problems or distracting habits.

- Reprint or recopy your notes on cards that are easy to read and handle; number them in order.
- Practice with your visuals—and your backups.

Present

- Take a deep breath, speak slowly, and make eye contact with your audience. Don't apologize.
- Use your notes to recall your talk, not to read.
- Concentrate on your audience—not yourself, your visuals, your notes, or outside distractions.
- Refer to, but don't read, visuals and handouts.
- Field questions confidently and directly.

Taking It Online

- Speaking
  http://departments.mwc.edu/spke/www/handouts.htm
  http://www.toastmasters.org/tips.asp

Tips for Collaborative Writers

Draft Collaboratively

- Organize parallel drafting, dividing up the project so that each person drafts a particular section.
- Try team drafting, assigning two writers for each section so one picks up when another gets stuck.
- Consider intensive drafting with a close friend or colleague, both working undisturbed and exchanging drafts or one talking as the other types.
- Exchange drafts as your group revises, but appoint one person as editor to integrate final drafts.

Revise Collaboratively

- Share your purpose and concerns with readers.
- Minimize apologies; everyone feels anxious about sharing a draft.
- Tape record responses, meet to discuss or take notes on comments, email, or annotate drafts.
- Recirculate a collaborative draft, or meet to revise.

Edit Collaboratively

- Revise first; prepare a clean draft for peer editors.
- Alert peer readers to concerns or recurring problems.
- Use familiar labels and symbols when you read drafts.

- Make clear, specific comments.
- Note possible errors, but let the writer make repairs.
- Look for patterns, repeating the same errors.

Taking It Online

- "Online Technical Writing: Strategies for Peer-Reviewing and Team-Writing"
  http://www.io.com/~hcexres/tcm1603/acchtml/team.html
- "Prof. David's Guidelines for Collaborative Writing"
  http://www.uncp.edu/home/vanderhoof/syllabus/colab-rt.html

Tips for Online Writers
Who Are Your Readers?

- Are they members of an online course conference, email correspondents, members of an electronic mailing list, participants in a newsgroup or Web forum, or random visitors to your Web site?
- What will readers expect of your course exchanges, messages, home page, or Web site?

What Might These Readers Expect You to Do?

- Follow netiquette, and adapt to group norms.
- Respect readers' time, interests, and privacy.
- Behave ethically online.

What Might You Try to Do in Your Writing?

- Consider what readers will expect, want, or need to find as they follow a thread or access your Web site.
- Focus briefly on essentials in each screen or message.
- Supply reliable information based on your expertise.
- Provide attachments, graphics, and other materials so that readers can easily access (or skip) them.
- Relate screens, supply options, and update so that your Web site remains current and easy to navigate.
- Identify and update useful links.
- Include email information so readers can respond.

What Form Should You Use?

- Lurk to observe expectations for messages and replies to conferences, mailing lists, or other groups.
- Follow course or workplace directions for attaching documents, graphics, or audio files.

- Analyze sample home pages and Web sites for ideas about design, navigation, and organization.

Taking It Online

- Netiquette
  http://www.fau.edu/netiquette/net/

Tips for Online Researchers

Find Resources Online

- Identify keywords related to your research questions.
- Try several search engines, especially those recommended by others.
- Use advanced search strategies.
- Follow links as you hunt for relevant sources.
- Print out or bookmark authoritative sites, pages, or links.

Screen Sources as You Search

- Be selective but flexible while you search.
- Measure sources against your research questions.
- Skip questionable sources that readers won't accept.
- Stay focused despite engaging—but irrelevant—links.
- Gather varied but reliable sources.
- Evaluate your search results as you work, and get expert advice from a librarian if needed.

Evaluate Potentially Useful Sources

- Assess the interests, possible motives, and reputation of the author, sponsor, or online publisher.
- Determine whether the source is current, well edited, and straightforward about its viewpoint.
- Check for logic, claims, and supporting evidence.
- Compare information across sources to verify accuracy, fairness, and consistency.
- Assess the relevance and reliability of information as your academic, work, or public readers will.

Taking It Online

- *The Good, the Bad, and the Ugly*
  http://lib.nmsu.edu/instruction/eval.html
- "Evaluation of Information Sources"
  http://www.vuw.ac.nz/~agsmith/evaln/evaln.htm

APPENDIX
Glossary of Manuscript Style

The alphabetical glossary that follows answers most of your miscellaneous questions about matters of form, such as margins, pagination, dates, and numbers. For matters not addressed below, consult the index, which directs you to appropriate pages elsewhere in this text.

Abbreviations

Employ abbreviations often and consistently in notes and citations, but avoid them in the text. In your citations, but not in your text, always abbreviate these items:

- Technical terms and reference words (anon., e.g., diss.)
- Institutions (acad., assn., Cong.)
- Dates (Jan., Feb.)
- States and countries (OH, CA, U.S.A.)
- Names of publishers (McGraw, UP of Florida)
- Titles of literary works (*Ado* for *Much Ado about Nothing*)
- Books of the Bible (Exod. For Exodus)

Accent Marks

When you quote, reproduce accents exactly as they appear in the original.

"La tradición clásica en españa," according to Romana,
remains strong in public school instruction (16).

Ampersand

Avoid using the ampersand symbol "&" unless custom demands it (e.g., "A & P"). In MLA, CSE, and CMS style, use *and* for in-text citations (e.g., Smith and Jones 213–14). In APA style use "&" within parenthetical citations (e.g., Spenser & Wilson, 1994, p. 73) but not in the text (e.g., Spenser and Wilson found the results in error).

Arabic Numerals

Both the MLA style and the APA style require Arabic numerals whenever possible: for volumes, books, parts, and chapters of works; acts, scenes, and lines of plays; cantos, stanzas, and lines of poetry.

Numbers Expressed as Figures in Your Text

Use figures in your text according to the following examples:

- All numbers 10 and above
- Numbers that represent ages, dates, time, size, score, amounts of money, and numerals used as numerals
- Statistical and mathematical numbers
- Numbers that precede units of measurement
- Numbers below 10 grouped with higher numbers

Number Use with Symbols

Use numerals with appropriate symbols (3%, $5.60); otherwise, use numerals only when the number cannot be spelled out in one or two words:

one hundred percent *but* 150 percent
a two-point average *but* a 2.5 average
one metric ton *but* 0.907 metric ton or 3.150 metric tons
forty-five percent *but* 45 1/2 percent *or* 45 1/2%

In business, scientific, and technical writing that involves frequent use of percentages, write all of them as numerals with the appropriate symbol (100%, 12%).

Numbers Expressed in Words in Your Text

Spell out numbers in the following instances:

- Numbers less than 10 that are not used as measurements
- Common fractions
- Any number that begins a sentence
- References to centuries

Numbers as Both Words and Figures

Combine words and figures in these situations:

- Back-to-back modifiers:

  twelve 6-year-olds *or* 12 six-year-olds, *but not* 12 6-year olds

- Large numbers (4 million)

Bullets, Numbers, and Indented Lists

Computers supply several bullet and number list styles whose indented lines begin with a circle, square, diamond, triangle, number, or letter. Use this feature to make a list stand out in your text.

Capitalization

Capitalize Some Titles

For books, journals, magazines, and newspapers capitalize the first word, the last word, and all principal words, including words that follow hyphens in compound terms (e.g., French-Speaking Islands). Do not capitalize articles, prepositions that introduce phrases, conjunctions, and the *to* in infinitives when these words occur in the middle of the title (for example, *The Last of the Mohicans*). Some scholarly styles capitalize only the first word of and proper names in reference titles and subtitles. Study the appropriate style for your field.

Capitalize the first word after the colon when introducing a rule, maxim, or principle and when introducing a quotation that is independent of your main sentence.

When introducing a list or an elaboration on the idea of the first clause, do not capitalize the first word after the colon.

Use capitals for trade names such as Pepsi, Plexiglas, Dupont, Dockers, Thunderbird, and Nikon.

Capitalize proper names used as adjectives *but not* the words used with them: Einstein's theory, Salk's vaccine.

Capitalize the names of departments or courses, but use lowercase when they are used in a general sense.

Department of Psychology but the psychology department

Capitalize a noun that denotes a specific place in a numbered series but not nouns that name common parts of books.

Comma

Use commas between items listed in a series of three or more, including before the *and* and *or* that precedes the last item. For example:

Reader (34), Scott (61), and Wellman (615–17) agree with
Steinbeck on this point.

Never use a comma and a dash together. The comma follows a parenthesis if your text requires the comma:

How should we order our lives, asks Thompson (22–23),
when we face "hostility from every quarter"?

The comma goes inside single quotation marks as well as double quotation marks:

> Such irony is discovered in Smith's article, "The Sources of Franklin's 'The Ephemera,'" but not in most textual discussions.

Figures and Tables

A table is a systematic presentation of materials, usually in columns. A figure is any nontext item that is not a table: blueprint, chart, diagram, drawing, graph, photo, photostat, map, and so on. Use graphs appropriately. A line graph serves a different purpose than a circle (pie) chart, and a bar graph plots different information than a scatter graph. Place captions above a table and below a figure. Here is an example:

Table 1
Response by Class on Nuclear Energy Policy

	Freshmen	Sophomores	Juniors	Seniors
1. More nuclear power	150	301	75	120
2. Less nuclear power	195	137	111	203
3. Present policy is acceptable	87	104	229	37

Sample table

Foreign Cities

In general, spell the names of foreign cities as they are written in original sources. However, for purposes of clarity, you may substitute an English name or provide both with one in parentheses:

Köln (Cologne)   Braunschweig (Brunswick)

Headings

Most papers require only major headings (A-level), but subheads are permitted. Also examine the chart at the top of the next page.

Indenting

Indent paragraphs five spaces or 1/2 inch. Indent block quotations (four lines or more) ten spaces or 1 inch from the left margin. If your block quotation is one paragraph, do not indent the first line more than the rest. However, if your block quotation is two or more paragraphs,

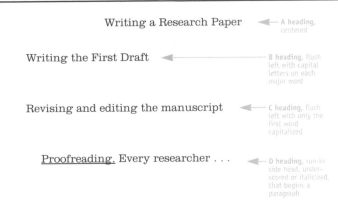

Writing a Research Paper ◀— A heading, centered

Writing the First Draft ◀—————— B heading, flush left with capital letters on each major word

Revising and editing the manuscript ◀— C heading, flush left with only the first word capitalized

<u>Proofreading.</u> Every researcher . . . ◀— D heading, run-in side head, under-scored or italicized, that begins a paragraph

indent the first line of each paragraph an extra three spaces or 1/4 inch. Use a five-space hanging indention for entries of the Works Cited page. Indent the first line of footnotes five spaces. Other styles (APA and CSE) have different requirements.

Margins

A basic 1-inch margin on all sides of each page is recommended. Place your page number 1/2 inch below the top edge of the paper and 1 inch from the right edge. Your software has a ruler, menu, or style palette that allows you to set the margins. *Tip:* If you develop a header, the running head may appear 1 inch from the top, in which case your first line of text will begin 1 1/2 inches from the top.

Monetary Units

Spell out monetary amounts only if you can do so in three words or fewer. Conform to the following:

$12 *or* twelve dollars
$14.25 *but not* fourteen dollars and twenty-five cents
$8 billion *or* eight billion dollars
$10.3 billion *or* $10,300,000,000
$63 *or* sixty-three dollars

Names of Persons

At the first mention of a person, give the full name (e.g., Ernest Hemingway or Margaret Mead) and thereafter give only the surname, such as Hemingway or Mead. (APA style uses the last name only in the text.) Omit formal titles (Mr., Mrs., Dr., Hon.). Use simplified names of famous persons (e.g., Dante and Michelangelo rather than Dante Alighieri and Michelangelo di Lodovico Buonarroti Simoni) when they are familiar. Use pseudonyms (e.g., George Eliot, Mark Twain, Stendhal). Use fictional names (e.g., Huck, Lord Jim, Santiago, Captain Ahab).

Numbering Pages

Number your pages in a running head in the upper right-hand corner of each. Depending on the software, you can create the head with the Numbering or the Header feature. See the sample papers in Chapter 8.

Roman Numerals

Use capital roman numerals for titles of persons (Elizabeth II) and major sections of an outline. Use lowercase roman numerals for preliminary pages of text, as for a preface or introduction (iii, iv, v). Otherwise, use Arabic numerals (e.g., Vol. 5, Act 2, Ch. 17, Plate 21, 2 Sam. 2.1–8, or *Iliad* 2.121–30), *except* when writing for some instructors in history, philosophy, religion, music, art, and theater, in which case you may need to use roman numerals (e.g., III, Act II, I Sam. ii.1–8, <u>Hamlet</u> I.ii.5–6).

Running Heads

Repeat your last name in the upper right corner of every page just in front of the page number. APA style requires a short title with the page number.

Shortened Titles in the Text

Use abbreviated titles of books and articles mentioned often in the text after a first, full reference. For example, after its initial appearance, *Backgrounds to English as Language* should be shortened to *Backgrounds* in the text, notes, and in-text citations.

Spacing

As a general rule, double-space all typed material in your paper—the body, all indented quotations, and all reference entries. Footnotes, if used, should be single-spaced, but endnotes should be double-spaced. APA style requires double-spacing after all headings and separates text from indented quotes and from figures by double-spacing. Use one space after commas, semicolons, colons, and periods. Use one space after punctuation marks at the end of sentences. Do not use a space before or after a dash.

Titles within Titles

For a book title that includes another title indicated by quotation marks, retain the quotation marks.

<u>O. Henry's Irony in "The Gift of the Magi"</u>

For an article title that includes a book title, use italics or underlining for the book.

"<u>Great Expectations</u> as a Novel of Initiation"

For an article title that includes another title indicated by quotation marks, enclose the shorter title in single quotation marks.

"A Reading of O. Henry's 'The Gift of the Magi'"

For an underscored book title that incorporates another normally underscored title, do not underscore or italicize the shorter title nor place it within quotation marks.

<u>Interpretations of</u> Great Expectations

Underscoring *(Italicizing)*
Titles

Use italics or underscoring for the titles of the following types of works:

TYPE OF WORK	EXAMPLE
book	*A Quaker Book of Wisdom*
bulletin	*Production Memo 3*
drama	*Desire under the Elms*
film	*Treasure of the Sierra Madre*
journal	*Journal of Sociology*
magazine	*Newsweek*
newspaper	*Boston Globe*
novel	*Band of Angels*
poem (book length)	*Idylls of the King*
short novel	*Billy Budd*

In contrast, place quotation marks around titles of articles, essays, chapters, sections, short poems, stories, songs, lectures, sermons, reports, and individual episodes of television programs.

Do not underscore the titles of sacred writings (Genesis, Old Testament); series (The New American Nation Series); editions (Variorum Edition of W. B. Yeats); societies (Victorian Society); courses (Greek Mythology); divisions of a work (preface, appendix, canto 3, scene 2); or descriptive phrases (Nixon's farewell address or Reagan's White House years).

Word Division

Avoid dividing words at the end of a line, even if it makes one line of text extremely short.

Glossary of Usage and Terms

This glossary includes matters of usage (words that writers often find confusing or difficult, such as *farther* and *further*), grammatical terms (such as *verb*), and rhetorical terms (such as *indirect quotation*).

a, an Use *an* before a vowel (*an old film*) or silent *h* (*an honor*) and *a* before a consonant (*a classic, a hero*)

accept, except *Accept* means "to take or receive"; *except* means "excluding."

Everyone **accepted** the invitation **except** Larry.

active voice (See **voice.**)

adverse, averse Someone opposed to something is *averse* to it; *adverse* conditions oppose achieving a goal.

advice, advise *Advice*, a noun, means "counsel" or "recommendations." *Advise*, a verb, means "to counsel or recommend."

He tried to **advise** students who wanted no **advice.**

affect, effect The verb *affect* means "to influence." *Effect* as a noun means "a result" and, rarely, as a verb means "to cause something to happen."

Because CFCs may **affect** the ozone layer with an uncertain **effect** on global warming, our goal is to **effect** changes in public attitudes.

aggravate, irritate *Aggravate* means "to worsen"; *irritate* means "to bother."

ain't Replace *ain't* in formal writing with *am not, is not,* or *are not.* The contractions *aren't* and *isn't* are more acceptable but are still informal.

all ready, already *All ready* means "prepared"; *already* means "by that time."

Sam was **all ready,** but the team had **already** gone.

all right Always spell this as two words, not as *alright.*

all together, altogether Use *all together* to mean "everyone"; use *altogether* to mean "completely."

We were **all together** on our plan, but it was **altogether** too much to organize by Friday.

allude, elude *Allude* means "refer indirectly"; *elude* means "escape."

allusion, illusion An *allusion* is a reference to something; an *illusion* is a vision or false belief.

a lot Even when spelled correctly as two words, not as *alot*, *a lot* may be too informal for some writing. Use *many* or *much* instead.

a.m., p.m. These abbreviations may be capitals or lowercase.

among, between Use *between* when something involves two things; use *among* for three or more.

> The fight **between** the two players led to a debate **among** the umpire and the managers.

amount, number *Amount* refers to a quantity of something that can't be divided into separate units; *number* refers to countable objects.

> The recipe uses a **number** of spices and a small **amount** of milk.

an (See **a, an.**)

analytical synthesis (See **synthesis.**)

and etc. (See **etc.**)

and/or Because *and/or* is imprecise, choose one of the words, or revise.

ante-, anti- The prefix *ante-* means "before" or "predating," while *anti-* means "against" or "opposed."

antecedent The noun or pronoun to which another word (usually a pronoun) refers.

anyone, any one *Anyone* is an indefinite pronoun; you may also use *any* to modify *one*, in the sense of "any individual thing or person."

> **Anyone** can dive, but the coach has little time for **any one** person.

anyplace Replace this term in formal writing with *anywhere*, or revise.

anyways, anywheres Avoid these versions of *anyway* and *anywhere*.

appositive A noun or pronoun that renames or stands for a prior noun.

appositive phrase An **appositive** (usually a noun) and its modifiers that rename or stand for a prior noun to add detail to a sentence.

> Ken and Beth, **my classmates,** won an award.

as, like Used as a preposition, *as* indicates a precise comparison. *Like* indicates a resemblance or similarity.

> Remembered **as** a man of habit, Kant, **like** many other philosophers, was thoughtful and intense.

as to *As to* is considered informal in many contexts.

> INFORMAL   The media speculated **as to** the film's success.
>
> EDITED   The media speculated **about** the film's success.

assure, ensure, insure Use *assure* to imply a promise, *ensure* to imply a certain outcome, and *insure* to imply something legal or financial.

> The surgeon **assured** the pianist that his hands would heal by May. To **ensure** that, the musician **insured** his hands with Lloyd's of London.

at In writing, drop *at* in direct and indirect questions.

> SPOKEN   Jones asked where his attorney was **at.**
>
> EDITED   Jones asked where his attorney **was.**

awful, awfully Use *awful* (adjective) to modify a noun; use *awfully* (adverb) to modify a verb.

He played **awfully** on that hole and sent an **awful** shot into the pond.

awhile, a while *Awhile* (one word) acts as an adverb; it is not preceded by a preposition. *A while* acts as a noun (with the article *a*) and is used in prepositional phrases.

The homeless family stayed **awhile** at the shelter because the children had not eaten for **a while.**

bad, badly Use *bad* (adjective) with a noun or linking verb expressing feelings, not the adverb *badly*.

because, since Use *since* to indicate time, not causality in place of the more formal and precise *because*.

being as, being that Write *because* instead.

beside, besides Use *beside* to mean "next to." Use *besides* for "also" (adverb) or "except" (adjective).

Besides being the firm's tax specialist, Klein would review nearly any document placed **beside** him.

better, had better Revise to *ought to* or *should* in formal writing.

between (See **among, between.**)

block quotation A quotation long enough to require separating it from the text in an indented block.

bring, take *Bring* implies movement from somewhere else to close at hand; *take* implies the opposite direction.

Bring more coffee, but **take** away the muffins.

broke *Broke* is the past tense of *break*, not the past participle.

DRAFT	The computer was **broke.**
EDITED	The computer was **broken.**

burst, bursted *Burst* implies an outward explosion: The boys *burst* the balloon. Do not use *bursted* for the past tense.

bust, busted Avoid *bust* or *busted* to mean "broke."

COLLOQUIAL	The van **bust** down on the trip.
EDITED	The van **broke** down on the trip.

but however, but yet Choose one word of each pair.

can, may *Can* implies ability; *may* implies permission or uncertainty.

Bart **can** drive, but his dad **may** not lend him the car.

can't hardly, can't scarcely Use these positively (*can hardly*, *can scarcely*), or simply use *can't*.

capital, capitol *Capital* refers to a government center, a letter, or money; *capitol* refers to a government building.

censor, censure *Censor* means the act of shielding something from the public, such as a book. *Censure* implies punishment or critical labeling.

center around Use *center on*, *focus on*, or *revolve around*.

choose, chose Use *choose* for the present and *chose* for the past tense.

cite, site   *Cite* means to acknowledge someone's work; *site* means a place.

Phil **cited** field studies of the Anasazi **site.**

clause   A word group with a subject and a verb. A **main** (independent) clause can stand on its own; a **subordinate** (dependent) clause begins with a subordinating word (*because, although, which, that*) and cannot stand alone.

Because he lost his balance, Sam fell on the ice.

climactic, climatic   *Climactic* refers to the culmination of something; *climatic* refers to weather conditions.

comma splice   Two or more sentences (main clauses) incorrectly joined with a comma.

comparative   The form of an adjective or adverb showing that the word it modifies is compared to one other thing. The comparative form adds *-er* or *more* (*faster, more adept*). (See **superlative.**)

compare to, compare with   Use *compare to* and *liken to* for similarities between two things. Use *compare with* for both similarities and differences.

Compared with the boy's last illness, this virus, which the doctor **compared to** a tiny army, was mild.

complement   A word (noun, pronoun, adjective) or phrase tied to a subject by a **linking verb** (*becomes, is, seems*). A **subject complement** describes or renames a subject: Nan seems **tired.** An **object complement** does the same for a direct object: Brad ate the pizza **cold.**

complement, compliment   *Complement* means "an accompaniment"; *compliment* means "words of praise."

The guests **complimented** the chef on the menu, which **complemented** the event perfectly.

compound modifier   Two or more words that work as a single modifier (***wood-burning*** fireplace).

compound object   Two or more objects joined by *and* or *both . . . and.*

compound subject   Two or more subjects joined by *and* or *both . . . and.*

compound word   A word made up of two or more independent words (such as *superman* or *father-in-law*).

conjunction   A word that joins two elements in a sentence. **Coordinating conjunctions** (*and, but, or, nor, for, yet, so*) link grammatically equal elements—compound subjects, verbs, objects, and modifiers. **Subordinating conjunctions** (*because, although, while, if*) create a subordinate clause.

conjunctive adverb   An adverb (*however, moreover, therefore*) that joins sentences or sentence elements, showing how they are related.

continual, continuous   *Continual* implies that something recurs; *continuous* implies that it is constant or unceasing.

The **continual** noise of the jets was less annoying than the traffic **continuously** circling the airport.

coordinate adjectives   Two adjectives, each modifying a noun on its own, separated by a comma. If the first modifies the second (which modifies the noun), they are **noncoordinate adjectives,** not separated by a comma.

coordinating conjunction   One of seven words (*and, but, or, nor, for, yet, so*) that link equal elements. (See **conjunction.**)

coordination A sentence structure using **coordinating conjunctions** to link and weight main clauses equally.

could of, would of Replace these, often pronounced as they are misspelled, with *could have* or *would have*.

couple, couple of In formal writing, use *a few* or *two*.

criteria *Criteria* is the plural form of *criterion*.

> PLURAL   The **criteria** were too strict to follow.

critical synthesis (See **synthesis**.)

curriculum *Curriculum* is the singular form. For the plural, use either *curricula* or *curriculums* consistently.

dangling modifier (See **misplaced modifier**.)

data Widely used for both singular and plural, *data* technically is plural; *datum* refers to a single piece of data. If in doubt, use the plural.

> PLURAL   These **data** are not very revealing.

different from, different than Use *different from* when an object follows; use *different than* (not *from what*) when a clause follows.

> Jim's tacos are **different from** Lena's; his enchiladas now are **different than** they were when he began to cook.

direct quotation A statement that repeats someone's exact words, set off by quotation marks. (See **indirect quotation**.)

discreet, discrete *Discreet* means "reserved or cautious"; *discrete* means "distinctive" or "explicit."

disinterested, uninterested *Disinterested* implies impartiality or objectivity; *uninterested* implies lack of interest.

disruptive modifier (See **misplaced modifier**.)

done *Done* is a past participle, not past tense.

> DRAFT   The runner **done** her best at the meet.
> EDITED   The runner **did** her best at the meet.

don't, doesn't Contractions may be too informal in some contexts. Ask your reader, or err on the side of formality (*do not*, *does not*).

double negative Avoid double negatives.

> DRAFT   The state **hasn't** done **nothing** about it.
> EDITED   The state **has** done **nothing** about it.
> EDITED   The state **hasn't** done **anything** about it.

due to To mean "because," use *due to* only after a form of the verb *be*. Avoid the wordy *due to the fact that*.

> DRAFT   The mayor collapsed **due to** fatigue.
> EDITED   The mayor's collapse was **due to** fatigue.
> EDITED   The mayor collapsed **because** of fatigue.

effect, affect (See **affect, effect**.)

e.g. Avoid this abbreviation meaning "for example."

> AWKWARD   Her positions on issues, **e.g.,** gun control, are very liberal.
> EDITED   Her positions on issues **such as** gun control are very liberal.

ellipsis A series of three spaced periods showing a reader where something has been left out of a quotation.

emigrate from, immigrate to People *emigrate from* one country and *immigrate to* another. *Migrate* implies moving about (*migrant workers*) or settling temporarily.

ensure (See **assure, ensure, insure.**)

enthused Avoid *enthused* for *enthusiastic* in writing.

especially, specially *Especially* implies "in particular"; *specially* means "for a specific purpose."

It was **especially** important to follow the **specially** designed workouts.

etc. Avoid this abbreviation in formal writing; supply a complete list, or use a phrase like *so forth*.

INFORMAL   The march was a disaster: it rained, the protesters had no food, **etc.**

EDITED   The march was a disaster: the protesters were wet and hungry.

eventually, ultimately Use *eventually* to imply that an outcome follows a series (or lapse) of events; use *ultimately* to imply that a final act ends a series of events.

Eventually, the rescuers pulled the last victim from the wreck, and **ultimately** there were no casualties.

everyday, every day *Everyday* (adjective) modifies a noun. *Every day* is a noun (*day*) modified by *every*.

Every day in the Peace Corps, Monique faced the **everyday** task of boiling her drinking water.

everyone, every one *Everyone* is a pronoun; *every one* is an adjective followed by a noun.

Everyone was dazzled by **every one** of the desserts.

exam In formal writing, readers may prefer the full term, *examination*.

except (See **accept, except.**)

expletive construction Opening with *there is, there are,* or *it is* to delay the subject until later in the sentence.

explicit, implicit *Explicit* means that something is openly stated, *implicit* that it is implied or suggested.

farther, further *Farther* implies a distance that can be measured; *further* implies one that cannot.

The **farther** they hiked, the **further** their friendship deteriorated.

faulty parallelism (See **parallelism.**)

faulty predication A sentence flaw in which the second part (the predicate) comments on a topic different from the one in the first part.

FAULTY   The **presence** of ozone in smog is the **chemical** that causes eye irritation.

EDITED   The **ozone** in smog is the **chemical** that causes eye irritation.

female, male Use these terms only to call attention to gender specifically, as in a research report. Otherwise, use *man* or *woman* unless such usage is sexist.

fewer, less Use *fewer* for things that can be counted, and use *less* for quantities that cannot be divided.

The new bill had **fewer** supporters and **less** media coverage.

first person Pronouns (*I*, *we*) for the person speaking. (See **person.**)

firstly Use *first*, *second*, *third* when enumerating points.

form The spelling or ending that shows a word's role in a sentence.

former, latter *Former* means "the one before" and *latter* means "the one after." The pair must refer to only two things.

fragment Part of a sentence incorrectly treated as complete.

freshman, freshmen Readers may consider these terms sexist. Unless you are using an established term (such as the Freshman Colloquium), use *first-year student*.

fused sentence Two or more complete sentences incorrectly joined without any punctuation; also called a **run-on sentence.**

genre The form or type of text to which a work conforms (play, novel, lab report, essay, memo).

get Replace this word with more specific verbs.

| INFORMAL | King's last speeches **got** nostalgic. |
| EDITED | King's last speeches **turned** nostalgic. |

go, say Some speakers use *go* and *goes* very informally for *say* and *says*. Revise this usage in all writing.

gone, went Do not use *went* (the past tense of *go*) in place of the past participle form *gone*.

| DRAFT | The officers **should have went** to the captain. |
| EDITED | The officers **should have gone** to the captain. |

good and In formal writing, avoid this term to mean "very" (*good and* tired).

good, well *Good* (an adjective) means "favorable" (a *good* trip). *Well* (an adverb) means "done favorably." Avoid informal uses of *good* for *well*.

got to Avoid *got* or *got to* in place of *must* or *have to*.

| SPOKEN | I **got to** improve my grade in statistics. |
| WRITTEN | I **have to** improve my grade in statistics. |

great Formally, avoid *great* as an adjective meaning "wonderful"; use it to mean "large" or "monumental."

hanged, hung Some readers will expect you to use *hanged* exclusively to mean execution by hanging and *hung* to refer to anything else.

have, got (See **got to.**)

have, of (See **could of, would of.**)

he, she Avoid privileging male forms.

helping verb A form of a verb such as *be*, *do*, or *have* that can be combined with a main verb.

hopefully Some readers may object when this word modifies an entire clause ("*Hopefully, her health will improve*"). When in doubt, use it only as "feeling hopeful."

however (See **but however, but yet.**)

hung (See **hanged, hung.**)

if, whether Use *if* before a specific outcome (stated or implied); use *whether* to consider alternatives.

If the technology can be perfected, we may soon have three-dimensional television. But **whether** we will be able to afford it is another question.

illogical comparison (See **incomplete sentence.**)

illusion (See **allusion, illusion.**)

immigrate to (See **emigrate from, immigrate to.**)

implicit (See **explicit, implicit.**)

incomplete comparison (See **incomplete sentence.**)

incomplete sentence A sentence that fails to complete an expected logical or grammatical pattern. An **incomplete comparison** leaves out the element to which something is compared; an **illogical comparison** seems to compare things that cannot be reasonably compared.

independent clause (See **main clause.**)

indirect question A sentence whose main clause is a statement and whose embedded clause asks a question. Treat these as statements, not questions.

Phil wondered **what the study would show.**

indirect quotation A quotation in which a writer reports the substance of someone's words but not the exact words used. Quotation marks are not needed. (See **direct quotation.**)

in regard to Replace this wordy phrase with *about.*

inside of, outside of When you use *inside* or *outside* to mark locations, omit *of: Inside* the hut was a child.

insure (See **assure, ensure, insure.**)

interpolation Your own words, marked with brackets, introduced into a direct quotation from someone else.

interrupter A parenthetical remark such as *in fact* or *more importantly.*

irregardless Avoid this erroneous form of *regardless.*

irritate (See **aggravate, irritate.**)

its, it's *Its* is a possessive pronoun; *it's* is a contraction for *it is.* Some readers object to contractions in formal writing.

-ize, -wise Some readers object to turning nouns or adjectives into verbs by adding *-ize* (*finalize, itemize, computerize*). Avoid adding *-wise* to words: "Weather-*wise*, it's chilly."

keyword A word in a database, catalog, or index used to identify a topic.

kind, sort, type Precede these singular nouns with *this*, not *these*. In general, use more precise words.

kind of, sort of Avoid these informal expressions (meaning "a little," "rather," or "somewhat") in academic and workplace writing.

latter (See **former, latter.**)

lay, lie *Lay* is a verb that needs a direct object (not the self). *Lie*, "place in a resting position," refers to the self; it takes the past tense form *lay.*

less (See **fewer, less.**)

lie (See **lay, lie.**)

like (See **as, like.**)

limiting modifier A word such as *only, almost,* or *just* that qualifies a word, usually the one that follows it.

linking verb A verb that expresses a state of being or an occurrence: *is*, *seems*, *becomes*, *grows*.

literally In both factual and figurative (not true to fact) statements, avoid *literally*.

DRAFT	Jed **literally** died when he saw the hotel.
REDUNDANT	Jed **literally gasped** when he saw the hotel.
EDITED	Jed **gasped** when he saw the hotel.

loose, lose *Loose* (rhyming with *moose*) is an adjective meaning "not tight." *Lose* (rhyming with *snooze*) is a present tense verb meaning "to misplace."

lots (See **a lot**.)

main clause A word group with a subject and a verb that can stand on its own as a sentence. (See **clause**.)

may (See **can, may**.)

maybe, may be *Maybe* means *possibly; may be* is part of a verb structure.

The President **may be** speaking now, so **maybe** we should listen.

media, medium Technically plural, *media* is frequently used as a singular noun to refer to the press. *Medium* generally refers to a conduit or method of transmission.

The **media** is not covering the story accurately.

The telephone is a useful **medium** for planning.

might of (See **could of, would of**.)

mighty In formal writing, omit or replace *mighty* with *very*.

misplaced modifier A modifier incorrectly placed relative to the word it modifies (its headword).

mixed sentence A sentence with a mismatched or shifted grammatical structure.

modifier A word or word group, acting as an adjective or adverb, that qualifies the meaning of another word.

modify The function of adjectives and adverbs that add to, qualify, limit, or extend the meaning of other words.

Ms. To avoid sexist labeling of women by marital status (not marked in men's titles), use *Ms.* unless you have reason to use *Miss* or *Mrs.* (as in the name of the character *Mrs. Dalloway*). Use professional titles when appropriate (*Dr.*, *Professor*, *Senator*, *Mayor*).

must of, must have (See **could of, would of**.)

nominalization A noun (*modernization, verbosity*) created from a verb (*modernize*) or adjective (*verbose*).

noncoordinate adjectives (See **coordinate adjectives**.)

nonrestrictive modifier (See **restrictive modifier**.)

nor, or Use *nor* for negative and *or* for positive constructions.

NEGATIVE	Neither rain **nor** snow will slow the team.
POSITIVE	Either rain **or** snow may delay the game.

nothing like, nowhere near In formal writing, avoid these informal phrases used to compare two things.

noun string A sequence of nouns used to modify a main noun (*multifunction modulation control device*) that may seem abstract or technical to readers.

nowheres Use *nowhere* instead.

number The way of showing whether a noun or pronoun is **singular** (one) or **plural** (two or more). Subjects and verbs must agree in number as must pronouns and the nouns they modify. (See **amount, number.**)

object The words in a sentence that tell who or what receives the action.

The class cleaned up **the park.**

of, have (See **could of, would of.**)

off of Use *off* instead.

OK When you write formally, use *OK* only in dialogue. If you mean "good" or "acceptable," use these terms.

on account of In formal writing, use *because*.

outside of (See **inside of, outside of.**)

parallelism The expression of similar or related ideas in similar grammatical form.

paraphrase To rewrite a passage in your own words, preserving the essence and detail of the original.

passive voice (See **voice.**)

per Use *per* to mean "by the," as in *per hour*, not "according to," as in *per your instructions.*

percent, percentage Use *percent* with numbers (*10 percent*); use *percentage* for a statistical part of something (*a large percentage of the budget*).

person The form that a noun or pronoun takes to identify the subject of a sentence. **First person** is someone speaking (*I, we*); **second person** is someone spoken to (*you*); **third person** is someone being spoken about (*he, she, it, they*).

personal pronoun A pronoun that designates persons or things, such as *I, me, you, him, we, you, they.*

phrase A word group without a subject, a verb, or both. (See **clause.**)

plagiarism The unethical or illegal practice of using another writer's words or text as your own without acknowledging their source.

plus Replace *plus* with *and* to join two main clauses. Use *plus* only to mean "in addition to."

possessive A pronoun (*mine, hers, yours, theirs*) or noun (*the bird's* egg) that expresses ownership.

precede, proceed *Precede* means "come before"; *proceed* means "go ahead."

predicate The words in a sentence that indicate an action, relationship, or condition—typically a **verb phrase** following the subject of the sentence. A **simple predicate** is a verb or verb phrase; to these, a **complete predicate** adds modifiers or other words that receive action or complete the verb.

prefix An addition, such as *un-* in *unforgiving*, at the beginning of a word. (See **suffix.**)

pretty Use *pretty* to mean "attractive," not "somewhat" or "rather" (as in *pretty good, pretty hungry*).

primary source Research material in or close to original form.

principal, principle *Principal* is a noun meaning "an authority" or "head of a school" or an adjective meaning "leading" ("a *principal* objection to the testimony"). *Principle* is a noun meaning "belief or conviction."

proceed (See **precede, proceed.**)

quote, quotation Formally, *quote* is a verb, and *quotation* is a noun. Some readers object to *quote* as an abbreviation of *quotation*.

raise, rise *Raise* is a transitive verb meaning "to lift up." *Rise* is an intransitive verb (it takes no object) meaning "to get up or move up."

He **raised** his head to watch the sun **rise.**

rarely ever Use *rarely* alone, not paired with *ever*.
real, really Use *real* as an adjective; use *really* as an adverb.
reason is because, reason is that Avoid these wordy phrases.
redundancy The use of unnecessary or repeated words.
reference chain A sequence of pronouns whose **antecedent,** the word to which they refer, is stated in the opening sentence of a passage.
regarding (See **in regard to.**)
regardless (See **irregardless.**)
relative clause A clause that modifies a noun or pronoun and begins with a **relative pronoun** (*who, whom, whose, which, that*).

Jen found a Web site **that** had valuable links.

respectfully, respectively Use *respectfully* for "with respect" and *respectively* to imply an order or sequence.

The senate **respectfully** submitted revisions for items 4 and 10, **respectively.**

restrictive modifier A **restrictive modifier** supplies information essential to the meaning of a sentence and is added without commas. A **nonrestrictive modifier** adds useful or interesting information not essential to the meaning and set off by commas.
rise (See **raise, rise.**)
run-on sentence (See **fused sentence.**)

says (See **go, say.**)
second person The pronoun (*you*) referring to the person spoken to. (See **person.**)
secondary source Research information that analyzes, interprets, or comments on primary sources. (See also **primary source.**)
sentence A group of words with both a subject and a complete verb that can stand on its own. (See **comma splice, fragment, fused sentence.**)
sentence cluster A group of sentences that develop related ideas or information.
set, sit *Set* means "to place"; *sit* means "to place oneself."
should of (See **could of, would of.**)
shift An inappropriate switch in **person, number, tense,** or topic.
since (See **because, since.**)
sit (See **set, sit.**)
site (See **cite, site.**)
so Some readers object to the use of *so* in place of *very*.
somebody, some body (See **anyone, any one.**)
someone, some one (See **anyone, any one.**)
sometime, some time, sometimes *Sometime* refers to a vague future time; *sometimes* means "every once in a while." *Some time* is an adjective (*some*) modifying a noun (*time*).

Sometime every winter, **sometimes** after a project is finished, the crew takes **some time** off.

sort (See **kind, sort.**)

specially (See **especially, specially.**)

split infinitive An infinitive is the base form of a verb paired with *to* (*to run*). Some readers object to another word placed between the two (to **quickly** run).

squinting modifier (See **misplaced modifier.**)

stationary, stationery *Stationary* means "standing still"; *stationery* refers to writing paper.

subject In a sentence, the doer or thing talked about, typically placed before a verb phrase. A **simple subject** consists of one or more nouns (or pronouns) naming the doer; to this a **complete subject** adds modifiers.

subject complement (See **complement.**)

subordinate clause A word group with a subject and a verb that is introduced by a subordinator (*because, although, that, which*). It must be connected to a main clause (which can stand alone). (See **clause.**)

subordinating conjunction A word (*because, although, while, if*) that introduces a subordinate clause, a word group with a subject and verb that cannot stand alone and must be connected to a main clause. (See **conjunction.**)

such Some readers will expect *that* to follow *such*.

The team solved **such** a complex problem **that** everyone cheered.

suffix An addition, such as *-ly* in *quickly*, at the end of a word. (See **prefix.**)

summary A concise restatement in your own words, boiling a passage or source down to essentials.

superlative The form of an adjective or adverb showing that the word it modifies is compared to two or more other things. The superlative adds *-est* or *most* (*fastest, most adept*). (See **comparative.**)

suppose to Use the correct form, *supposed to*, even though the *-d* is not always heard in pronunciation.

sure, surely Formally, use *sure* to mean "certain." Use *surely*, not *sure* as an adverb.

He has **surely** studied hard and is **sure** to pass.

sure and, try and Write *sure to* and *try to* instead.

synthesis The distilling of separate elements into a single, unified entity. For a research paper, an analytical synthesis relates summaries of several sources while a critical synthesis presents conclusions about a variety of perspectives, opinions, or interpretations.

take (See **bring, take.**)

tense The form a verb takes to indicate time—past, present, or future tense.

than, then *Than* is used to compare; *then* implies a sequence of events or a causal relationship.

Lil played harder **than** Eva; **then** the rain began.

that, which In formal writing, use *that* when a clause is essential to the meaning of a sentence (restrictive modifier) and *which* when it does not provide essential information (nonrestrictive modifier).

theirself, theirselves, themself Replace these with *themselves* to refer to more than one person and *himself* or *herself* to refer to one person.

them Avoid *them* as a subject or to modify a subject, as in "*Them* are fresh" or

"*Them* apples are crisp." Replace with *they, these, those,* or *the* with a noun (*the apples*).

then (See **than, then.**)

there, their, they're These forms sound alike, but *there* shows location, *their* is a possessive pronoun, and *they're* contracts *they* and *are.*

Look over **there. Their** car ran out of gas. **They're** starting to walk.

third person Pronouns (*he, she, it, they*) that indicate the person or thing spoken about. (See **person.**)

thusly Replace this term with *thus* or *therefore.*

till, until, 'til Some readers will find *'til* and *till* informal; use *until.*

to, too, two These words sound alike, but *to* is a preposition showing direction, *too* means "also," and *two* is a number.

Ed went **to** the lake **two** times and took Han **too.**

toward, towards Prefer *toward* in formal writing.

transitional expression Expressions (*therefore, in addition*) that link one idea, sentence, or paragraph to the next, helping readers relate ideas.

try and, try to (See **sure and, try and.**)

ultimately (See **eventually, ultimately.**)

uninterested (See **disinterested, uninterested.**)

unique Use *unique,* not *most* or *more unique.*

until (See **till, until, 'til.**)

use to, used to Write *used to,* even though the *-d* is not always clearly pronounced.

verb The word in a sentence that expresses action (*jump*), occurrence (*happen*), or state of being (*be*).

voice A verb is in the **active voice** when the doer of the action is the subject of the sentence and in the **passive voice** when the goal or object of the sentence is the subject.

wait for, wait on Use *wait on* for a clerk's or server's job; use *wait for* to mean "to await someone's arrival."

well (See **good, well.**)

went (See **gone, went.**)

were, we're *Were* is a verb; *we're* is a contraction for "we are."

where . . . at (See **at.**)

whether (See **if, whether.**)

which (See **that, which.**)

who, whom Though the distinction between these words is disappearing, many readers will expect you to use *whom* for an object. Err on the side of formality, or rewrite.

who's, whose *Who's* is a contraction for "who is"; *whose* shows possession.

-wise (See **-ize, -wise.**)

would of (See **could of, would of.**)

yet (See **but however, but yet.**)

your, you're *Your* is a possessive pronoun; *you're* contracts "you are."

If **you're** taking math, you'll need **your** calculator.

abbrev	incorrect abbreviation	¶	paragraph
add	information needed	p, punc	punctuation error
agr	error in agreement	⌃	comma
apos	apostrophe error	no ⌃	no comma
art	incorrect article	; :	semicolon, colon
awk	awkward construction	'	apostrophe
cap	capital letter needed	" "	quotation marks
case	incorrect pronoun form	. ? !	end marks
clear	clearer sentence needed	( ) [ ]	parentheses, brackets
coh	coherence needed	— … /	dashes, ellipses, slashes
coord	faulty coordination	prep	preposition error
cs	comma splice	pr ref	pronoun reference error
cut	unneeded material	proof?	evidence needed
dev	development needed	reorg	reorganize
discrm	discriminatory	rep	repetitious
dm	dangling modifier	sent	sentence revision needed
dneg	double negative	shift	shift
emph	emphasis needed	sp, spell	spelled incorrectly
focus	focus needed	sub	faulty subordination
frag	sentence fragment	t, tense	wrong verb tense
fs	fused sentence	trans	transition needed
gap	explanation needed	und	underlining (italics)
hyph	hyphen (-) needed	us	error in usage
inc	incomplete sentence	var	sentence variety needed
ital	italics (underlining)	verb	incorrect verb form
lc	lowercase letter needed	wc, ww	word choice, wrong word
link	linkage needed	wordy	too many words
log	faulty reasoning	⌃	insert
mixed	mixed sentence	⌿	delete
mm	misplaced modifier	⌒	close up space
modif	incorrect adjective or adverb	∿	transpose letters or words
num	incorrect number	#	add a space
//	parallel elements needed	X	obvious error

Index

Abbreviations, 216–218, 245
Abstracts, 34, 40
  databases containing, 44
  writing of, 107–108
Academic communities, 2
  critical reasoning in, 7
  documenting sources for, 55
  issue identification in, 16–17
  research in, 39
  style and, 12
Academic models, 89–95
Academic readers' expectations, 12
Academic sources, 82–83
Academic thesis, 6, 8
Academic writers, tips for, 237
Accent marks, 245
Accuracy, 88
ad hominem fallacy, 22
Adjectives, 179–187
  coordinate, 206
Adverbs, 179–182
Advocacy Web site, 47
Age, and biased language, 132
Agreement, 170–174
  pronoun-antecedent, 174
  subject-verb, 171–173
Amounts (number), 218–219
  abbreviations for, 217
Ampersand, 245
Analogy,
  false, 22
  using, 158–159
Analyses, 7, 34
Annotated bibliography
  and summary notes, 107
  preparation of, 108–111
Annotations, 40
Apostrophes ('), 209–210
Appeals, logical and emotional, 21–22
Applied sciences, source materials
  for, 62

Appositives, 205
Arabic numerals and symbols, 246
Argument, constructing an, 16–22
Argumentative thesis, 6, 8
Argument papers, academic model, 93
Article
  scholarly, 84–85
Assignment, understanding
    sources, 81–82
Audience, 1–2, 37
Audiovisual collections, 43, 66,
Augustine, 140
Authority, 87–88

Background, 8
Begging the question, 22
Bias
  identify in source, 51, 72
  in language choices, 131–132
Bibliographic databases, 44
Bibliographies, 42
Biographies, to evaluate authors, 84
Block quotations
  for poetry, 56–57
  for prose, 56
Blogs, 47
Body of paper, 134
Borrowing from sources
    correctly, 76–79
Browser, 45
Bullets, 247

Capitalization, 214–216, 247
CD-ROM
  as source of topics, 29
Character, use in argument, 157–158
Cicero, 140
Circular reasoning, 22
Claim, 21
Clause, 164

Clear sentences, 183–186
  editing for, 184
  recognizing unclear sentences, 184
Clustering, 4
Code-shifting, 199
Coherence, 129
Coherent paragraph, 9–10
Collaborative revision, 5
Collaborative writers, tips for, 241–242
Colons (:), 207, 208
Commas (,), 202–206, 247–248
  series and, 205–206
Comma splice, 166–168
Community of readers and writers, 1–5.
  See also Academic communities;
      Public communities; Work
      communities
  style in, 11–13
Community style, 11–12
  distance, 11
  formality, 11
  language, 11
  writer's stance, 11
Comparative form of adjectives and
      adverbs, 235–236
Comparative study, academic
      model, 93–94
Comparisons, 182
Complete sentence, 164
Compound modifiers, 220
Conciseness, 196–198. *See* also
      Wordiness
Conditional hypothesis, 32
Conducting research, 37–60
      finding library and database
          resources, 42–44
      finding Web and Internet
          resources, 44–47
      integrating and crediting
          sources, 54–60
      planning and, 37–41
      reading and evaluating
          sources, 48–54
Conjunctive adverbs, 207
Contractions, 210
Coordinate adjectives, 206
Coordinating conjunctions, 202
  commas preceding, 202
Coordination, 193–196
Correct forms, 174–182
  adjectives and adverbs, 179–182
  comparisons, 182
  pronouns, 177–179
  verb, 174–177
Counterarguments, presenting, 20
Cover page, 34
Critical reading, 3
Critical reasoning, 6–7
Currency, 88

Dangling modifiers, 188–189
Dashes, 223, 224
Data, 21
Databases, 43–44
  containing abstracts, 44
Data-warrant-claim reasoning, 21
Dates, abbreviation of, 217
Dialect, 198
Diction, 11
Dictionaries, 42
Direct quotation notes, 103–104
Disability, non-biased language, 132
Discipline, language of, 61–63
Disrespectful language, 199
Documentation of sources, 55
  academic community and, 55
Document design, 13–16
  sample documents, 15–16
Documenting, 58–59
Documenting sources for audience, 55
  academic, 55
  public, 55
  work, 55
Documents, designing for readers, 13–16
  laying out document, 14
  planning document, 13
  sample documents, 15–16
  using type features, 14
  using visuals, 15
Drafting the paper, 4, 121–161
  field of study, 121–124
  focusing argument, 124–127
  humanities, 122
  inquiry, 124
  negotiation, 124
  persuading, 124
  physical & medical
      sciences, 123–124
  social sciences, 122–123
  unity of coherence, 129
  verb tense, 129
DVD
  as source of topics, 29

Editing, 4, 5
  final manuscript, 136–137
  with a computer, 137
Electronic addresses, 227
Electronic book catalogs, 28
Electronic mailing lists, 46
Electronic messages and postings, 46
Electronic notes, 41
Electronic research, 41
Electronic sources, using, 28–29
  as source of topics, 28
  CD-Rom, DVD, VHS, 29
  electronic book catalogs, 28
  library databases, 28
  World Wide Web, 28–29

Ellipses (...), 225
E-mail (email) (electronic mail), 46
    gathering data from, 63-64
E-mail discussion groups, 86
    as source of topics, 27
Emotion, as form of argument, 157-158
Encyclopedias, 42, 85-86
Enthymeme, 30, 31-32
ergo propter hoc, 21
Ethnic identity, terminology used, 132
Evidence, 7, 8, 19-20
    quotations as, 8
Examples, 8
Experiments conducting, 67-69
    notes from, 85
Explanation, in research proposal, 34

Fallacies, 21
False analogy, 22
Faulty cause-effect relationship, 21-22
Field report, 94
Field research, 39, 61-69
    notetaking, 108
Field sources, 39
Figures and tables, 248
Focused freewriting, 4
Focused paragraph, 8
Foreign cities, in MLA style, 248
Formality, 11
Formal outline, 4
Fragments, 163-165
Freewriting, 4, 25
Full-text databases, 43-44
Fused sentences, 166-168

Gender, and biased language, 131-132
Generalizations, 7
General search engines, 45
General subject narrowed to working
        topic, 33
General thesis, 6, 8
Generating ideas, 24
Gerunds, 234
Given/new method, 152-154
Government documents, 43, 65
Graphs, 15

Headings, 14, 248
Headword, 188
History,
    academic model, 90-91
Homophones, 223
Humanists, source materials for, 62-63
Humanities
    academic sources, 82
Hyphens (-), 219-221
Hypothesis, 30, 32-33

Ideas,
    generating, 24-30
    organizing, 89-99
Illogical comparison, 187
Incomplete comparison, 187
Indefinite pronouns, 173, 235
Indexes, as research tools, 42
Indexing databases, 44
Indirect questions, 226
Individual Web site, 47
Infinitives, 234
Information, 7, 8
Informational Web site, 47
Informative thesis, 6, 8
Inquiry turned in writing, 54
Internet, 45
    discussion group, as source of
                topics, 27
    sources, 44-47
Interpolations, 224
Interpretations, 7, 18
Interview, 85
    evaluation, 85
    gathering data from, 63
    notes from, 63
Introduction, writing of, 132-133
Introductory expressions, commas
        following, 203
Irregular verbs, forms of, 234
Issues, identifying, 16-17
Italicizing/underlining, 213-214
Italics, 251

Journal entries, 4
Judgments, 7

Keywords, 25
    research community and, 38-39

Laboratory investigations, academic
        model, 94
Language, 11
    biased, avoidance of, 131-132
    choices, 198-199
    community style and, 11
    dialects, 198
    of discipline, 129
    disrespectful, 199
    sexist, 131-132
Lanham, Richard, 147
Lecture, gathering data from, 65
Letters (of alphabet), with words
        hyphenating, 220
Library books, 29
Library database, 28
    as source of topics, 28

Library research, 42–43
  search strategies, 39, 43–44
Library sources, 39
Limiting modifiers, 189
Literature, academic model, 90
Local e-mail discussion group, 27
Logical arguing, mapping, 157–158
Logical fallacy, 21–22
Logical reasoning, 20–22

Magazines, 86
Main clause, 194, 229
Mapping, logical, 157–158
Marginal comments, 3–4
Margins, 249
Metaphor, using, 159–160
Metasearch sites, 45
Microform collections, 43
Misplaced modifiers, 188–189
Mixed structures, 186–188
Models (patterns), academic, 89–95
Modifiers, 188
Monetary units, 249
Mood, of verb, 176

Names of persons, 249–250
Newsgroups, 46
Newspapers, 86
Nominalizations, 184
Nonrestrictive modifiers, commas
    with, 203, 204
Note cards, 41
Notes, 101–119
  academic models of, 101
  annotated bibliography, 108–111
  effective, 102
  field research, 108
  paraphrase, 105–106
  personal, 102–103
  quotation, 103–104
  review of literature, 111–119
  summary, 106–108
Note taking, 41
Noun string, 184
Numbering of pages, 250
Numbers
  arabic, 246
  roman, 250
Numbers, figures, and symbols, 246
Numerals, 218–219

Observation, gathering data
    from, 67–69, 85
Online catalogs, 43
Online databases, 43
Online periodicals, 42

Online researchers, tips for, 243
Online sources, 39. *See also specific*
    types of source, e.g., Books
  evaluating, 48, 50–54
  search strategies, 39, 44–45
  Web and Internet, 45–47
Online writers, tips for, 242–243
Organizing ideas and setting
    goals, 89–99
Outlines, 4
  sentence, 99
  topic, 98–99
  writing, 97–99

Pace, reading, 160–161
Pages, 45
Paradigms (academic models), 89–99
Paragraphs, 8–10
  coherent, 9–10
  development of, 10
  focused, 8
  plain, 148–156
Parallelism, 192–193
Paraphrase, 48
Paraphrase notes, 105–106
Paraphrasing, 48–49
Parentheses, 223, 224
Parenthetical expressions, commas
    with, 203, 204
Participles, verbal phrases and, 233
Passive voice, 130, 154–156
Patterns for paragraph development, 10
Peer review, 137–138
Period(s) (.), 226
Periodical indexes, 42
Periodicals, 42
  see also Magazines; Newspapers
Personal ideas, as source of
    topics, 24–25
Personal interview, as source of
    topics, 27
Personal notes, 102–103
Persuasion, 34
Persuasion papers, academic pattern, 93
Persuasive style, 156–161
Pie charts, 15
Philosophy
  academic model, 91
Phrase(s), 25, 229
Physical sciences, source materials
    for, 61–62
Plagiarism, 54, 71–80
  avoiding, 57–58, 73–75
  common knowledge exceptions
      to, 75–76
  honoring property rights, 73
Planning, 4
Possessive nouns, 209

Possessive pronouns, 234
post hoc, 21
Prefixes, 220
Primary sources, 40, 81-83, 104
Printed document with visuals, 59
Problem paragraph, 50
Pronoun reference, 168-170
Pronouns, 177-179, 234
  personal, 234
Proofreading, 4, 5, 138
Proper adjectives, 215
  capitalization of, 215
Proper nouns, 215
  capitalization of, 215
Propositions, 7
Public address, gathering data from, 65
Public communities, 2
  critical reasoning in, 7
  documenting sources for, 55
  research in, 39
  style and, 13
Public readers' expectations, 13
Public writers, tips for, 238-239
Punctuation
  apostrophes, 209-210
  brackets, 224
  colons, 207, 208
  commas, 202-206
  dashes, 223, 224
  document design and, 13-16
  in electronic addresses, 227
  ellipses, 225
  hyphens, 219-221
  parentheses, 223, 224
  periods, 226
  question marks, 226
  semicolons, 207-208
  slashes, 225
Purpose, 2
Purpose statement, 34

Query, in search strategy, 46
Questioning, 49-50
Question marks, 226
Questionnaires, gathering data
    from, 66-67
Questions, 26, 50
  to refine a topic, 26
Quotation marks, 221-213
  for emphasis, 213
Quotations, 8
  block, 56-57
  in-text citations, 104
  primary sources, 104
  research papers and, 55-57
  secondary sources, 104
Quotations, using, 55-57
  block quotations for poetry, 56-57

block quotations for prose, 56
guidelines, 56

Racial identity, terminology used to
    describe, 132
Radio, gathering data from, 66
Rationale, for the project, 34
Readers (audience), 1-2
  tips for, 239-240
Reading to writing, moving from, 3-4
  reading critically, 3
  turning reading into writing, 3-4
Ready references, 42
Reasoning critically, 6-7
Reasoning logically, 20-22
  data-warrant-claim reasoning, 21
  logical and emotional appeals, 21-22
Reasons, developing, 19-20
Recommendations, 7
Red herring, 22
Reference books, as source of topics, 30
Reflexive pronouns, 235
Relative pronouns, 195, 235
Relevance, 87
Religion
academic model, 91
Research, planning and conducting,
    37-41
  developing research questions, 39
  developing search strategies, 39-40
  identifying keywords, 38-39
  keeping track of sources and
      notes, 41
  pulling research materials
      together, 41
  recognizing research
      communities, 37-38
  recognizing research topics, 38
  selecting resources for working
      bibliography, 40
Research communities,
    recognizing, 37-38
Research databases, 43-44
Research journal, 25
Research materials, pulling together, 41
Research methods, 35
  budget, 35
  materials, 35
  timetable, 35
Research notebook, 41
Research-oriented Web site, 47
Research proposal, drafting, 33-35
  writing detailed proposal, 34-35
  writing short proposal, 33-34
Research questions, 38, 39
  in search strategy, 39
Research strategies, 37-41
Research topics, 38

Resource databases, 44
Resources. *See* Documentation; Online
    sources; Sources
Restrictive modifiers, commas with, 204
Review of the literature, 35, 111–119
Revising, 4, 5
  rough draft, 136–138
Roman numerals, 250
Rough draft, revision of, 136–138
Rough thesis, 5
Running heads, 250

Sample documents, 15–16
Scholarly article, 84–85
Scholarly books, 83–84
Sciences, source materials for, 82–83
Scientific analysis, academic
    model, 94–95
Search engines, 45,
Searching efficiently, 46
Search strategies, developing, 39–40
Secondary sources, 40, 81–83, 104
Semicolons (;), 207–208
  series joined by, 208
Semidrafting, 4
Sentence(s), 229–231
  capitalization for, 214–216
  clarity of, 183–186
  complete, 164
  conciseness in, 196–198
  coordination in, 193–196
  fused (run on), 166–168
  misplaced modifiers in, 188–189
  mixed structures in, 186–188
  parallelism in, 192–193
  subject and verb position
    in, 171–173
  subordination in, 193–196
Sentence fragment, 164–165
Sentence outline, 99
Sentence, in paragraphs
  point, 149
  support, 149
  topic, 148–149
  transitional, 148
Series (grammatical)
  commas in, 205–206
Sexist language, avoidance of, 131–132
Sexual orientation, use of term, 132
Shortened titles in text, 250
Simile, use of, 158–159
Sites, 45
Slashes (/), 225
Social sciences
  academic style, 130
  source materials for, 61, 82
Source materials
  avoiding plagiarism, 73–75
  bias identification, 72

  credibility of, establishment
    of, 71–72
  evaluation of, 87–88
  finding the best, 83–87
  primary, 81–83
  secondary, 81–83
Sources
  citing. *See* Documentation
  evaluating, 50–54
  plagiarism and, 54, 57–58
  primary, 40
  searching for. *See* Search strategies
  secondary, 40, 81–83, 104
Sources
  field, 39
  library, 39
  online, 39
  primary, 40
  secondary, 40
Sources, integrating and crediting, 54–60
  avoiding plagiarism, 57–58
  deciding what to document, 58–59
  documenting sources for
    audience, 55
  integrating sources into text, 57
  presenting sources, 59–60
  using quotations, 55–57
Sources, presenting, 59–60
  printed document with visuals, 59
  Webbed documents, 59–60
Sources, reading and evaluating, 48–54
  evaluating online sources
    critically, 51–54
  evaluating sources critically, 50–51
  evaluating sources for bias, 51
  evaluating sources for credibility, 51
  summarizing and
    paraphrasing, 48–49
  synthesizing and questioning, 49–50
  turning inquiry into writing, 54
Sources and notes, keeping track of, 41
  electronic notes, 41
  note cards, 41
  research notebook, 41
Spacing, 250
Speakers, tips for, 240–241
Special collections, 43
Specialized encyclopedias, 42
Spelling, 221–223
  numbers, 219
Squinting modifier, 189
Statement of qualification, 35
Statistics, 8
Strategic questions, 4
Style(s)
  community style, 11–13
  grand, 240
  persuasive, 140, 156–161
  plain, 140, 141–156

Style and strategy, matching to
community of readers, 11–13
adjusting to community's style, 12
recognizing community's
expectations, 12–13
recognizing community's
style, 11–12
Subject, focusing, 24–30
Subject-verb agreement, 171–173
Subordinate (dependent)
clause, 164, 194, 229
Subordination, 193–196
Subordinators, 195
Suffixes, 220
Summarizing, 48
Summary, 48
Summary notes, 106–108
Superlative form of adjectives and
adverbs, 235–236
Supporting evidence, developing, 19–20
Surveys, gathering data from, 66–67
Synthesis, 49
Synthesizing, 49–50

Table of contents, as source of topics, 29
Tables, 15, 248
Tables of information, 15
Talking with others, as source of
topics, 27
Internet discussion group, 27
local e-mail discussion group, 27
personal interview, 27
Television
gathering data from, 66
Tense, 129. *See also* Verb tenses
Tentative thesis, 19
Terminology, 26–27
Tests, 85
conducting, 67–69
notes from, 85
Textbooks, as source of topics, 29
Thesis, 4, 39
academic, 6, 8
argumentative, 6, 8
development of, 5–6
general, 6, 8
informative, 6, 8
Thesis sentence, 30
in outline, 96–97
Thesis statement, 5, 18–19, 30–31
argumentative, developing, 18
counterarguments, 20
creating and revising, 18–19
reasons and supporting evidence
for, 19–20
Third person, writing in, 130
Title(s)
of books, as source of topics, 29
within titles, in MLA style, 250–251

Titles (of people), abbreviations of, 217
Titles (of works), quotation marks for,
212–213
Tone, in writing, 157–158
Topic(s), finding scholarly, 2, 23–35
drafting research proposal, 33–35
generating ideas and focusing
subject, 24–30
writing thesis, enthymeme, or
hypothesis, 30–33
Topic outline, 98–99
Topic sentence, 8–9
Topic shift (faulty predication), 186
Trade books, 85
Transitional expressions, 207
semicolons and, 207–208
Type features, document design, 14
typefaces, 14
type size and weight, 14

Underlining. *See* Italicizing/underlining
Underscoring, 251
Understanding the assignment, 81–82
Uniform Resource Locator (URL), 45
Unity of writing, 129
Unnecessary shifts, 190–192
in person and number, 190–192
in tense, 191–192

Value judgment, 18
Verb(s), 174–177, 231
active or passive, 233
agreement with subject, 171–173
contractions of, 210
infinitives, 234
participles, 233
Verbals, 233
Verb tense(s), 231–233
active voice, 231–233
for MLA & CMS styles, 129
VHS, as source of topics, 29
Visuals, using, 15

Warnings, 7
Warrant, 21
Web and Internet resources, developing
online search strategy, 44–45
finding, 44, 45
searching efficiently, 46
using, 47
Webbed document, 59–60
Web discussion forums, 46
Web sites. *See* World Wide Web sites
Word choice. *See* Diction
Wordiness, 197
Work communities, 2
critical reasoning in, 7

documenting sources for, 55
issue identification in, 16-17
research in, 39
style and, 12-16
Working bibliography, 40
Working outline, 4
Workplace writers, tips for, 238
World Wide Web, 28-29
  as source of topics, 28-29
  evaluating sources on, 48, 50-54
  permission to publish
    material, 79-80
World Wide Web sites, 42, 44-47
  advocacy, 47
  evaluating sources on, 48, 50-54
  individual, 47, 86-87
  informational, 47
  locating sources on, 44-46
  research-oriented, 47
  sponsored, 85
  using resources on, 47
Writer's stance, 11
Writing
  coherence of, 129
  in language of discipline, 129
  notes, 102

tense of, 129
unity & coherence, 129
with style, 139-161
Writing clearly, 183-199
  clear sentences, 183-186
  conciseness, 196-198
  coordination and
    subordination, 193-196
  dangling and misplaced
    modifiers, 188-189
  language choices, 198-199
  mixed structures, 186-188
  parallelism, 192-193
  unnecessary shifts, 190-192
Writing correctly, 163
  agreement, 170-174
  comma splices and fused
    sentences, 166-168
  correct forms, 174-182
  fragments, 163-165
  pronoun reference, 168-170
Writing process, 4-5
  discovering and planning, 4
  drafting, 4
  revising, editing, proofreading, 4-5
Writing situation, understanding, 2-3